WHAT MEN CALL TREASURE

WHAT MEN CALL TREASURE
The Search for Gold at
VICTORIO PEAK

David Schweidel and Robert Boswell

Cinco Puntos Press
El Paso, Texas

FIRST EDITION
10   9   8   7   6   5   4   3   2   1

Library of Congress Cataloging-in-Publication Data

Schweidel, David, 1954-
    What men call treasure : the search for gold at Victorio Peak / by David
Schweidel and Robert Boswell. — 1st ed.
        p. cm.
    ISBN 978-1-933693-21-7 (alk. paper)
    1. Doña Ana County (N.M.)—Gold discoveries. 2. Victorio Peak
(N.M.)—Gold discoveries. 3. Treasure troves—New Mexico—History—
20th century. 4. New Mexico—Gold discoveries. 5. Noss, Doc, d. 1949.
6. Noss, Babe, d. 1979. 7. Adventure and adventurers—New Mexico—
Biography. 8. Delonas, Terry. 9. Noss, Babe, d. 1979—Family. 10. New
Mexico—Biography. I. Schweidel, David. II. Title.

    F802.D6B67 2008
    978.9'66—dc22

                                                            2008011634

―――――

Cover design by Sergio Gomez
Book design by Vicki Trego Hill

What men call treasure…the gods call dross.
—James Russell Lowell

————

Contents

Part I

Part II

Part III

Part IV

Part V

Appendix

PART I

(Overleaf) The road to Victorio Peak.

1

A Postmodern Treasure Story

This is a land of illusions and thin air. The vision is
so cleared at times that the truth itself is deceptive.
—John C. Van Dyke

Treasure Island opens with the arrival of a mysterious stranger at the Admiral Benbow, a coastal inn run by the Hawkins family. The stranger—Billy Bones—strolls in singing about dead men and rum. His tales of pirates walking the plank or swinging by the neck fascinate young Jim Hawkins, as does his request to keep an eye out for a "seafaring man with one leg." The one-legged man does not appear at the inn, but two others come calling. The first is Black Dog, a "pale, tallowy creature" missing two fingers. Billy Bones runs him off. The second is Blind Pew, a sightless beggar in a tattered cloak who gives Bones a death summons—the "black spot." Shortly after Blind Pew leaves, Billy Bones dies from a sudden stroke and Jim Hawkins discovers among the man's possessions a treasure map.

This is the correct way to start a treasure story.

The characters should have names like Billy Bones, Black Dog, and Blind Pew. Several should be missing significant body parts. Death must be summoned no later than chapter three. And the hero ought to be a brave and lively kid in possession of a map or a wild tale or a genie's bottle.

Our treasure story opens in a therapist's office on a balmy evening in the

Neverland of Southern California. Colorful names, wild tales, and the summoning of death all eventually find a place in the narrative, but they don't occupy the same space they hold in *Treasure Island*. They can't. The world has changed too much since Robert Louis Stevenson penned his yarn.

Yet whatever else the treasure of Victorio Peak may be, it is a *story*. It starts out as a pre-modern saga about a hero wishing to be restored to his rightful fortune (the sort of plot Shakespeare liked to borrow), and ends up a postmodern fable about a gay Jehovah's Witness putting together a team of dreamy romantics (many of whom are openly homophobic) and taking on Congress, the United States Army, and finally a mountain, all in response to a fiercely unlikely legend passed along in a single family from generation to generation like a bad gene.

The mountain in question might be more accurately described as a hill. Victorio Peak rises a scant five hundred feet from the floor of the Hembrillo Basin in southern New Mexico. The high desert in these parts plays host to mesquite, catclaw, and ocotillo; rattlesnake, roadrunner, and mule deer. Rain is rare; the summer heat, vicious; and the parched desert air possesses an eerie clarity. This is mirage country. Not far from here, a Franciscan friar mistook a jumble of adobe huts for a glittering city of gold and set the modern history of the Southwest on its course.

Victorio Peak stands in the middle of the *Jornada del Muerto*, loosely translated as "Dead Man's Trail." From the sixteenth century to the nineteenth, the Jornada was the deadliest stretch of the *El Camino Real*, the principal route from Mexico City to Santa Fe. For more than four hundred years, virtually every trading caravan between Old Mexico and New risked falling prey to the Jornada's nasty heat, dry water holes, and roving Apaches. One of those Apaches, Chief Victorio, lends the peak its name. He and his men defeated the U.S. Cavalry in a battle fought near the base of the peak in 1880. Treasure enthusiasts speculate that Victorio was protecting a hoard of gold and jewels hidden within the mountain, the plunder accumulated from centuries of Apache raiding, though no historian has ever endorsed this view.

In November of 1937, according to legend, unlicensed foot doctor Milton Ernest "Doc" Noss found his way inside Victorio Peak. A few months later, the story goes, he returned with his wife, Ova "Babe" Noss. Over the course of several visits, Doc ventured further and further down a succession of narrow walkways, squeezing through bottlenecks and fording an underground stream. Eventually, he discovered a series of small, interlinked caves and one large cavern that purportedly contained a treasure of fabulous proportions. The system of caves, according to Doc and Babe, held Spanish armor, statues of saints, swords, a crown, a chest of jewelry, twenty-seven skeletons, and an estimated 16,000 gold bars of various types, from primitively smelted cigar-shaped bars to uniform gold bricks stacked in boxes stamped with the Wells Fargo imprint.

Eyewitnesses have signed sworn statements declaring that they saw Doc Noss bring gold bars and other artifacts out of Victorio Peak. One witness claims to have gone with Doc into the treasure room. Doc and Babe's descendants admit that Doc was a bit of a con man who went on to traffic in fake gold bars, but the original discovery, they insist, was the real thing.

The truth has proved difficult to determine. Even the undisputed facts are subject to conflicting interpretations.

Doc and Babe did their best to keep the treasure a secret. The Gold Reserve Act of 1934 made it illegal for private citizens to own gold in any form other than coin or jewelry, and Doc feared that if he reported his find, the government would confiscate it. In the fall of 1939, in an effort to improve access to the treasure, Doc hired a mining engineer to set off a dynamite blast at the worst bottleneck. The explosion collapsed the series of walkways and blocked the passage to the treasure room. In the family's version, Doc was furious that the mining engineer had used too much dynamite; the alternative is that Doc intentionally destroyed the passage to keep anyone from learning that the peak contained no treasure. Certainly, a buried fortune in gold served as a potent lure to attract investors. By December 4, 1941, when Doc and Babe's Cheyenne Mining Company held its first meeting at the peak, they had raised enough money to begin excavation, which was scheduled to commence the following Monday. But Pearl Harbor was attacked, and the U.S. Army annexed Victorio Peak and the surrounding desert for missile-testing purposes.

Doc and Babe had to wait till the end of World War II to resume their treasure hunt. In 1947, Doc left Babe for another woman, Violet Boles of Polaski County, Arkansas. In 1949, he returned to New Mexico with a plan to sell the last of the bars he had hidden near the peak to Texas oil man

Charley Ryan. When the deal went sour, Ryan killed Doc with a gunshot to the temple. The day before Doc's death, the family says, he and Babe reconciled, a contention that may have been intended to strengthen Babe's claim to the treasure. She and Violet Boles Noss wrangled over possession of Doc's maps and other effects while a Las Cruces jury acquitted Charley Ryan of murder.

For the next six years, the federal government and the state of New Mexico battled in court to decide who had legal jurisdiction over the area that included Victorio Peak. Babe took advantage of the dispute to conduct excavations whenever she could scrape together enough money. In 1955, the federal government won its suit and evicted Babe for the last time.

The tale of the treasure, however, refused to die.

In 1958, four airmen stationed at nearby Holloman Air Force Base crawled into a foul-smelling cave in Victorio Peak where—as they later swore in lie detector tests—they discovered stacks of dust-covered gold bars. To prevent others from taking the gold, they collapsed the passageway leading to the cave. Subsequently, in partnership with Holloman's judge advocate general, they badgered the army for permission to recover the treasure. In 1961, the army authorized a search—classified Top Secret. When Babe learned from a local rancher that the army was jumping her claim, she contacted the state land office and managed to have the search suspended. The army maintained that no treasure had been located, but rumors flourished that soldiers had carted off a fortune in gold.

In 1963, the army consented to a three-month excavation conducted by the Gaddis Mining Company of Denver, Colorado, under the auspices of the State Museum of New Mexico. After ninety days, with the Gaddis crew insisting they were on the verge of a breakthrough, the army refused the museum's request for an extension. In addition, the army censored the museum's report, deleting all references to the army's own search and all statements suggesting the possible presence of treasure. Among locals, gossip spread that the army had helicoptered several tons of gold from the peak to a ranch in Texas belonging to President Lyndon Johnson.

The Victorio Peak saga went national in 1973 when John Dean, testifying at the Watergate hearings, mentioned that F. Lee Bailey had sought help from the Nixon administration in a matter involving "an enormous amount of gold." Bailey was quoted in newspapers around the country the next day: "Give me a helicopter and half an hour and I'll find 292 bars of gold." The flurry of publicity and the resulting pressure on the army eventually led to Operation Goldfinder, a ten-day survey organized by professional treasure hunter Norman Scott in 1977. Scott brought in an expert in ground-penetrating radar from the Stanford Research Institute to test sites specified by seven claimants. The expert, Lambert Dolphin, quickly debunked five of the claims, but found evidence to support Doc's original account. "The radar immediately confirmed the existence of a large, now inaccessible cavern directly under the summit of the mountain," Dolphin reported. "The radar also showed cracks and fissures around the summit in the vicinity of the Doc Noss shaft which seemed to confirm the Noss account that he had at one time entered the cavern from the summit."

The army denied requests from Scott and Dolphin to conduct a thorough search.

Even though the reliability of ground-penetrating radar was suspect, and even though a cavern—if it existed—might hold no treasure, the legend of Victorio Peak had become a monument of something more than stone and earth: it had the power of *buzz*. *The New York Times*, *The Washington Post*, *Time*, *Newsweek*, and "Sixty Minutes" all covered Goldfinder. Dan Rather stood atop the windswept peak, grinning like a scarecrow and trumpeting Doc Noss's treasure.

If Victorio Peak could capture the interest of the general public, it could also dominate the lives of those closest to its tantalizing promise. Babe's daughter, Dorothy Delonas, called the treasure a curse. Dorothy's son Terry grew up with the story ingrained in his imagination. The question of what lay buried in Victorio Peak nagged at Terry for decades. Eventually, he decided to follow the mystery to its logical—or illogical—conclusion. Despite his many reasonable doubts, he believed in the family legends. The sincerity of his faith would inspire others to believe. Terry entertained romantic visions, but he went about his quest in a manner befitting his times: he incorporated.

The story of Terry Delonas and his pursuit of phantom treasure is rooted in the desert, land of illusions and thin air. Like any good mystery, it refuses to be solved. Instead, it offers an eye-of-the-beholder experience—a glimpse of a glittering vista that might be gold or dried mud, miracle or mirage. Many of Terry's supporters see his story as an old-fashioned adventure, with Terry as reluctant hero—Hamlet in a suit, out to avenge the death of his step-grandfather, reclaim the family fortune, and restore his grandmother's good name. We, the authors, spent years trying to tell the story just that way, but such narratives, we discovered, are no longer possible. It was like trying to chronicle the rise of an honest politician who succeeds thanks to intelligence, kindness, and integrity: the world long ago turned past that conception of itself, and it has kept on turning. Even if the actual events were to match up identically with the old-fashioned story-line, the reader—and the characters—would view the experience through a warped lens.

Terry's implausible and seemingly impossible mission has morphed into a postmodern fable encompassing conspiracy theories and conquistadors, Kaposi's sarcoma and a vacuum cleaner the size of an Airstream, along with Doc and Babe as characters in a screenplay, weird walk-ons from Miss U.S.A. and Santa Claus, writer's block, a dowser from the Department of Defense, acts of Congress, acts of stupidity, acts of (something like) God, and a mountain that is and is not a hill, is and is not a metaphor.

2

Swinging Bachelor

Where gold goes, blood follows.
—Ova "Babe" Noss

1983

"Since I was five, I knew. I didn't know what it was, but I knew I was different. I'd go down to the Kingdom Hall several times a week. I felt like an impostor. I wouldn't read certain passages of the Bible—St. Paul's condemnation. I'd get shaky and fear that God would strike me dead. By the time I was twenty, I hated myself. I prayed thousands of hours. *Don't make me this way.* I never got an answer. I stayed celibate until I was twenty-nine and a half."

The therapist's office was located in what southern California realtors call a "transitional neighborhood." A district of winding streets and elegant bungalows had been invaded by office buildings. The unadorned concrete boxes and their asphalt lots abutted green lawns with catalpa trees and bougainvillea. The old houses and new buildings, standing side-by-side, looked absurd, the discreet and dignified holding hands with the coarse and commercial.

The season was autumn, the weather warm and unusually humid. The trees had not yet lost their leaves. On the third floor of one of the ugly buildings, Terry Delonas sat in a dimly lit office, facing an attractive middle-aged woman with razor-cut hair—his therapist. Because the air conditioning was broken, she had moved the chairs next to an open window, but the room felt muggy. The window let in the sounds of a baseball game on the radio. Terry focused for a second on the announcer's familiar voice. He had never visited a therapist before.

The sky outside the window was almost black, but lights shone from below. He guessed the game was coming from a Spanish-style house with a red roof and greenish vapor lamp above a curving brick driveway. From this height, he could see the pattern of new buildings among the old houses, the dark cubes blocking the flickering lights of the city beyond, hulking over the neighborhood. He studied this pattern while the therapist waited for him to continue. The new structures had intruded into the quiet residential area like antigens invading a bloodstream, mammoth and predatory. They would prevail, of course. It might take years, but the neighborhood would die.

He wondered what he should say next. He felt compelled to tell the truth, and the truth was complicated. "I was raised to believe in a spirit world," he said, a declaration that sounded bizarre, even to him. The therapist didn't change her expression, but the quality of her attention seemed to change. She became more alert and perhaps slightly wary. He began describing Clovis, New Mexico.

Situated at the intersection of two highways, ten miles from the Texas line, the town of Clovis cultivated the conservative values of the Texas panhandle, as well as the panhandle accent. The train stopped in Clovis, and people driving the interstate might pause there for a meal, but the real commerce had always revolved around cattle, cowboys, and oil. It was a dusty, ugly little town, Terry explained.

The therapist, of course, offered nothing of her own background. The artificiality of their conversation momentarily derailed him. He felt, in part, like a salesman making a pitch. In question was the legitimacy of his desire to die. Would the therapist buy his reasons? He resisted the impulse to exaggerate, to play to expectations. Terry wanted to be neither defensive nor boastful. He wanted to get at the truth. The baseball game drifted in, the voice of Vin Scully, rising and falling with anecdotal inflection.

"Every Jehovah's Witness is considered a minister," he said. "Even the children. When I was a boy, I went with my mother door to door to hand out the *Watchtower* and testify for God. By the time I was ten, I had six suits—and we weren't a wealthy family." Members of the faith believed the Second Coming had already occurred. Christ, reborn as a spirit, had begun an invisible reign as earth's unrecognized king. One day he would lead a battle against Satan for the redemption of the world. "If you're a Jehovah's Witness," Terry said, "Satan isn't a metaphor. He's flesh and blood." According to the writings of the church, Satan would eventually be defeated by Christ, and one thousand years of divine rule would follow. The dead, during this time, would rise and live again as human beings. They would be given a second chance at salvation.

The therapist wanted to know whether Terry's faith had made him an outcast.

"That's not the word I'd use," Terry said, "but to be a Witness means you acknowledge no authority but God. You can't salute the flag or serve in the military or even pledge allegiance. I wouldn't say 'outcast,' but it does single you out."

Ridicule, the therapist suggested, was one of the hazards of believing in anything. The radio grew louder, a beer commercial between innings. She offered to close the window.

"It doesn't bother me," Terry said, and then he expressed his thanks for being seen on short notice. He was often effusive in his gratitude, an attribute largely sincere yet partly affected. In this case, he was genuinely grateful but he was also using his gratitude to change the subject. "I can tune things out pretty well," he continued. "Things that bother me, I put in a little compartment I don't have to look at. It works well for me." He gave a slight lift of one shoulder and grinned, a self-mocking smile that acknowledged the present failure of the strategy. "Most of the time it works."

The therapist nodded again and waited, unimpressed, it seemed, by either the gratitude or the stalling. She had been recommended to him by a stranger, someone from his health club who recognized that he was in crisis and suggested he get help. "My family means a lot to me," he said. "*Kin* is what my mother calls family. I always liked that. Kinfolk." He could hear the word in his mother's mouth, and it made him sad. "My grandmother called family *blood*. She used to say, 'If he ain't blood, don't trust him.' I was close to my grandmother." He wanted to explain how the difference between his mother and grandmother was captured in *kin* and *blood*, but he didn't know that he could put his finger on it. Besides, what did it matter? In the past few days, fear had become a constant and debilitating companion, but something in his character would not let him show it. He had ironed his shirt before coming over and trimmed his mustache.

"Witnesses don't believe in heaven," he said. "Not the way it's pictured by other Christians. We believe God will create a perfect world here on earth."

The therapist wanted to know what that meant. What was the definition of a perfect world?

He admitted that he was unsure. He knew that it would be peaceful and dominated by love. There would be no poverty or injustice. All people would live as brother and sister. "There will be no homosexuals. Our teachings are very clear about that."

The therapist encouraged him to go on.

"Jehovah's Witnesses are good people," he said. "Deliciously pure in the doctrine they've developed to live together without racism or class consciousness. Just don't be gay. You can be an alcoholic, a wife-beater, and they'll try to help you. But if you're gay, you've gone too far."

The therapist nodded. She made an incomplete gesture with her mouth. She might have begun to bite her lip. She specialized in gay clients, and Terry worried that he had offended her. He shifted to free his back from the sweaty shirt and the adhesive leather of the chair. Lifting himself slightly, he could see once again the shapes of the nearby office buildings scattered among the houses. The glow of the distant city limned the buildings with reflected light and lent them a semblance of dignity.

"I grew up in rural New Mexico," Terry said, "not Southern California. Some things aren't negotiable. Some things can't be put in a compartment—not forever, anyway." He shook his head slightly. "I've spent my life denying who I am." The statement seemed to him both true and an exaggeration. "One day I'd be wearing a suit, talking about God on somebody's doorstep, and the next day I'd be at school trying to act like one of the guys. People in my family speak with a country accent, but my brother and I taught each other to talk like the voices on the radio. We didn't want to be hicks."

Terry tried to describe the extent to which he had faked his life—at school, at home, even with his friends. He had become an expert at deception, at blending in. He had always known he was faking, even before he knew he was gay. The pretending created a distance, not only between Terry and his family, but within Terry. "When I lived in Santa Fe—before I'd ever had sex—I'd go out with gay men and conduct what I thought of as interviews. I wanted to get a profile of who was gay and why. I wanted to see where I fit in. I'd listen to their life stories, offer a little half-baked counseling, and tell my story. It was a kind of intimacy."

The therapist asked what he had learned from those interviews.

"I never talked to anyone who had a choice," he said. "All but one had fought a tough battle against it."

"Does your family know your sexual preference?"

"No," Terry said. "They think I'm a bachelor. They still believe in that notion of a *swinging bachelor*." He smiled at that. "I love them," he said. He loved them, but he was not like them, did not even want to speak as they did. He had strong religious convictions, but he could not maintain those convictions without betraying himself. "One part of me always seems to contradict another part. I play one kind of character with my family. That's all they know of me."

"With therapists, you play the calm and composed type."

"My grandmother actually encouraged me to pretend," he said. "Not that she understood what I was going through. She just thought I was timid." For her own reasons, she had wanted him to be brave. She had taught him to make believe that he was courageous. She cultivated courage through the simple denial of doubt. "The problem is that I'm always acting as if there was someone watching me," Terry said, "a witness to my every move." The room fell silent. The baseball game had ended. The quiet itself seemed a presence. "This feeling that I don't want to live anymore has been getting stronger and stronger."

"Terry," the therapist said softly. "Have you been diagnosed with AIDS?"

He shook his head. "I'm not sick," he said. "I can't be very much at risk." He had not lived the promiscuous life that had enthralled many of his friends. He still thought of the disease as *Gay Plague*. "If the church finds out I'm gay, I have to go before the elders. If I don't repudiate my sexuality, I'm banned for life. *Disfellowshipped*, we call it. My family wouldn't even be able to talk to me. I can't live with that."

The therapist waited until she was certain that he had nothing else to add. "Suppose you really were going to kill yourself. Is there anything you'd want to do first?"

The question surprised him, but not the answer that sprang to mind. "My grandmother was my closest friend," he said. "She and her husband found something—a treasure—and then they lost it. It's complicated, and it all happened a long time ago, but they had it and then they lost it, and she spent the rest of her life trying to get it back. People didn't believe her. They thought she was strange—a liar, a *character*."

"But you believed her."

"It would have been easier if she had forgotten about it. But she couldn't." He tried to explain how the treasure had made her life extraordinary but spoiled it at the same time. "I went out there once—with her—to the mountain where the treasure is buried. Seven years ago. She brought her scrapbook. For forty years she'd been trying to get the treasure back. They would never let her do it."

"Is this something you could do?" the therapist asked.

"Just like that?"

"You tell me," she said.

He could not meet her gaze. In the back of his bedroom closet, beneath a stack of shirts and pants he no longer wore, a cardboard box held the few tangible links he had to the treasure—photographs of his grandmother from the 1930s, a video tape of her telling the story, trial transcripts, personal letters, and declarations from men who swore before God that they had held in their hands ancient bars of gold. The prospect of pursuing the treasure thrilled and daunted him. Outside the window of the therapist's office, the city's flickering lights had grown brighter as the neighborhood darkened, a trick of perspective. The nearby buildings no longer clashed. Darkness blurred the distinctions that moments ago had seemed obvious.

Terry would not be diagnosed with AIDS for another three years. By then his project would have an office and letterhead stationary, a core of volunteers and investors who had put up thousands of dollars. He would feel unable to quit. His purpose, despite the prospect of dying, would remain unchanged: reach the mountain, find the treasure, learn the truth.

3

Soon to Be a Major Motion Picture

Never play cards with a man called Doc.
—Nelson Algren

May 1993—David Schweidel

My first novel hadn't sold.

My second novel hadn't sold *yet*.

I didn't have the heart to start a third, which was why, when the call came, I said yes.

The caller was Robert Boswell, a friend of ten years. We'd climbed the pyramids of Palenque together, dated the same redhead. Boz was married now, a professor of creative writing at New Mexico State University, author of four books—all, unlike mine, published. His latest had just gotten good reviews, including one in his local paper, which was probably why the treasure hunters had asked him to consider writing about their project. Boz wondered if I might be interested. Maybe we'd collaborate. Even if there was no book in it, he said, a treasure hunt sounded like fun.

I flew to El Paso a few days later. Boz drove me up to Las Cruces. The treasure hunters had provided video tapes with segments on the treasure from "60 Minutes" and "Unsolved Mysteries." We watched the videos and jotted down questions for Terry Delonas.

Our experience in journalism was not extensive. Boz had seen *All the President's Men*—twice, he insisted—and I'd taken "Intro to News Writing" as an undergrad. What I remembered from the class was how someone had walked in during the first lecture and shot the instructor with blanks. When the instructor clutched his heart, fake blood spurted from a vial stashed in his breast pocket. He collapsed to the floor, students gasped, and then he jumped up and said, There's your story. We were all sitting at typewriters; we had fifteen minutes to type our accounts. The most interesting thing, I told Boz, was how much the accounts differed. The shooter was described as a man and as a woman; as small and as hulking; as clean-shaven, as masked; as wearing a hat, as bareheaded; as firing three shots, one shot, two shots; as leaving immediately, as pausing to make sure the gun had done its work. It was a useful lesson in the vagaries of memory. People could believe they were telling the truth and still be wrong. And if that happened after fifteen minutes, what about after fifty years?

You can't trust memory, I said.

Especially mine, Boz said. His memory had gone fuzzy when his first child was born. Now he had two. My memory remained unimpaired.

We compiled a long list of questions for Terry Delonas, but it didn't include the big one: *Are you a con?* We'd have to trust our instincts, journalistic or not.

The following afternoon, a few hours before our interview with Terry, Boz dropped me off at a modest ranch-style house in a quiet Las Cruces neighborhood. While he administered a master's exam at the university, I would play reporter. A small sign on the front door displayed the logo of the Ova Noss Family Partnership. Armed with an empty notebook and a pair of new Bic pens, I knocked.

I don't remember who answered the door, but I do remember the sense of entering an alternate universe—not that the people appeared alien or abnormal, but their world seemed to have a different spin. Everything revolved around Victorio Peak. A scale model of the peak, encased in Plexiglas, occupied a corner of the sparsely furnished living room. Clippings filled one wall: *People Magazine, The New York Times,* an editorial from the local paper headlined "Is There Really Gold in Them Thar Hills?" Someone showed me to the office in the back room, where a fax machine was spitting out a fax, a telephone was ringing, and stacks of papers covered the desks, the photo-copier, and much of the floor. I left my notebook in my pocket. My goal was to fit in. The army required paperwork from anyone seeking access to the peak; I filled out the necessary forms, which were faxed to White Sands Missile Range and later placed atop one of the many stacks, to be filed, eventually, with everyone else's forms.

The woman in the office reminded me of my second-grade teacher—steady, efficient, with a hint of motherly concern. I suppose I was looking for the Moonie glint, but she seemed altogether unvarnished, friendly but not too friendly, more like a farmer than a fanatic. She introduced me to the grand dames of the project, the mother of Terry Delonas and his aunt, and I soon found myself sitting in a lawn chair in the living room, sipping lemonade and chatting about the weather with Dorothy Delonas and Letha Guthrie, both in their seventies, both polite but wary. Dorothy was a small woman who carried herself in a way that accentuated her smallness. She wore dark glasses. I pegged her as someone who battled depression. Letha was more expansive. She launched into an account of her first trip to Victorio Peak, and I slipped out my notebook and started scribbling notes. The larger story held no shape for me yet; I had no idea where this episode might fit, but Letha seemed to enjoy having her words written down, and after a while Dorothy added a bit about eating cold spaghetti and hiding a gold bar in her tent. When I asked a question, they both nodded and smiled, and it occurred to me that they appreciated being taken seriously, *and so did I*. If they were witnesses to legendary events, then I was a savvy journalist, and vice-versa.

We talked for more than an hour, excavating history or sharing a delusion, until friends of theirs arrived, an elderly couple with close ties to the treasure story. Out they all went to an early dinner, unlikely to attract special attention at the restaurant, yet in the universe of Victorio Peak, they were stars.

I read the clippings on the living room wall, noted the dop kits in the bathroom, the single mattresses on the bedroom floors. "Is There Really Gold in Them Thar Hills?" To pursue the treasure was to risk public ridicule. To write about the pursuit seemed to pose less of a risk.

• • •

In Las Cruces in late May, sunset lasts for hours. While Boz and I interviewed Terry Delonas, the sky outside the living room window turned from pink to purple to black. Terry answered our questions in a soft, clear voice. He had the effortless good manners of someone taught from birth to *behave*. His age was 44, but he looked younger, slender and boyish, neatly dressed in olive-drab slacks and matching shirt, with dark hair cut short and olive skin. He impressed me first for what he was not: not slick, not pompous, not in love with the sound of his own voice. He wore no gold chains, no ring that I remember. His crooked lower teeth gave his smile an innocent quality. He came across as gentle and sincere, the ultimate good boy, always polite, always attentive, with just enough mischief not to be boring. And he seemed to understand what would appeal to a pair of fiction writers: strong characters, vivid action, quirky details. He told us about his appearance at the Pentagon, his adventures in Congress, the time the commanding general of White Sands Missile Range showed up on his doorstep in full-dress uniform. When he spoke of his step-grandfather, he managed to convey a degree of reasonable doubt in Doc's more outlandish claims; but when he spoke of his grandmother, his voice thickened with emotion. She was the obvious source of his faith.

Near the end of the interview, three treasure hunters trudged in, dirty and exhausted. They had flights the next morning, home for Memorial Day weekend. One headed for the shower, one sprawled on the floor, one held up two garbage bags stuffed with laundry. You're looking at all I own, he said. This is clean. This is dirty.

Terry encouraged us to interview the treasure hunters. They'd just driven in from the peak; we were going out there in the morning. You'll see, the one with the laundry promised.

Shortly before we left, Terry described his first time at the peak. If you hear the freaky music, he said, you know you're supposed to be there.

The slim choice of restaurants open after nine o'clock led us to a place with gloomy lighting and vinyl upholstery.

What do you think? Boz asked.

He's no con, I said.

We talked about Terry over overdone steaks—his calmness, his focus, a certain ascetic quality, almost monkish. He hadn't mentioned a sweetheart. He slept on a single mattress. Boz asked if I'd spotted his Halcyon on the bathroom counter. I hadn't, but an anti-depressant made sense. Terry's project had grown into a million-dollar venture, with million-dollar headaches. And he was living in the same house as his mother.

Think he's gay? I asked.

Could be, Boz said.

Does it matter?

No.

The next day we saw. We stood at the top of Victorio Peak and heard the freaky music.

Could we translate that music into words?

Sure. Why not? We'd write something quick and easy. The kind of book you'd buy at the airport and bring to the beach. A blockbuster, soon to be a major motion picture, with Tom Hanks as Terry and Tommy Lee Jones as Doc. If the treasure hunters hit the jackpot, so would we. If they came up empty, well, a downer ending might have a certain literary charm. Either way, I had little to lose. I was almost forty. No book to my name. I could take a leave of absence from my half-time job, sublet my place in Oakland, kiss my sweetheart goodbye. She'd understand. We'd lived apart before. Besides, I'd grown up in the Southwest. I loved the desert. And maybe Boz's publishing success would rub off. That's why I said yes. I can't speak for Boz.

PART II

(Overleaf) Babe Noss with artifacts from Victorio Peak.

4

Petition

But his heart was in a constant, turbulent riot.
—F. Scott Fitzgerald

1988

Poised on the threshold of his makeshift office, Terry Delonas hesitated. A package lay on his desk. He'd stepped out just long enough to buy lunch, which he carried now in a brown paper bag. He'd been gone ten minutes at the most. Either the courier had timed the delivery perfectly while Terry's back was turned, or the package had simply materialized while he was away. Coincidences affected Terry. He attributed this sensitivity to his conservative Christian background. He couldn't divorce himself from the belief that even the most commonplace events held deeper meaning.

He stepped into the project office and shut the door behind him, purposely avoiding the Federal Express envelope, maneuvering around his desk as if the package held a bomb. Though he'd been waiting for the delivery since morning, there was no reason to rush now.

He settled in the far corner of the room on a black vinyl chair, absently running a finger over the electrical tape he'd used to mend its seams. He unwrapped his sandwich and put the waxed paper in the sack. It was three in the afternoon and he hadn't eaten since breakfast.

In that windowless office with the door shut, no one could possibly observe him, yet Terry behaved self-consciously, presenting the appearance of composure to the empty room. Most of his life he'd been content to listen, to observe from a safe distance. He'd grown up a timid child in a family unwieldy with personality. Pursuing this project had forced him to work against an essential element of his character, and the effort had propelled him into a sustained state of agitation, a chaotic emotional tumult. Fear bred images of failure, nightmares wherein he forgot an important detail and destroyed the project. But an equal portion of the agitation arose from a seemingly boundless optimism. Ostentatious scenes unreeled in his mind—fantasies of wealth, daydreams of redemption.

He let none of his internal commotion show, even in the privacy of his own company. By this time tomorrow, he would be through the worst of it—the presentation at the Pentagon to the Secretary of the Army. His flight to Washington was scheduled to leave Los Angeles early the next morning. In the Federal Express envelope, a petition awaited his attention. Between now and his presentation, he would have to study it closely. But first he would eat lunch. He would deny his inner havoc by taking time with the sandwich. The arrival of the package during the few moments he'd vacated the office was merely happenstance, he told himself, a coincidence that meant nothing.

The small room where he sat had previously served as storage space in the offices of Advanced Media Productions. Alex Alonso, the company's founder and principal video engineer, let Terry use the room without charge. Like virtually everything else connected with the project, the tiny office appeared more impressive at a distance. Alex answered calls in Terry's absence—making it seem that the project employed a secretary. When he told callers that Terry couldn't come to the phone, he didn't explain that Terry was a few blocks away at his real job, eking out a living.

Terry had thanked Alex for the office in a formal letter of welcome: "Congratulations on your decision to join the Ova Noss Family Partnership. I guarantee it will ruin your life."

Alex had responded with characteristic good humor. "Certain relatives have made predictions about my future," he had said, "but this is the first time anyone's put it in writing."

Ruin was an extreme word, Terry thought now. How many lives had the treasure ruined? *Consumed*, certainly, but *ruined?* He eyed the cheap bamboo blinds that covered not a window but a square of beige wallpaper, appraised the blonde desk and matching chair salvaged from an old elementary school, assessed the industrial gray carpet of his melancholy office. To address the Secretary of the Army, he'd compiled testimonials, gathered evidence, constructed a logical, no-nonsense argument. He'd hired Norman Scott, an experienced professional treasure hunter, to accompany him. Scott was the opposite of timid. He'd successfully lobbied the army before, and his tough-guy bluster would permit Terry to be reasonable and accommodating. Terry was passionate about the project but he knew better than to ride the passion. Passion had to remain below the surface, underneath the skin of things.

As he sat in the corner eating his sandwich, the peace of mind he pretended to possess became, for the moment, real. Then the door to his office swung open. Alex Alonso stuck his head in. "I saw the Fed Ex guy cruise through," he said. "How's it read?"

"I haven't opened it yet." Terry waved his sandwich as explanation.

Alex produced an exaggerated frown. He was twenty-four years old, and Advanced Media Productions was the seventh company he'd founded or co-founded; it wasn't in his nature to let the envelope lie unopened. He yanked the tab on the packet and began studying the petition. He often shot video for movie studios, and he had both the good looks and theatrical manner associated with the industry. The contortions his face went through while he read the petition could have come straight from a sit-com. Terry tried to laugh, but Alex's scowl made him nervous.

Finally, Alex waved the sheath of papers and said, "Who *wrote* this?"

Terry put the sandwich down. The calm interlude was over. "Norman Scott," he said. "Why?"

Alex made another face. "Is *analyzation* a word?"

"What? *Anal* what?"

"*Analyzation*, as in 'the analyzation of the material suggests…'"

"No," Terry said calmly, "that's not a word." His stomach clenched. Already he wished he had not eaten. "*Analysis* is what he means. Let me see."

"He uses it all over the place." Alex pecked at the page with his finger. "How about *blarring?* Ever heard of that?"

"I can't believe this," Terry said, scanning the page.

"The type's crooked," Alex went on, sweeping his hand over the manuscript. "I think *blarring* is supposed to be *blaring*, but what he really means is *glaring*."

Terry shook his head sadly, but when he spoke he sounded almost amused. "My family has been trying to get the army's attention for fifty years, and now I have to go to the Pentagon with this."

"If you ask me, that would be a *blarring* error," Alex said. "If you ask me, we should perform some *analyzation* on this, and type it over before your flight. When do you leave?"

To get to LAX in time for his departure, Terry had to leave Irvine by 5:45 in the morning.

"I know a guy who can type really fast," Alex said.

Terry flipped to the end of the petition: one hundred fifty pages. He estimated that a third of it was made up of photocopied documents, which left one hundred pages to revise and re-type. Writing style was unlikely to be of serious concern to the army, but he was acutely aware that many considered his project ridiculous. He didn't want anything under his control to diminish its credibility.

He sighed, the riot in his blood in full swing, and handed Alex the phone. "See if your friend can come over." He tossed the remains of his sandwich in the trash, opened his desk drawer, and groped inside for his emergency bottle of Halcyon. What he found instead was a chocolate bar. Terry didn't eat chocolate—it triggered migraines—but he'd purchased the bar that morning from a co-worker at American Savings and Loan.

Alex waved the pages of the petition dramatically. "We're going to need major caffeine," he said. "And a decent printer, some good bond paper..."

Terry handed him the chocolate bar. "Here," he said, "caffeine." He began investigating the drawer once again. "Call your friend, but give me the petition." He located the bottle of Halcyon. In the years to come, whenever people talked about the excitement of the project, he would recall the long night in a made-over closet, eating anti-depressants and editing Norman Scott's swaggering prose.

The petition consisted of nine parts.

Part I was a letter from Norman Scott requesting permission to conduct a ninety-day search of Victorio Peak. The letter established that Scott had interviewed more than three hundred people, including, in his words, "actual living witnesses of the events stated herein." Through a Freedom of Information Act request, Scott had obtained records from the U.S. Mint, the Department of the Treasury, the Secret Service, the FBI, the Land Office of the State of New Mexico, and several other government agencies. A thorough search, the letter contended, would settle the controversy that had plagued the army ever since it annexed Victorio Peak. Even if no treasure was found, Scott argued, the legend could finally be "put to bed."

Part II of the petition, a report prepared by the State Museum of New Mexico, recounted Doc Noss's discovery of the treasure, which included "gold bars, a chest of jewelry, Spanish armor, swords, crowns, the statues of several saints, and Wells Fargo chests." According to the report, "Noss also reported that there were twenty-seven skeletons in the room, and later he brought one out to prove it." The report described the 1939 explosion that blocked access to the treasure, and the army's subsequent annexation of the area.

Part III of the petition presented sworn statements from six men who had seen gold removed from Victorio Peak, starting with Joe Andregg, a retired Los Alamos electrician who helped Doc Noss in 1938:

> When I was a young boy about fourteen years old…I worked for Doctor M.E. Noss at Victorio Peak in the San Andres Mountains…. He was bringing gold and coins out of a shaft at the top of Victorio Peak. My job was to stand watch for him, to ride with him, feed the animals, do the chores, and to help with the…work on his mining claim.

Melvin Rueckhaus, a retired Albuquerque attorney, described a meeting with Doc Noss:

> Doc had found some intriguing metal bars but was afraid to come forward with them because of the Gold Act of 1934, which prohibited private citizens from owning more than two ounces of gold…. [H]e had seven bars and was interested in finding out [their contents] without official analysis…. I referred him to a pawnbroker named Jack Levitt…. Somehow a meeting was arranged at the pawnshop on 4th Street with a prospective purchaser, a Catholic priest. I went to Doc's hotel room and there he showed me seven, what appeared to be, *dore* bars of gold—*dore* meaning normal or semi-refined gold. The bars were less than a foot in length, less than three inches in breadth, and coming down to almost a vee on the bottom, blackish in color. I cannot guess the weight and did not do so at the

time.... Levitt insisted that [a] bar be sawed in order that any decent karat test could be given. Doc pulled out a knife and cut off a piece of gold without any trouble. Levitt...showed...the gold content of the interior area tested would be between eighteen and twenty karats.

Tony Jolley, an Idaho ranch owner, worked with Doc briefly in 1949, the night before Doc was killed.

[We] drove east out of Hatch [New Mexico] across the desert. We stopped at a windmill and took a shovel and dug up twenty bars of gold. Having been a prospector and familiar with what gold looked like, I became curious and asked Doc what the deal was with the gold bars. He told me that he had a partner that was flying in the next day and that he learned that his partner was going to take the gold and just keep going with it and that he wouldn't get anything out of it and that he wanted me to help him bury it so the man could not get hold of it. We took the gold to a basin on east of the well and went past a ranch house close to a place that Doc told me was an old Spanish fort that was built to fight the Indians and buried it. We then went back just past the ranch house around to the left and up the hill as if going to start up on a peak which I learned several years later was Victorio Peak. There I saw and counted ninety similar bars...

Jack Woods, a bulldozer operator who had been hired by Ova Noss to put in a road to Victorio Peak in 1949, described a gold bar she had shown him:

It looked like a large Baby Ruth candy bar, approximately nine inches long, two inches wide, with rough exterior, dark in color. With [Ova Noss's] permission, I cut a small sliver off the bar with my pocket knife.... Later on I was told by a jeweler in El Paso that it was gold.

The final two statements came from Air Force Captain Leonard Fiege and Airman Tom Berlett, who claimed to have discovered a cave full of gold bars at Victorio Peak in 1958. Both men passed lie detector tests administered by the U.S. Secret Service.

The cave was large enough to stand up in until I [Fiege] came to a small opening about thirty inches around. I shined my light into this hole and it looked like it opened up into a large shaft on the other end. I climbed through on my stomach and entered the large part of the shaft again. This shaft led into the main cavern. The dust was too thick and the air was foul and hard to breathe, so I sat down on what I thought was a dust-covered pile of rocks.... I started inspecting this area. The pile of so-called rocks was not rocks but smelted gold in bars about the size of a house brick.... With my flashlight I saw three piles of this gold all lined up and another pile off to the left that was partly covered by the wall of the cave that had fallen in.... I found it impossible to see farther than about fifteen to twenty feet because of the dust in the air. It was like headlights on a car shining into dense fog. I started getting sick again and made my way back out.... Tom [Berlett] and I handled the gold and thought about taking some of it out, but decided against it because we were not familiar with laws that governed the claiming of this gold. We might lose it all if we took it out now, so we decided to go back in and cover this area up so nobody could find it.... We caved in the roof and walls to make it look like the tunnel came to a dead end. Then we left.

Part IV of the petition documented the major attempts to recover the treasure—the army's clandestine operation in 1961, the Gaddis Mining Company excavation in 1963, and Norman Scott's Operation Goldfinder in 1977—and explained why each attempt had failed: inadequate funding, primitive technology, limited time.

Part V described recent advances in treasure-hunting technology. Dr. Lambert Dolphin, whose survey of the peak during Operation Goldfinder had substantiated key elements of the Noss claim, highlighted recent refinements in ground-penetrating radar and expressed his eagerness to participate in a more sophisticated search:

[During Operation Goldfinder] I made a thorough study of all accessible areas on and around the Peak using a ground-penetrating radar. The radar immediately confirmed the existence of a large, now inaccessible cavern directly under the summit of the mountain...and the radar also showed cracks and fissures around the summit in the vicinity of the Doc Noss Shaft which seemed to confirm the Noss account that he had at one time entered the cavern from the summit....

Part VI listed other claimants who had come forward over the years and summarized the current status of their claims. Scott argued that the army could maintain its impartiality by permitting each claimant to appoint a representative to observe the proposed search. In the event of a discovery, a court would decide the rightful owner.

Part VII included an assay of a gold bar Doc Noss had purportedly removed from the peak; a 1949 report from the New Mexico Bureau of Mines and Mineral Resources stating that the Noss claim was "certainly worthy of further investigation"; a letter from author David Chandler detailing the tonnage of gold mined within a sixty-mile radius of Victorio Peak; a letter from Dr. Oren Swearingen describing a map of Victorio Peak that had belonged to Doc Noss; a letter from the Commissioner of Public Land of the State of New Mexico declaring that the state had no objections to the proposed search; and a letter from the Governor of New Mexico approving the venture.

Part VIII—"Theory of Origin"—proposed possible sources of the treasure inside Victorio Peak: Indian mines predating the Spanish conquest of New Mexico; Spanish mines including the Lost Mine of Padre Larue; and plunder taken by the Apaches from caravans traveling the Jornada del Muerto and from later raids on miners, settlers, and stagecoaches.

Norman Scott concluded the petition in Part IX with a flurry of underlining:

> When you analyze the efforts of the other three entries, including the 1977 attempt by Expeditions Unlimited, they were <u>not conclusive</u>, they were not of <u>sufficient time or breadth</u>, and the state of the art technology had <u>not been developed</u> to the point to which it is today to determine the <u>existence of material</u> in the caverns.
>
> Therefore at this time we are in a position to <u>conclusively, once and for all, establish or refute</u> the legend by <u>implementing</u> the suggested proposal.
>
> Your respectful consideration would be greatly appreciated.

Judy Holeman, Terry's work associate and friend, left American Savings and Loan of Irvine at 5:30 and drove the few blocks to the offices of Advanced Media Productions. The weather was perfect, the late afternoon sun still bright on the stucco walls but low enough that her Toyota cast a long shadow across the pavement. Three years earlier she'd moved to California after a lifetime in the Midwest, where she and a business partner had owned and operated a bowling pro shop. A tall, friendly woman with a ruddy complexion and a bowler's build, Judy was forty-seven years old with three grown children and a husband now eight years in the grave. The project had excited her from the moment she learned of it. She'd become one of its first investors.

For the sum of twelve hundred fifty dollars, she'd purchased a quarter of a percentage point in the net value of the recovered treasure. A risky investment, even for a savings and loan officer, but if Terry's step-grandfather was on the level, and if the U.S. Army permitted a search, and if the treasure hadn't already been stolen, and if the value of gold remained steady—her twelve hundred fifty bucks could return five million.

As she parked outside the offices of Advanced Media Productions, the somber voice of a local newsman came over the car radio announcing that indictments were expected shortly for Lieutenant Colonel Oliver North and former national security advisor John Poindexter on charges that they had sold weapons to Iran and used the profits to fund the Nicaraguan contras. A correspondent in Washington speculated that the trial of these men would involve testimony from many of the highest-ranking officials in the government.

Judy waited to turn off her engine until the newsman switched to sports, his voice equally grave as he reported spring training scores. She hurried inside, where she discovered Alex Alonso sprawled across the carpet, a mess of papers before him. Terry sat in the black vinyl chair shaking his head and writing carefully in the margins of a sheet of paper. At the cluttered desk, a young man she didn't recognize typed on a computer keyboard at an inhuman pace.

"We're having to do a little rewrite of Norman's petition," Terry said. He described the bombastic prose and substandard usage, the spelling errors and grammatical snafus.

"I should have guessed." She settled on the couch, took a pen from her purse, and snatched a section of the report off the desk. "He was supposed to get it to us a month ago."

Despite Norman Scott's deficiencies as a writer, his hiring had moved the project out of the realm of fantasy. He'd put Terry's ambitious plans into action. The petition's off-kilter English and crooked type were just part of the price. Three years earlier, Terry had written a letter seeking Scott's assistance. It was Scott who had successfully badgered the army to authorize Operation Goldfinder in 1977, and he and Terry had met briefly.

> We have not spoken for many years, but since I have just finished viewing much of the video footage of the expedition, I feel as though we have just recently parted company.
> I must comment now that during that '77 effort, you did an amazing job of

dealing with the insistent press, anxious claimants, cumbersome military restrictions, fading memories, high hopes, and desert winds. I could wish that my grandmother, Ova, had been better informed and advised of your qualities and been able to finance the effort personally at that time. Anyway, belated congratulations and thanks for the much that was accomplished without a closer association.

Terry went on to remind Scott that his grandmother had reserved all her legal rights and placed the army on notice that she would some day present her own request for entry. The Ova Noss Family Partnership was now pursuing such a request.

> The Ova Noss Historical Research Institute and Archives has accomplished much research and documentation during the past many years by building on the vast amount of first-hand information and materials left by my grandmother, Ova, and working on expeditions with my aunt, Letha Guthrie.
>
> It may well be that the time is now right to complete the work of opening Victorio Peak and closing the mystery of the elusive treasure together. Please advise me of your current interest in the matter at your convenience.

The Ova Noss Historical Research Institute had two members—Terry and Judy—and its archives consisted of video and audio tapes they had made or copied, as well as the hodge-podge of artifacts that Terry's Aunt Letha had accumulated, but Terry understood the value of fancy titles. Scott signed a contract with the Ova Noss Family Partnership on October 1, 1987. Now, just five months later, he had arranged a meeting at the Pentagon with the Secretary of the Army.

"This guy really loves to *interface*," Alex said. "Hardly any *talking* or *writing* —it's all *interfacing*." The rapid tapping of keys in the background sounded like rain on a metal roof.

It was 2 a.m. Terry sat on the floor with his back against the desk reading the final section of the petition. "Norman is not a stylist."

The typist asked a question, his hands still gliding across the keyboard. "Where did you get the money for this trip to D.C.? Some big moneybags?"

"No," Terry said. "The investors are all just people who have a few thousand dollars."

"Who *had* a few thousand dollars," Judy corrected.

"Then I could be one," the typist said. "I had a few grand once."

Terry barely smiled. He was exhausted.

By the time they completed the editing, Alex had tracked down a laser printer that belonged to the father of the girlfriend of his ex-roommate. His comment seemed to sum up the night: "Who needs money when you have ex-roommates?"

Twelve hours later, Terry Delonas exchanged a quick handshake with Secretary of the Army John Marsh in a Pentagon hallway. Secretary Marsh lingered a moment to admire the sword Terry was carrying, an artifact Doc Noss had removed from Victorio Peak. Marsh was polite but perfunctory. One of his assistants, he explained, would preside over Terry's meeting.

Marsh had played football at the University of Virginia with one of Norman Scott's former classmates, retired colonel Charlie Mott. By means of this connection, Scott had arranged the meeting, and he stood now with Terry in the Pentagon hallway, along with William E. Casselman II, a Washington attorney Mott had recommended. Marsh quickly disappeared down the hall, leaving Terry, Scott, and Casselman waiting for an escort.

Casselman, aged forty-six, had served as deputy special assistant to President Nixon and as general counsel to President Ford. He towered above the other two, a big man in an elegantly tailored suit. It had to be an advantage for a lawyer to be that tall, Terry thought, although Casselman did not work through intimidation, relying instead on soft-spoken logic, an almost bashful insistence on reason. His physical presence and intellectual shrewdness permitted him to forego belligerence.

Scott didn't have this luxury. Short and heavy through the middle, Scott linked his hands over his large western belt buckle, a posture that made his undersized jacket cowl at the neck. The cuffs of his pants curled under his heels. It seemed to Terry that Scott pugnaciously rejected anything not in accordance with the way he saw the world—including, evidently, the size of his own belly and the length of his own legs. He had been in the treasure recovery business for over twenty-five years, conducting projects for the National Geographic Society, the Florida Oceanographic Society, the governments of Jamaica and the Bahamas, and the Smithsonian.

Terry stood between the unlikely pair. He wore a typical banker's suit, off-the-rack but handsome and well-fitted, meticulously pressed. According to the research he had done, the sword he carried had been made in the early

1800s in the Central European city of Klingenthal, in what was now Czechoslovakia. French cuirassiers had carried Klingenthal swords, and one theory for the presence of gold in Victorio Peak was that some of Maximilian's men had fled Mexico with stolen gold and died in the Jornada del Muerto. The sword was in perfect condition, complete with an elegant scabbard. It had caused trouble with airport security. "You can't carry weapons onto a commercial airliner," the security man had said, as if Terry had missed the past twenty years and didn't know the rules of the air. "It's an artifact, an antique," he'd patiently explained. "I can't check it like luggage." Ultimately, the pilot had agreed to keep the sword in the cockpit.

Terry had run into similar trouble with the Pentagon security screeners. They hadn't wanted to let him into the building with a weapon, however ancient, but once again he had prevailed by means of steady, logical, friendly persuasion. The sword was the most dramatic and impressive of the Victorio Peak artifacts that had remained in the family's possession, and Terry wanted physical evidence of the treasure that the army representative—whoever wound up seeing them—could hold in his hands.

Besides, Terry reasoned, a sword would appeal to a military man.

Presently, a uniformed officer appeared. Assistant Secretary John W. Shannon had reserved a conference room for their meeting. This was good news, Casselman said as they followed the officer down the hall. He spoke so softly Terry had to cock his head to hear. If they were seeing Shannon, then they were being taken seriously.

"Oh, they're going to take us seriously," Scott said. "Don't you have any doubts about that."

For reasons Terry couldn't readily articulate, Scott's insistence disturbed him. His grandmother had once sued the army for a billion dollars in an attempt to regain access to Victorio Peak. Terry wanted to work in a different fashion, cultivating good will and appealing to reason. He worried even now—especially now—that he would not have a real opportunity to present a logical argument. He had decided to start at the top because his grandmother had failed in several attempts to win cooperation from the various commanders of White Sands Missile Range. Whoever was in charge there now would follow the Pentagon's orders, Terry assumed. Top-down authority—wasn't that how the army worked?

The escort opened the door to the conference room. Within this austere chamber sat more than a dozen taciturn men, each in formal military regalia or a conservative suit, each armed with a pen and a yellow legal pad. To Terry, the men appeared vaguely annoyed, as if he'd kept them waiting for hours. His stomach seized and his mouth went dry, but outwardly he displayed his characteristic calm. A glance at his watch indicated that he was on time.

Casselman leaned close and whispered into Terry's ear a single word: "Lawyers." He said it as if each of the men bore an identifying mark on his forehead.

Assistant Secretary Shannon was fifty-four years old, recipient of the Bronze Star and the Legion of Merit medal, as well as a Distinguished Civilian Service Award from the Department of the Army, and an Outstanding Public Service Award from the Department of Defense. Terry was too nervous to be impressed. What struck him, even while he was being introduced to Shannon, was the enormous tension in the room, the unspoken animosity.

As soon as Terry handed the petition to Shannon, an aide snapped to attention, marched over, snatched the document, and sprinted out of the room—to make copies, presumably, but the utterly somber nature of the mad rush struck Terry as farcical.

He began his presentation with the story of the discovery. The audience of unsmiling lawyers inspired him to call his step-grandfather *Doctor* Noss. He chose not to mention *Doctor* Noss's lack of a medical degree or his criminal record. The sword passed from hand to hand while Terry described how the treasure was found and how it was lost. He had never told this story without getting a good response—until now. The stoic landscape of military lawyers unnerved him. "In the petition," he said, "you'll find affidavits that substantiate my grandparents' story—eyewitness accounts." He paused. No one yet had a copy of the petition. The presentation was going badly.

"None of the previous expeditions to recover the gold has been thorough," he said. "None has recognized the scope of the challenge, and none has employed the kind of high-tech equipment necessary for a scientific study. The Ova Noss Family Partnership has secured the financial backing necessary for the work and has acquired the technological expertise to achieve the task." One advantage of having rewritten the petition the night before was that Terry could lead the Pentagon lawyers through the document without looking at a copy. "White Sands Missile Range no longer actively uses the area surrounding Victorio Peak," he went on. "All we're asking for is ninety days." He felt like a man dropping stones down a well without hearing the answering splash. Even a cough would have been welcome.

He presented a short video that reiterated parts of his argument and included interviews with family members and key participants in the saga. Then he argued that resolution of this issue would benefit the army and the country in four specific ways.

First, the army would no longer be bothered by people illegally sneaking onto the range to conduct unsanctioned excavations at Victorio Peak.

Someone finally spoke. The army, Shannon said, was not aware of any trespassing problem.

Terry was so grateful for the response, his face erupted in a wide and inappropriate smile. "There have been fifty-seven recorded illegal entries in the past three years," he said, "all people attempting to investigate Victorio Peak—and who knows how many more that went unnoticed."

Shannon whispered something to an aide and asked Terry to continue.

The second benefit was historical. "Even if all we do is *dis*prove the story, we will have closed the book on one of the Southwest's most famous legends," Terry said.

Third, the partnership would pay taxes on any treasure recovered, so the government would receive a share of the wealth.

The fourth benefit Terry phrased with particular care. He didn't want to threaten the army with bad publicity, but he wanted to imply the possibility. "This project is likely to receive national attention," he said. "The army's cooperation could generate some very positive press." He alluded to the persistent rumors that the army had stolen the treasure. "We all know how damaging rumors can be," he said. "The army's cooperation could lay those rumors to rest."

Scott then explained that there were no other active claimants. He spoke briefly but emphatically of his qualifications to lead such a project.

Shannon asked a few questions about feasibility and liability—all simple to answer.

Terry sensed a peculiar letdown—as if the army had prepared for worse. Perhaps they expected him to threaten a lawsuit or leak a dark secret to the press. Perhaps, reeling from the Iran-Contra affair, they were relieved that he just wanted to look for the treasure. Or maybe his imagination was overheating.

After an hour and fifteen minutes, the meeting closed with this promise from Assistant Secretary Shannon: "The army will take your request under advisement."

"What does that really mean?" Terry asked Casselman as they shuffled from the room. "Is there some undercurrent I'm missing?"

"To take a request under advisement? It can mean anything."

"They'll have to respond in some fashion," Norman Scott said. "We're not going to be ignored. I won't permit it."

"They're putting us off," Terry said, but he voiced this complaint inside the walls of the Pentagon. He couldn't help but feel that getting there was an accomplishment. "At least we have their attention. For the past twelve years, they've had a policy of no entry whatsoever, and now they're going to consider it."

Despite himself, he imagined the army capitulating, the Secretary of the Army shaking his hand as flashbulbs popped and reporters shouted questions. The image would taunt him in the difficult months ahead.

5

Clovis Boy

Any story told twice is fiction.
—Grace Paley

1958

The number one record was "At the Hop" by Danny and the Juniors, but it did not appear on the jukebox of the Busy Bee Diner in Clovis, New Mexico. Jerry Lee Lewis's "Great Balls of Fire" also missed the cut, but you could hear the Everly Brothers harmonize on "Bird Dog" or Conway Twitty croon "It's Only Make Believe."

Terry Delonas, an impeccably well-mannered ten-year-old, bussed tables at the Busy Bee for his father. Gus did not care for rock 'n' roll. Even the Silhouettes' big hit "Get a Job"—an edict close to Gus's heart—got no play time at the diner.

The Busy Bee had not been capriciously named. Gus worked long days and his family worked with him. Terry's mother Dorothy managed the cash register and Terry's older brother Jim washed dishes. The brothers worked weekends during the school year and every day during the blistering summers.

The Busy Bee was known for good food and low prices. The building itself was long and narrow with a solid mahogany counter running its entire length and high "gangster" booths lining the opposite wall. The restaurant could accommodate four hundred people, which made it the best place to hang out in all of Clovis. Terry spent a good portion of his childhood in the Busy Bee.

The Delonas family was strict and hard-working. Gus and Dorothy permitted the boys to watch "The Rifleman" and "Wagon Train," but Gus disapproved of the smart-aleck attitude in "Maverick," and Dorothy thought "Peter Gunn" unsavory. However, there was one diversion to which the boys were permitted unlimited access: their grandmother, Babe.

Babe lived on the edge of town in a dilapidated house trailer augmented by two add-on cabana rooms constructed of plywood and tin siding. Mornings, when Terry and Jim dropped by, their grandmother would offer them greasy eggs and heavy pancakes drowned in white Karo syrup. "Grub," she called it, and neither boy questioned her choice of words. An extremely direct and often critical woman, Babe was not easy to be around. While the trailer remained in a constant state of upheaval—her many papers and files covered every available surface—she tolerated no sloppiness in the boys' appearance, and her pronouncements on the subject were seldom issued with tact. "Tuck your shirt in, you look like a pig," she would say, and the boys would quickly do as they were told.

Jim, less meticulous in his appearance than Terry, grew reluctant to visit, but the attraction for Terry never dimmed. Babe had something to offer that seemed more alive and lively than Jerry Lee Lewis, more wild and western than "The Rifleman"; she had stories—true stories—about adventures so outrageous and a treasure so enormous that Terry could barely comprehend the possibilities. He had to keep coming back to hear the tales again because some part always seemed to escape him, and he wanted to embrace the entire saga, to possess it, to make it *his*. But each time he listened, there would be a new detail to consider, yet another episode to take into account. Terry could never get hold of the chronicle; it eluded his grasp.

That same year, on the other side of the planet, Nikita Khruschev assumed power in the Soviet Union, an event the Clovis newspaper failed to report. A Russian-born author, Vladimir Nabokov, had American readers buzzing over his scandalous, magnificent *Lolita*, a novel that could not be purchased anywhere near Clovis. The introduction of the Bank Americard ignited a revolution in the spending habits of the American public, but no business in Clovis accepted plastic. Life in Clovis, New Mexico, was as dull as tap water. Little wonder that Terry Delonas grew obsessed with the story of his grandparents' discovery, a treasure of such magnitude as to rewrite history, as to make even an ordinary boy in a dusty desert town part of the greater human adventure.

Ova Noss was not a large woman, but something in her manner suggested tenacity and strength, as well as an intemperate and precarious disposition. She possessed a stoutness of spirit that took on dimension in her walk, in the decisiveness of her stare, in the tone of her speech. She tended to grow large in memory, so that a person returning to see her might be momentarily startled that she did not occupy the whole doorway.

Her hair had turned gray in middle age, and she piled it high on her head. She rode a horse like a man and shot a rifle better than all but the most skilled marksmen. She felt no compunction about calling a person a liar or a coward, whether that person was a cowboy or a four-star general, a respected historian or a timid ten-year-old.

Terry was her favorite grandchild, perhaps because, as he later put it, "I was the only one who really liked her." He would visit her before school and after. Weekends, he often spent the night on her lumpy couch. When strangers bearing maps came to consult about mining claims and treasure trove law, Babe would call Terry and tell him to hurry over. "Some folks showed up I want you to meet," she might say. "I won't decide if they're fools till you get here."

She became the center of his world, and her stories became his gospel. For Terry, the story of treasure buried in Victorio Peak was not a tall tale. It was not an entertainment. It was his legacy.

Time would reveal it to be a very demanding legacy, one that would leave him and his family open to derision, one that would strip down his life to an uncomfortable bareness. But he foresaw nothing of that future in 1958, sitting in Babe's decrepit trailer, listening attentively to an irascible woman tell incredible stories—stories that would become the map by which he plotted his future.

"Doc and I was out with some friends hunting mule deer," Babe began, standing over the dinette booth in the cramped trailer. The boys had stopped in to see her Saturday morning before reporting to work. "It was raining some, and our tent wasn't what you'd call waterproof."

Jim rose from the table almost immediately. Thirteen years old and almost as many years weary of his grandmother's stories, he launched into a litany of excuses for leaving.

"Finish them eggs," Babe said.

Jim bent over the table and scooped a last large, runny bite into his mouth, muttering good-bye while he fingered the yolk off his chin. He hurried past Babe, ducking as if she might take a swipe at him.

Terry encouraged her to continue the story.

She plopped down in the seat Jim had vacated. "November seven, nineteen hundred and thirty-seven, that was the day Doc first found the opening to the cave. It ought to be a national holiday, but nobody knows the whole story but me." After a purposeful pause, she added, "And you."

Terry beamed at her. The manipulation was transparent to him even then, but he didn't care.

"Some of our blood know the facts," she said, "but nobody really has that *gut* knowing but us."

Terry nodded enthusiastically. What she said was precisely accurate—his faith in the story inhabited not just his mind, but his body. He believed such visceral knowledge to be an unmistakable sign of truth.

"We went to the Hembrillo Basin out there with some other couples. It was cloudy and cool, the kind of day you come to appreciate in the desert."

"I thought it was raining," Terry said.

Babe leaned forward and stared at him. He couldn't tell whether she was trying to remember the weather or preparing to snap. "You ever known it to rain when it wasn't cloudy?"

"No, ma'am," he said.

"All right, then." She resettled herself in the chair and started again.

Babe's companion on the hunting trip was her second husband and the great love of her life, Milton Ernest "Doc" Noss. She described him as handsome and tall, with dark hair, three-eighths Cheyenne by blood, a foot doctor by trade. They had met in Oklahoma City in 1933, and Babe had become his nurse. The Great Depression struck no state harder than Oklahoma, and they moved first to Texas and then to New Mexico. It never occurred to Terry to inquire about Doc's medical credentials, and Babe didn't volunteer information on the subject. Terry would be an adult before he discovered that Doc had been run out of Texas for practicing medicine without a license.

Nevertheless, Doc had a busy practice in Hot Springs, New Mexico. "The town was full of bath houses," Babe explained, "and people came in there crippled, and they was hunting all kinds of doctors to treat this and that. There was plenty of foot-troubled people in Hot Springs, so Doc got plenty of practice."

He was a fastidious man, insisting on a neatly pressed shirt, the crease in his trousers sharp and straight. Terry liked this aspect of his grandfather, and he sometimes wore one of his suits to Babe's trailer for no reason but to emulate Doc.

"We drove most of the way out there," Babe continued. She and Doc and two other couples had camped near a little spring in the Hembrillo Basin, a rocky piece of New Mexico's high desert rimmed with modest mountains and populated with scrub trees, cactus, and yucca. Cotton-woods grew near the spring. It was a cool autumn day that may or may not have been rainy. Doc slipped away to hunt deer and was late returning. "We had to eat before sundown on account of the bugs," Babe explained, adding that Doc and his bulldog had almost missed dinner. That night, in the privacy of their tent, Doc revealed that he had found something un-usual that he didn't want the others to know about. He had climbed a pyramid-shaped peak in search of deer. At the top of the mountain, he discovered an opening partially covered by a rock. He crawled into the hole, inching his way down through the narrow space around a huge boul-der, striking matches now and again to look for snakes. After descending approximately thirty-eight difficult feet, he came to a little room, almost large enough to stand in. Without a lamp, he couldn't explore the room properly, but the discovery excited him.

He and Babe did not immediately return to the Hembrillo Basin. The long drive crossed rough terrain—stretches where a vehicle could get stuck in soft sand to its axles, rocky ground that could puncture a tire or crease an oil pan. Besides, they didn't want to appear too anxious to get back to the canyon. Already they were leery of attracting attention.

A few weeks after Doc found the cave, they drove back out in his step-van. They parked west of the basin and hiked over the rim. Two small moun-tains rose from the center of the bowl, Victorio Peak and Geronimo Peak, each about five hundred feet high from base to summit.

"We climbed to the top of Victorio Peak," Babe said. "We was on the highest point." Doc moved the rock that covered the entrance, and again he crawled inside the opening and descended to the little room. Equipped with a miner's lamp, he could see that there were paintings on the wall—Indian pictographs.

Babe followed him down. The descent was cramped and difficult, and there was barely space for the two of them at the bottom. A big boulder lay at one end of the room, covered by what Babe called a rat's nest. "You know, sticks and grass and hay," she said. "Enough to fill a washtub."

Terry interrupted her. "What did the Indian paintings look like?"

Babe shook her head. "I didn't pay close attention. I thought it was poor art."

Together, Babe and Doc shoved the boulder to one side. They discovered, in the limestone wall, an opening just large enough for a person to wriggle through—"a bottleneck," Babe called it—about two feet wide, eighteen inches high. Doc crawled through first. The hole in the solid limestone wall opened, after only a few feet of tight space, on what appeared to be a narrow shaft. By the dim light of his carbide lamp, Doc could make out the top of a wooden pole leaning against the wall directly beneath him. The pole had notches on either side—a crude kind of ladder that led down into the darkness. He tried to grab the pole, but it leaned against the wall beyond his reach. He shimmied back into the little room.

"Take a look for yourself," he said, his voice steady, but his eyes betraying that he had discovered something important. "Be sure and get your fill," he added, handing her the miner's lamp, "'cause from now on you're gonna be up top—with a rifle, standing guard. I don't know what's down here, but we're gonna find it."

Babe crawled into the hole. It was an even tighter fit for her. She made it to the shaft and stared down at the ladder. The silence and the dark expanse beyond the weak beam of her lamp brought to mind the term "bottomless pit." She took a deep breath before inching her way back through the bottleneck.

To get his feet onto the ladder, Doc would have to wriggle through the bottleneck on his stomach, feet first, extending his legs into the shaft until he could bend at the waist and lower his feet to the pole. If the pole didn't hold his weight, he would fall to whatever lay below, and—if he survived—

he'd have no way to get back out. He decided to postpone this descent until he had a good rope.

The climb up and out of the little room was more strenuous than Babe anticipated, and she was exhausted when she reached fresh air. The afternoon sun shone brightly on the canyon. It came as a shock—she had expected it to be much later.

Far below, Doc yelled, "You out?"

"Yeah, I'm out. I ain't gonna fall and crush you."

"Can't be too safe," he called back.

Babe chuckled at this, but as she surveyed the canyon again—the brush and cactus, the stunted trees, the dry creek bed, the cottonwoods near the spring—it struck her that they would need to be careful.

They waited almost a month to return to the peak. Doc carried a rope down into the room decorated with Indian paintings and anchored it around a boulder. He backed through the bottleneck on his stomach, holding tightly to the rope with one hand.

Babe stayed above with a rifle and a box of supplies, guarding the entrance. She shoved the rock back over the opening, leaving a small gap. Around her ankle, Doc had tied a clothesline, and they had worked out yanking signals; two quick tugs meant that he was coming up, and she should push the rock off the hole. She sat with the rifle across her lap, watching the canyon for movement, waiting.

Doc slithered backwards on his belly into the bottleneck until his legs were through and he could bend at the waist. Then he scraped the toe of one boot down the rock wall to locate the top notch of the pole ladder. He eased himself down slowly, shifting his weight from the rope to the ladder. The pole cracked, and he began falling, the rope burning his hands before he could regain a tight grip on it. His body banged the rock wall. He hung from the rope and gasped for breath. The pole was too brittle to support him.

Down below, the rope trailed off into darkness. He could lower himself the length of the rope easily enough, but what would be waiting for him? Even if there was a floor to stand on, would it support his weight? He climbed hand over hand back up to the opening. Pulling himself into it, he scraped his hands and chest, and by the time he had tugged himself through the bottleneck, his bleeding palms ached.

Terry interrupted his grandmother to pose a question. "Why didn't he wear gloves?"

"You can bet he did from then on," Babe said, "but at that time we didn't have no idea what we was getting into." She shook her head forcefully, her bouffant quivering like gelatin. "We didn't have good light either," she said. "Not like they have nowadays. You couldn't see past your own hands, and if your nails were dirty, you couldn't see them. You might think you was in a big cave, but when you took a step you'd see the wall's right in front of your nose. Doc had to take it slow. But before he climbed up, he tied a big knot in one end of the rope and sent it flying back down the shaft. It hit bottom, and by tugging on the rope, he was able to figure that it was about a twenty-five foot drop." Babe smiled. "That Doc could figure things out."

They returned to the peak in late December, but again Doc failed to get to the bottom of the shaft. "Ain't many men would even have tried," Babe added defensively. Snow covered the Hembrillo Basin in January, and they waited out the cold weather. Doc didn't want to leave a trail in the snow.

They would return several times before, in March of 1938, Doc actually lowered himself all the way down the shaft and onto the dirt floor below. He wore a vest with zippered pouches for his compass, tape measure, and any rocks or artifacts he might want to haul out. It would be a difficult climb, and he'd need both hands. From the opening at the top of the peak to the floor of the painted room was roughly thirty-eight feet. The drop from the bottleneck to the bottom of the shaft was just as he'd figured before, twenty-five feet. At the bottom of the shaft was a long and narrow cave running east-west through the middle of the mountain.

Unlike the walls, which were solid limestone, the floor of the cave was made of dirt, and sloped downward as Doc cautiously moved to the east, feeling for openings along one wall and then the other. After a few yards, the walls grew even more narrow, pinching together, and Doc thought he might have to turn sideways or crawl. According to his tape measure, he had covered more than sixty feet when his lamp revealed another solid rock wall, a dead end—or so it appeared at first. Before stepping to the wall, Doc got on his hands and knees. He crawled to the edge of a large hole in the cave floor. His heart beat heavily. Had he been paying less attention, he might have tumbled into the opening.

He lay on his belly and shone the light into the hole. The slanting floor he'd been hiking down was made of dirt and rock wedged between the limestone walls. The floor of the walkway appeared to be about four feet thick. Underneath the hole lurked dead air and darkness.

After considering the problem a few minutes, he took off his shirt. He tied the miner's lamp to one sleeve and lowered it slowly into the opening. The lamp illuminated another dirt floor several feet below.

Doc raised the lamp and put his shirt back on. He tossed a rock the size of his fist through the hole. It hit the dirt below with a reassuring thud, but he wished he had better evidence of the solidity of the next walkway. He lowered himself through the hole and dropped onto the dirt floor. This walkway sloped downward and to the west, a zag to the first one's zig. At the end of this walkway was another hole, and Doc dropped through it, marching east again, continuing downward.

Babe had trouble describing the walkways. She had never seen them herself and based her description entirely on Doc's words. He had explained that the cap of Victorio Peak was made of solid limestone, but there was a crack in it, a fissure that ran all the way down the cap, deep into the mountain. When they crawled through the bottleneck, they entered this fissure. The dirt walkways were wedged between the walls of the fissure and angled downward from west to east, then east to west. As far as Doc could tell, the walkways had been formed naturally. Their surfaces were smooth, while the bottoms were rocky and rough, which suggested that they had been altered by hand—or by foot, by the movement of people back and forth. He reckoned that water could have done the smoothing, except that the cave was conspicuously dry.

The earthen walkways zigzagged down the deep crack in the limestone like switchbacks down a mountain road. The final walkway ended at the bottom of the limestone fissure. Doc estimated that he was about two hundred feet below the opening where Babe stood guard with a rifle. The fissure ended in a slant of rock—shale, Doc decided, not limestone. He had reached the bottom of the limestone cap. Gingerly, he stepped onto the sloping shale and immediately lost his footing, sliding down a few feet to the opposite wall.

The miner's lamp went out, and Doc sat in the heart of the mountain in the middle of a great darkness. It took him only a moment to relight his lamp. It was then, sitting on his butt, appreciating the dim light, that he spotted the tunnel and got up to investigate. Nothing but a dark hole, a black maw in the shale that went beneath the limestone. He fell to his knees— not to pray, but to crawl inside the tunnel's mouth.

Babe was not inclined to worry about Doc. "If ever there was a man could take care of himself, it was Doc," she told Terry.

The boy glanced at the electric clock that sat on top of the refrigerator. He was almost late for work, but Jim would let their parents know where he was. "Trapped," Jim would say, but Terry did not feel trapped by his grandmother's story, although he did feel the closeness of the cave's walls.

"But that day I got scared," she said. "He'd been gone so long, I was half thinking what to say at his funeral." She had watched the sun move across the Hembrillo Basin. She'd spotted deer near the spring, seen a coyote chase a rabbit across the dry creek bed. In the afternoon, she'd spotted hunters. It hadn't been bad entertainment, watching the deer elude them, silently cheering the hunters' dejected march out of the canyon.

As dusk approached, she grew frightened. She would have to decide whether to try to climb down after him—she had no light but matches—or hike to the truck and drive for help. Really, though, that was no decision. She knew Doc wouldn't want her showing the cave to anybody, no matter what. Her choices became clear: she could wait for him, she could go after him.

She waited. The sun set and she built a fire. It was early enough in spring that the chill set in quickly. She ate jerky and heated a can of beans. She reminded herself of all the scrapes Doc had been in and how he'd survived them. Yet she knew that trouble had a way of catching up with people. She ate her beans and watched the basin for movement.

It was well after dark when she felt the clothesline tug. "Good god," she said when he finally crawled out.

He was layered in dirt, and his shoulders slumped from fatigue. His shirt carried circles of sweat at the armpits and beneath his neck. His knees were muddy.

"You made a campfire," he said. "People could see."

"There ain't a person in this basin. I looked it over so many times today I can tell you how much each tree growed."

Doc crawled over next to the fire, his arms trembling under the weight of his body. He unbuttoned his vest, then unzipped a long inside pocket. "Look here." He pulled out an old leather bag.

"It looked like a horse's feed bag," she told Terry. Inside the leather pouch were silver coins. "Old foreign money," Babe explained, "like you never seen before." She held a kitchen spoon and unconsciously rubbed her thumb over the spoon's silver declivity. "That was the first of the treasure," she said. "I can still remember holding it in my hands."

Terry, too, could feel the coins, cool and metallic, on his palms, and could also feel the surge of excitement, the rush of elation as they began to understand the proportions of their discovery.

"I ain't got a one of them coins now." Babe set the spoon on the table. "At the time, all we could see was that the coins—and the other things he brought out—would stake us to a better operation. We didn't see reason to save any when we had a whole mountain full of treasure just waiting for us to come get it." She whisked away Terry's plate. He had finished eating twenty minutes earlier.

"Anyways," she went on, ambling over to the sink, "we kept going back. Doc couldn't make the trek down and back more than once in a day. Took too long, and he got wore out."

In the next several months, Doc would carry up jewels, Spanish style stirrups, a sheathed sword, ancient papers, clothing. He told Babe there was a labyrinth of caves and tunnels circling around a huge central chamber— "the treasure room," he called it. An underground stream crossed one of the caves, while another cave was filled with human skeletons, their bones scattered about, as if by a wild animal. The only way Doc could determine the number of dead was by counting the skulls.

The tunnels that extended from the room were "large enough to drive a train through," he reported, and in one he found an old ox cart. There were several stacks of black metal bars. "Ricks of pig iron," he told Babe. He found knives with jeweled handles, elaborately decorated swords, trunks containing velvet and lace, metal boxes holding letters mailed from Europe, religious statues, gold crosses, wooden crates filled with precious gems.

He lugged out a gold crown that Babe later cleaned in her kitchen sink. She was standing at the trailer's sink as she recounted this episode, and

Terry tried to imagine her scrubbing a priceless crown instead of his dirty breakfast plate.

"I took it to a jewelerman in El Paso," she said, "and when he seen it, he started talking to us real polite. The crown had two hundred forty-three diamonds and one big pigeon-blood ruby." Later, Doc would haul out ancient armor—a breastplate with chain mail—covered in cave droppings. Babe and her daughters took the armor to a radiator shop and had it dipped in solution to clean it.

She asked a number of times for Doc to bring up one of the bars of pig iron, and he finally complied. "That's the last one of them things I'll ever tote out of there," he said to her when he climbed from the opening. He dropped the bar on the ground near her feet. "I pretty near threw it down two or three times, it's so heavy." He encouraged her to pick it up. "Go on," he said. "Feel the heft of it." It was so heavy she could barely lift it. However, she noticed that the bar had been scuffed by the rocks, and the black had scraped away from one corner. Beneath the black, the bar was yellow.

"Look at this," she said.

Doc studied it. He took his knife and scraped away more of the black. When he pressed the knife-blade against the bar, it made a deep groove.

"If this is gold," he said, "and all that other down below, we can call John D. Rockefeller a tramp."

This was Terry's favorite part of the story, and it was all he could do not to cheer.

On his next trip down into the mountain, Doc counted the stacks of bars—the width of each stack, multiplied by the length, times the height. He estimated that there were sixteen thousand gold bars in Victorio Peak.

"Yes sir," Babe said, surveying her mealy trailer, "if I met a Rockefeller even today I'd call him a tramp."

Terry did not doubt her word. "Grandma," he said, "I've got to get to the diner."

She nodded. "It's good for a boy to work." She glanced at the clock on the refrigerator. "But you ain't all that late. Wait one more minute."

Terry recognized this as a command, not a request. He remained seated while she slipped out of the kitchen. The tale of the discovery of the treasure was only a small part of Babe's story, but it accounted for a large part of

Terry's fascination. The later chapters were full of mistakes, betrayal, bad timing, and the worst kind of luck. Doc had tried to widen the passage with dynamite; the explosion had caused a cave-in; and he'd spent the rest of his life—a life cut short by a bullet—trying to get back to the treasure room.

Now and again Terry felt the righteous indignation of a prince denied his throne, but more powerfully he felt for his grandmother, how her life, which could have installed her in a mansion, had left her instead in a rundown trailer in Clovis, New Mexico.

"We just got to find a way back to the peak," Babe called from the other room. "Me and you, Terry boy. Crack that mountain open, and the world'll see we ain't fools. You're the one gonna help me do it. It's in your blood."

Although there was no one in the room to see him, Terry nodded, agreeing, promising not to let her down.

Soon he would run to the Busy Bee. His father would not mind that he was late. Gus put little stock in the gold tales, but he believed in the importance of family. In fact, he had a surprise for Terry. The jukebox man had come, and Gus had permitted him to add Terry's favorite song, the current Elvis Presley hit. Gus had not changed his mind about rock 'n' roll, and he had not been convinced to carry the song because of its enormous popularity. He'd added it because his son loved both Elvis and Babe, and Elvis's big hit of 1958 was "Hard Headed Woman." It was an irony even Gus could not resist.

In the years to come, Terry would discover that the hard-headed woman he idolized had left things out of the story she told him, omitting the fact that Doc had been to prison, that he had eventually left her for another woman. And Terry would hear strange variations of the story from his relatives, as well as documented criticisms of Doc's character, the shady circumstances surrounding Doc's fatal shooting, sworn testimony that Doc was nothing but a con man. For the remainder of his life, Terry would hear experts scoff at the story of Doc's treasure, but he would also hear the powerful timbre of conviction in his grandmother's voice, the plaintive note of loss.

At age ten, in Babe's tiny kitchen, Terry had no reason to question any aspect of the story.

"Here you go," Babe said, stepping through the doorway. She held in her hands the sheathed sword Doc had taken from Victorio Peak. "Take it," she said. "Grip it yourself."

Terry accepted it from her. His hands did not tremble, but there was a trembling inside him, as if a membrane between his imagination and the actual world had burst.

"You like the feel of that?" Babe asked him.

Terry nodded.

"That's pure history you're holding," she said. "Your family history and world history both."

He ran his hands up and down the gray metal several times, so that later, while he bussed tables at the Busy Bee, listening to the jukebox and imagining the mountain, he could cup his hands over his face and breathe in the metallic scent of his destiny.

6

Gridlock

*If each day you travel halfway
closer to your destination,
you will never reach it.*
—*Zeno's Paradox*

1988

On April 28, seven weeks after the Pentagon promised to take his request under advisement, Terry drove to White Sands Missile Range to meet with the commanding general. The early morning sun glinted off the haphazard array of old rockets mounted like trophies on metal stands just inside the entrance to the base. Rascal, Matador, Honest John, Hawk—the whitewashed missiles reminded Terry of a bygone era when houses had fallout shelters, schools held duck-and-cover drills, and most red-blooded American boys loved to play war.

The base—founded on February 20, 1945, a day after the U.S. Marines raised the flag on Iwo Jima—owed its existence to the fear that America lagged behind Germany in the field of rocket science. Though the German surrender appeared imminent, Army Intelligence nonetheless wished to close the gap. The sparsely populated Tularosa Valley provided an ideal site to test missiles. A cadre of German scientists led by Werner von Braun relocated after the war to White Sands, which grew into the world's largest missile range, covering more than 4,000 square miles, including the small promontory known as Victorio Peak.

Terry's grandmother had tangled with almost every general who'd commanded the base. As Terry presented his driver's license, vehicle registration, and proof of insurance to a taciturn sergeant at the visitor's office, he remembered his Aunt Letha's account of calling on General Eddie with Babe back in 1952:

> We had no gold. All we had was a story, and the sword. We must have sounded like a couple of nuts. General Eddie said, "If you can prove to me that there's gold out there, I'll let you on." So, like two stupnagels, we got everyone who had seen the gold to make a notarized statement. We took them to Eddie. He said: "If anyone digs that gold out there, it's going to be me or the army."

Babe had enlisted the support of Senator Dennis Chavez of New Mexico, who wrote a letter to General Eddie asking him to grant access to the peak. The senator's son took Babe and Letha to see the general a second time. He again refused to help—but the story had a kicker. Babe swore forever after that on the map of the base hanging in Eddie's office, Victorio Peak was circled in red, and inside the circle someone had written "Noss Treasure."

Terry regarded the story as part fact and part paranoid exaggeration. He expected no trouble from the current general. Unlike Babe, who bowed to no one, he would show the general respect. That's why he'd worn a conservative suit. That's why he'd brought along Norman Scott and Lambert Dolphin, recognized experts in their fields. Besides, the Assistant Secretary of the Army had already advised the general to cooperate.

If that wasn't good enough, Terry carried a secret weapon in his inside jacket pocket. Scott had received a call the week before from a man offering to sell photographs of a secret digging operation currently in progress at the peak. The man had motorcycled to the rim of the Hembrillo Basin and taken the photographs using a telephoto lens. After haggling over the price, Scott had met with the man and acquired the photos. Our ace in the hole, he'd called them. Terry now gave them a little pat before entering the general's conference room, where a dozen White Sands personnel and three representatives from the Pentagon sat at a long table.

In the middle of introductions, General Thomas John Paul Jones strode into the room in combat boots and camouflage fatigues, his shaved head gleaming. Six foot four, a two-star general who'd started as a private, he aimed his chin at Terry and clenched both hands into fists. "How dare you go over my head?" he yelled.

Under less stressful circumstances, Terry might have found the question amusing, given the dizzying height of the general's head—but there was nothing funny about the general's profanity-laced tirade. He castigated Terry for not coming to him first. This was a local matter. It should have been handled locally. Instead, Terry had sneaked behind his back to the Pentagon. Spit flew from the general's mouth when he uttered the word *Pentagon*. Terry attempted to speak, but the general drowned him out.

He had two volumes, Terry discovered, "loud" and "screaming." Worse yet, he was charging Terry for this tongue lashing. ONFP would receive a bill for each participant's time: the general, his second-in-command, the judge advocate general, the base's civilian attorney, civilian financial officer, civilian environmental officer, and all the others. When it occurred to Terry that the meter was running, he wondered what would happen if he pulled out the photographs and informed the general that he was notifying the press of the illegal treasure hunt underway at Victorio Peak.

Fear held him back, not only fear *of* the general, but fear *for* the general—the bulging veins in his neck looked ready to pop. Terry wanted cooperation, not a stroke. The photographs would lose their value once he released them to the press. Any chance of smooth relations with the army would be shot.

He sank meekly into his padded leather chair and listened to Jones rant. Norman Scott, meanwhile, tapped the eraser of his pencil on a copy of the petition as if he were nothing but bored. Then he fiddled with the piece of silver bullion he wore on a chain around his neck, a memento from a treasure he'd recovered off the coast of Jamaica. Terry appreciated this show of impatience. For all his bluster, Scott had the nerve Terry lacked.

Jones ended his forty-five minute diatribe with a surprise announcement. "I'm going to approve your request," he said. Terry's elation lasted less than a second. "But I'm going to make your life hell."

The general's antagonism seemed strangely personal to Terry. He'd felt animosity from the Pentagon lawyers, but not like this. At the Pentagon he was a nuisance; at White Sands Missile Range he seemed to pose a threat. He couldn't help wondering if Babe's improbable tales of generals stealing treasure held any truth. He turned to Norman Scott. "I need a word with the general. In private. Can you set it up?"

A few minutes later, in the privacy of the general's office, Terry laid out the photographs he'd brought.

Remarkably, Jones didn't scream. "I'll look into this immediately."

Jones followed up on his promise by helicoptering out to the peak that afternoon with one of the Pentagon representatives. Terry drove out with Scott and Dolphin. No one spoke on the hike up to the shaft that Babe had excavated after Doc's death. Camouflage netting now covered the opening. An air compressor and a generator sat nearby, along with electric cable, air ducts, shovels, pickaxes, and dynamite.

Norman Scott pulled aside the netting. "Shall we?" he asked, but Jones refused to permit anyone to climb down the shaft.

"There's nothing going on here," he said. "I'll take care of it."

Despite the obvious contradiction between the two statements, Terry trusted Jones to halt the digging. His surprise and embarrassment were unmistakable. If the photographs accomplished nothing else, at least they'd induced him to lower his volume for a while.

Terry flew back to California with a new sense of urgency. The meter was running. When Norman Scott asked for a 50% raise, Terry could almost hear the click. ONFP paid Scott close to $5,000 a month, plus expenses, which typically mounted to another $5,000. Terry's own expenses—travel, telephone calls, etc.—might add $1,000 more to the total. The meeting at White Sands would cost an estimated $2,000.

Luckily, Craig Harrison kept finding investors.

Terry had met Craig not long after testing HIV positive. Terry had needed a place to live, and Craig had rented him the back room of his house in Newport Beach. Craig, too, had recently tested positive. Terry was one of the few people he told. Craig was flamboyantly gay, but he kept his disease in the closet—though he did drag Terry along to more than one bizarre doctor in pursuit of a miracle cure.

Handsome, graceful, creative, Craig was a master of presentation. Terry had seen him buy a 79-cent gift and spend $11 to wrap it. As maitre d' at the Irvine Hilton, he made small talk with hundreds of people a night. He loved to have the best story in town, and the Victorio Peak saga had entertained hundreds of diners. Now and then someone would be more than entertained. "How can I invest?" That's when Craig would introduce Terry.

No one could invest until Terry explained the risks. He liked to meet with potential investors on weekends, when the conference room at American Savings and Loan was free. He'd bring in Ralph Monroe to talk about the possible origins of the treasure. Ralph was 71 years old, measured, deliberate, the antithesis of Craig. Terry admired his combination of devout faith and worldly sophistication. A law school graduate and certified public accountant, he'd worked for Howard Hughes and balanced the books for the Los Angeles Country Club.

"I'm no historian," Ralph would tell potential investors, "but I do fancy myself a student of history."

He'd start with the seven cities of gold, recount the mysterious disappearance of the Aztecs' great riches, describe the caravans that traveled through the treacherous Jornada del Muerto, mention the legend of Padre Larue and the rumors of Maximilian's lost treasure, and conclude with the daring exploits of Chief Victorio.

Then Terry would hand over a copy of the "Confidential Private Placement Memorandum," a two-page description of the limited partnership agreement, which was still being finalized. He would read aloud the "Risks Inherent in Salvage Operation":

(a) Certain uncontrollable variables.

(b) No known method of assessing the probability of locating a cavern. No assurance that treasure remains in the cavern or that whatever remains in the cavern will be salvageable or of significant value.

(c) No guarantee that the Secretary of Army will issue a permit to ONFP.

(d) No guarantee that a treasure was actually discovered by Doc and Ova; and no guarantee that such a treasure, if discovered, was not subsequently removed.

(e) No guarantee that Ova has not signed away her rights to such a treasure or that a court may assign rights to the treasure to the State of New Mexico, Federal Government, the Government of Mexico, the Mescalero Apache tribe, or individuals who may convince the Court of their superior rights thereto.

(f) No guarantee that environmental or other agencies may not interfere with the work contemplated by ONFP.

(g) Imponderable risks.

(h) Safety hazards on site, no guarantee of suitable insurance coverage.

(i) No guarantee that if treasure recovered, adequate security will be provided.

(j) Subject to unknown and unpredictable expenses.

The paradoxical effect of emphasizing the risks, Terry had already discovered, was that it seemed to make people *more* eager to invest, as if accepting the risks somehow proved their shrewdness and courage.

"Don't give us your house payment," Ralph would say. "This has to be money you can afford to lose."

Terry would close by outlining the three phases of the project. During Phase I, before the petition had been presented to the army, a one-percent interest in the project had cost $5,000. During Phase II, the current phase, a one-percent interest cost $10,000. Phase III would begin when and if the army granted permission for a search. One percent would then cost $80,000.

"According to our lawyer in Washington," Terry would say, "we're on the fast track to Phase III."

Not everyone who heard the pitch invested, but so far enough money had trickled in to pay Scott on time—most months. A Santa Ana financial consultant had promised to bankroll the project once all the bureaucratic hurdles were cleared. A consortium of businessmen from Oklahoma City had also expressed interest in the project, but they, too, preferred to wait and see, despite the financial incentives of investing before the next phase began.

Meanwhile, the meter was running and Terry feared that the project might go broke just as success came in sight. In September, Terry terminated Scott's full-time contract. Scott threatened to pursue a permit on his own.

"What I do from now on is my affair," Scott said in a telephone conversation with Ralph Monroe, "and what you do is your affair. Those two may be in conflict with one another."

"That would be unfortunate," Ralph said.

"I could be doing something with the army," Scott went on, "and you could be doing something with the army, and the poor army could see a divided force, and—"

"That would be unfortunate," Ralph said again.

"I don't want to get into a pissing contest," Scott said.

"This is the time to work together and get the job done," Ralph said. "You stand to benefit handsomely in every way, as I'm sure you recognize."

"Providing I'm involved in the project," Scott said.

"Well, yes, you are!" Ralph said. "Of course you are!"

The two of them reached an uneasy truce, but afterwards Ralph counseled Terry not to trust Scott. *A gorilla on a chain*, Ralph called him. Terry liked the phrase but not the added worry.

When the Assistant Secretary of the Army invited Terry back to the Pentagon in mid-October—seven months after he'd filed the petition, seven long and expensive months—he felt less jubilation than relief. Riding to the meeting with Bill Casselman, he compared the army's decision-making process with the bumper-to-bumper traffic. "Gridlock is a way of life around here."

Casselman agreed about the traffic but not about the army. "If they approve our petition today—and we have no reason to believe they won't—it will set a land speed record. Seven months is the blink of an eye in bureaucratic time."

Terry clasped his hands on top of the briefcase in his lap and tried to adjust to the sluggish pace. Negotiations with General Jones and his staff at White Sands had certainly set no speed record. Jones insisted that ONFP contract all work through the base. Terry had objected because the base would charge far more than any civilian contractor. Jones also insisted that ONFP reimburse the base directly for all expenses incurred. Terry had agreed to this condition. It didn't matter to him whether ONFP's checks went to Washington or White Sands, as long as the charges were reasonable. His concession, unfortunately, had failed to sway Jones, who refused to budge on the contracting issue. He could only hope that Jones's cooperation would improve once the army okayed the project.

Terry and Casselman arrived at the Pentagon just seconds before the meeting was scheduled to begin. An escort ushered them directly into Assistant Secretary Shannon's office. Shannon was joined by only one lawyer this time, Gordon Hobbs, whom Terry remembered because of his resemblance to Truman Capote. Hobbs had attended the first meeting at White Sands and helicoptered to the peak with General Jones. He carried himself like the ultimate bureaucrat—gray suit, gray hair, gray skin. There was no sign of flashbulbs, popping or otherwise, but Terry didn't care as long as the army let the project go forward.

Hobbs opened the meeting with a bland recitation of the specifics of Terry's request. The army, he concluded after fifteen minutes, had no objection in principle to a search of Victorio Peak.

"No objection in principle?" Terry repeated.

"However," Shannon said, "there are some serious concerns that must be resolved before a search could proceed."

"The reimbursement issue," Hobbs said.

"That's no problem," Terry said. "We'll pay whoever you want us to pay. We don't expect a free ride."

The problem, Hobbs explained, was that under current law no mechanism existed to permit the base to accept direct payment for administrative expenses.

Bill Casselman cited Department of Defense Regulation 3200-11, which General Jones himself had mentioned several times.

"Inadequate," Hobbs said. "Our staff, after careful review, has determined that the regulation is inadequate for your purposes."

"You may wish to seek legislation," Shannon said.

"But this is just a minor technical point," Terry said.

"The army is in favor of permitting a search," Shannon said. "Once the issue is resolved."

The meeting ended, and Terry didn't ask Casselman for clarification until they were once again in the car. He couldn't reconcile the sympathetic tone with the discouraging words.

"Did they tell us yes?"

"No."

"Did they tell us no?"

"Yes."

"How big a deal is legislation?"

"We need an act of Congress," Casselman said. "An act of Congress for a personal project, an individual agenda." He hit the brakes as the car ahead stopped abruptly. The traffic was as congested as before.

How would Babe have handled this news? Terry wondered. Not meekly, he felt sure. Something in his stomach seemed to sink and keep on sinking. For a moment he was transported to the waiting room outside the Special Diseases unit of the Orange County Health Clinic. A counselor called his name and invited him to a tiny office to hear the results of his AIDS test. As soon as he saw the counselor—corduroy sports coat with elbow patches, bad haircut, apologetic half-smile—he knew the worst. "Have you ever been suicidal?" the counselor asked. "Do you have family or friends in the area?" The counselor said that only 30% of those who tested positive would go on to contract AIDS.

A horn honked behind them. Casselman's car had come to a stop, though the light ahead was green. The intersection looked like a parking lot.

"I guess they knocked us off the fast track," Terry said. "No land speed record."

"We still have options," Casselman said.

Terry appreciated the note of optimism, but it didn't alter the truth: he was stuck with the meter running, and the click in his ears sounded deafening.

7

Goldfinder

You talk about a godforsaken place. This is it.
—Dan Rather

1977

Seventy pairs of taillights bobbed toward Victorio Peak in the chill March dawn. The last pair belonged to a green Dodge van carrying the crew of KENW, the public broadcasting station in Portales, New Mexico. As the outline of the San Andres Mountains slowly emerged from the darkness and dust, the driver of the van offered advice to the reporter and the cameraman. The driver was a part-time student at Eastern New Mexico State with no experience in journalism, but he kept suggesting questions to ask, shots to look for, possibilities, angles. This twenty-eight-year-old sophomore, who had convinced KENW to cover Operation Goldfinder, probably knew more about the coveted treasure than anyone except Babe Noss, but there was one crucial gap in his knowledge. He'd never set foot on Victorio Peak. Soon, though, unless the army turned him back, Terry Delonas would enter the realm of his dreams.

If not for the Watergate break-in, Operation Goldfinder might never have been permitted. The break-in begat the hearings of the Senate Select Committee on Presidential Campaign Activities, and the hearings begat the nationally televised testimony of Presidential counsel John Dean. On June 25, 1973, while detailing events surrounding the cover-up, Dean mentioned a fragment of lunchtime conversation between Attorney General John Mitchell and White House chief of staff H.R. Haldeman.

> Mr. Mitchell raised the fact that F. Lee Bailey…had a client who had an enormous amount of gold in his possession and would like to make an arrangement with the government whereby the gold could be turned over to the government without the individual being prosecuted for holding the gold. Mitchell was addressing his request for assistance to Haldeman but Haldeman was non-responsive and the matter was dropped.

Those few sentences—comprising less than a paragraph of Dean's 245 pages of testimony—could hardly have been more peripheral to the Watergate scandal, but the next day *The Washington Post* published a story headlined "Attorney Can't Get U.S. to Take Gold." Newspapers around the country quoted F. Lee Bailey: "Give me a helicopter and half an hour and I'll find 292 bars of gold." The flamboyant attorney, defender of the Boston Strangler and author of *The Defense Never Rests*, estimated the total amount of hidden gold at one hundred tons, with a value of more than 250 million dollars.

Four months earlier, in February of 1973, Bailey had contacted the White House seeking permission for his clients to enter an unnamed military base, recover an unspecified amount of gold, and turn it over to the government. In exchange, the government would pay an amount equal to half the gold's value, tax free, and guarantee immunity for any crimes related to its recovery. When a White House aide had asked for a sample of the gold, Bailey's clients produced a small, cigar-shaped bar about seven inches long, dotted with bubbles. The chief of the laboratory of the Bureau of the Mint assayed the bar himself. The matter was treated as strictly confidential. When the aide informed Bailey of the results—the bar, apparently of antique origin, contained sixty percent gold and forty percent copper—Bailey enthusiastically repeated his initial proposal and gave the aide a second bar to assay. Three days later the general counsel of the Department of the Treasury informed Bailey that any gold found on U.S. government property belonged to the U.S. government and could not be acquired by trespassers. Furthermore, the second bar had proven to contain no gold. A Treasury agent returned the bars to Bailey's public relations consultant. Columnist Jack Anderson wrote about the stalled negotiations in his Washington Merry-Go-Round column, but the government had remained intransigent until John Dean's brief reference to "an enormous amount of gold."

Before Dean, the Victorio Peak treasure had attracted mostly regional attention. The Watergate spotlight transformed it into national news. For those who wished to believe, it was easy to equate publicity with proof. Watergate bestowed a kind of credibility on the legend. Other claimants, including Babe Noss, asserted their rights to the treasure, and the demand for a search intensified, despite government opposition.

In July, two Treasury agents visited the office of F. Lee Bailey's public relations consultant and accused him of violating the Gold Reserve Act. The agents confiscated not only the bar that had assayed sixty percent pure but also the bar that contained no gold. Bailey lodged a protest, but the bars were never returned.

The U.S. Army, meanwhile, steadfastly denied the existence of any Victorio Peak treasure. At a press conference in August of 1973, the commanding general of White Sands Missile Range referred to a report issued by the State Museum of New Mexico in 1961: "The geologist concluded in his report that no caverns such as claimed by Doc Noss were revealed." What the general failed to mention was that the army had heavily censored the report. Originally it had concluded that the existence of such caverns was quite likely.

Upset by the army's misrepresentations, the writer of the report, archeologist Chester Johnson, furnished the *Albuquerque Journal* with both the censored and uncensored versions. A comparison revealed that all references to the army's own treasure-hunting activities had been deleted. The *Albuquerque Journal* ran an eight-part series on Victorio Peak that generated great interest throughout New Mexico and convinced F. Lee Bailey to bypass the federal government and try his gold bar diplomacy on New Mexico governor Bruce King.

Bailey presented Governor King with a bar that assayed to 63% gold, 33% copper, and 1% silver. A contract was soon signed in which Bailey's clients agreed to give the State of New Mexico a fourth of their share of the treasure—described as "certain valuable treasure trove, mineral deposits, bullion, coins, historical artifacts and precious or semi-precious stones and unmined precious mineral deposits"—and the State of New Mexico agreed not to prosecute any of Bailey's clients for possession of gold or artifacts removed from the Victorio Peak area. The clients themselves were not named in the agreement, but Bailey placed a list of their names and social security numbers in a safe deposit box in the Bank of Santa Fe.

The agreement rankled the other claimants. Babe Noss filed a billion-dollar lawsuit, contending that the agreement violated her constitutional rights by depriving her of personal property without due process. She didn't win her case, but the judge did order the parties to "go forth to the site of the treasure," recover it, and place it in the custody of a court-appointed receiver until the merit of the claims could be determined.

The U.S. Army, however, continued to deny all parties entrance to the site. Consequently, the State of New Mexico sued the U.S. Army, asking the federal district court in Albuquerque for access to the treasure. In a decision that pleased no one, the court ruled that the army had no right to search for treasure on White Sands Missile Range, the State of New Mexico had no right to search for treasure on the range without the army's permission, and no claimant had the right to search for treasure on the range without the permission of both the state and the army.

The claimants—by this time seven had emerged—pressured the government to relent. Senators Stuart Symington and Thomas Eagleton wrote letters to the Department of the Army on Babe's behalf. Representative George Mahon of Texas wrote letters on behalf of one of Doc Noss's former partners, Roscoe Parr, who swore that Doc had left him a map and detailed instructions for locating the treasure. Violet Yancey—the former Violet Boles, Doc's second wife—filed her own suit against the government. Jesse James III claimed that the treasure had belonged to his notorious grandfather. The Mescalero Apaches claimed that the treasure had belonged to Chief Victorio and his tribe. Air Force captain Leonard Fiege claimed rights to the cave full of gold bars he and three other men had discovered at Victorio Peak in 1958. F. Lee Bailey and his group also persisted in their efforts to win permission for a search. Bailey was quoted in the December 18, 1975 issue of *Rolling Stone*:

> My clients saw some people take two tons of gold from White Sands Missile

Range in two Jeeps and a truck. This was reported to the Assistant Secretary of the Treasury, and no action was taken. They are not enforcing the law.

A state land office memo written in March of 1976 referred to a widely circulated rumor that "eleven tons of gold went out of White Sands Missile Range" on March 10, 1976 by TWA Swiss Air to Credit Swiss in Zurich, Switzerland, supposedly shipped out of Albuquerque International Airport, possibly through Chicago. No one, not even an embittered baggage handler, substantiated the allegation.

Nevertheless, the rumors and endless legal wrangling finally convinced the Department of the Army that demand for a treasure hunt would not subside. A tactical surrender was called for, but to whom should the army surrender and on what terms? If all the claimants were set loose on the peak at once, the potential for chaos would be enormous. The army wanted an orderly process, a dignified search that wouldn't turn into an embarrassment.

Enter Norman Scott. Even before John Dean's momentous snippet of testimony, Scott had been pursuing the treasure of Victorio Peak. In a letter to the state land office, he'd sought official permission to conduct "a sophisticated scientific search." Scott had contacted the various claimants and offered to finance the recovery of the treasure in exchange for a small percentage of their interest in it. When the Department of the Army reluctantly acknowledged seven qualified claimants, Scott recognized the problems the army faced and presented himself as the solution.

First, he was a professional treasure hunter with years of experience. The army didn't know how to organize a search of Victorio Peak, but he did. Second, he was impartial. Each of the claimants would tell him where to look, and he would search there. It didn't matter to him which claimant was right, as long as he received a modest share of the recovered treasure. Third, he was scientific. Throughout his negotiations with the army, Scott emphasized his commitment to science and technology. He invoked the power of "sophisticated instrumentation" unavailable to previous searchers and enlisted the services of geophysicist Lambert Dolphin, recognized as an expert in the field of ground-penetrating radar.

Scott offered the army the reassuring promise of professionalism and objectivity. The army accepted his proposal and—optimistically or sarcastically—dubbed the venture "Operation Goldfinder." A clue to which attitude prevailed can be found in a letter from the Department of the Army responding to Scott's request to bring in a bulldozer and backhoe. This was not the sort of sophisticated instrumentation the army envisioned for a "six-day electronic search." Aggravating the army even further, Scott sought permission to widen the search's scope. "It serves no purpose whatsoever to go in and look at only one site," he argued. The army's reply suggests the extent of their exasperation.

> The fact is that we never believed that any claimant knew or knows the locations of the legendary treasure. We recognize as qualified for a permit those claimants who told a plausible story concerning their knowledge of the treasure location. Another way of saying it is that the most convincing liars were recognized as qualified claimants, plus those who believed their gold fantasies...

> Upon further reflection we have just about concluded it might be to the Army's advantage to have you represent any and all persons who claim to know the location of the treasure.... If you...find only dry holes, as you almost certainly will, then the Army will be justified in refusing for the next decade or so to issue a treasure trove permit to anyone, on the grounds that the legend has been effectively debunked.

Babe Noss accused the army of permitting a slapdash search to prevent a thorough one. She refused to participate without a guarantee that her right to negotiate a future search would be preserved. She never agreed to let Norman Scott represent her, but she did ultimately decide not to block the expedition in court.

Almost four years after the Watergate hearings drew national attention to Victorio Peak, the combination of F. Lee Bailey's clout, Norman Scott's canny self-promotion, and the persistence of Babe Noss wore the army down. Operation Goldfinder would go forward—with restrictions. The army authorized the search for only ten days, confined exploration to a few designated areas, and limited each claimant group to three entrants per day. As if to dramatize the lack of official support, the army sent bulldozers to the peak soon after the search was approved, caved in all known openings, and sealed them with steel doors.

· · ·

Military police stopped the convoy three miles short of Victorio Peak at a windswept stretch of desert designated as HEL site. HEL was one of those obscure acronyms so pleasing to the military mind. Civilians assumed the name was Hell Site. The army had installed portable toilets, temporary power lines, and a trailer, but these amenities only accentuated the harsh impression. "The most forbidding terrain we've ever been in," Dan Rather would tell viewers of "Sixty Minutes."

On the first morning of Operation Goldfinder, even Terry Delonas found it difficult to appreciate the beauty of the desert. The temperature hovered at twenty-seven degrees and he felt as though he'd swallowed a glacier. MPs scrupulously searched each entrant and checked under the hood of every vehicle, reporters swarmed from interview to interview, and Terry's grandmother trumpeted her frank opinions to anyone who would listen—mainly Terry and the KENW crew.

"It's a liar's convention," Babe told the skinny young reporter. "Rigged to fail."

Babe's attorney quietly counseled Babe not to offend the army. An ill-chosen remark printed in a major newspaper could jeopardize her chances of returning to the peak under more favorable circumstances.

"I didn't get to be eighty-one by talking careful," Babe said.

"You can't muzzle mama," her daughter Letha chimed in.

The attorney, David Daar, turned to Terry, urging him to shield Babe from the press.

"That's why I'm here," Terry said. Nearby, the grandson of Jesse James was explaining to a pair of reporters that his grandfather had not been killed by Robert Ford in 1882 but saved by the Knights of the Golden Circle, a fraternal order whose purpose was to finance the rebirth of the Confederacy. "I just don't want her lumped in with..." Terry glanced at Jesse James III, and Daar mouthed the word *crackpots*.

While the tedious inspections of each vehicle dragged on, the White Sands public information officer issued warnings about the dangers of poisonous snakes and unexploded twenty millimeter shells. When an MP took Babe's picture, Terry asked Daar if he thought it was for surveillance purposes. Daar responded that Terry was the one member of the family he counted on *not* to be paranoid.

"I'm just afraid someone may try to throw me out," Terry said.

"Don't worry," Daar said. "You're bending the rules, not breaking them."

Terry had hooked up with KENW to circumvent the army's limit of three entrants per claimant group. As he fretted about the ethics of impersonating a journalist, the real reporters suddenly flocked toward Norman Scott, who had climbed onto the bed of a pickup truck with a battery-powered megaphone. The goal of Operation Goldfinder, Terry heard Scott say, was to investigate the likelihood of all the various claims using scientific means. Scott called the mountain "Vicky Peak," which reminded Terry of customers at the Busy Bee who'd called his mother "honey" or "sweetheart" even though they didn't know her—an unwarranted familiarity. The reporters, though, seemed mesmerized by Scott. Terry watched them scribble in their notebooks, then turned back to his grandmother, resplendent in her purple pantsuit, her bouffant seemingly impervious to the wind.

His first view of Victorio Peak came from the rim of the Hembrillo Basin, behind the wheel of his van, through a windshield caked with dust. He set the emergency brake, jumped out of the van, and loped to the edge of the rim. The peak jutted up from the floor of the basin like nothing else he could imagine. Though he'd seen it before in grainy black-and-white photographs, he felt unprepared for its presence. It was smaller than he'd expected, yet it made an enormous impact. He wanted to compare it to something, describe it to himself in words, but all he could do was look, and for a second he seemed to rush toward the peak, as if he were peering through a zoom lens, and then he became aware of the real distance, aware of the wind and dust, sunlight glinting off what looked like rockets scattered across the floor of the desert. The back of his neck went numb. He thought of the *Twilight Zone*, the freaky music, that strange but familiar sense of encountering the uncanny.

When Lambert Dolphin of the Stanford Research Institute looked at Victorio Peak, he saw a geological marvel, the result of a seventy-million-year-old coincidence. Dolphin was trained to think in geological time. He had an international reputation in ground-penetrating radar and a mind agile enough to make the leap 290 million years into the past, to the Virgilian Age, when the Hembrillo Basin had been a tropical lagoon and the fossilized remains of ancient sea creatures slowly formed a limestone reef much like the atolls found in the Pacific Ocean. Eventually, over millions of years, the lagoonal sea receded, faults and fractures broke the single reef in two, tectonic shifts pushed the two reefs farther apart, and then, seventy million years ago, the event that Dolphin described as an incredible coincidence occurred. Volcanic activity sent molten rock up through a crack in the earth's surface to form a wall twenty-five feet wide and seven miles long, a wall that just happened to cut right through the middle of one of the reefs—dividing the mountain now known as Victorio Peak almost precisely in two. This wall, composed of the igneous rock diorite, was impermeable to water. It functioned as a kind of dike that trapped the water on one side of the reef. The seepage of this trapped water through the fractured limestone created voids, perhaps even a cavern where treasure could be hidden.

Dolphin liked to compare Victorio Peak to the Pyramid of Cheops, where he'd conducted his first experiments in ground-penetrating radar. The peak stood about as tall as the Egyptian pyramid—480 feet—and seemed equally mysterious. The biggest visible difference was the shape of the top. Instead of rising to a point, the massive limestone crown was split in half by the dike, and the northern half had partially collapsed. Viewed from a distance, Victorio Peak lay as open to interpretation as an ink blot in a Rorschach test. Some people thought it resembled a cowboy hat, cropped in the middle and dented on the side. Others thought it resembled the hemispheres of the brain. Dolphin saw it as a bioherm reef bisected by a diorite dike, with significant slumping in the northern half.

The most powerful single instrument for finding underground cavities was ground-penetrating radar, in Dolphin's not unbiased opinion. Unfortunately, it hadn't worked in Egypt. The Giza limestone of the Pyramid of Cheops had a high clay content that collected heavy moisture and absorbed the radar signals within a few feet of the surface of the pyramid. Some scientists believed that the effective range of ground-penetrating radar would always be limited to a few feet, but Dolphin had predicted that it would perform better at Victorio Peak.

With the help of an assistant, Dolphin began to take readings at a limestone outcrop on the northwest face of the peak which several people, including Air Force Captain Leonard Fiege, had indicated as the location of Soldier's Hole. The army had insisted that Dolphin "find" this site, even though army bulldozers had caved in the opening just a few months earlier. Using a resistively loaded dipole antenna, Dolphin bounced radar signals of 150 megahertz against various subsurface targets. The amplitude and delay time of the echoes were registered on a wide-band oscilloscope powered by a 300-watt portable battery pack. Dolphin's assistant took Polaroid photographs of the oscilloscope screen to provide a record of each reading.

Meanwhile, at the base of the peak, Terry Delonas wandered from group to group, checking out the various claimants and reporters. He'd already met Dan Rather and the "Sixty Minutes" crew. They'd interviewed Babe in Las Cruces the day before Goldfinder began. Rather had been surprisingly soft spoken. Terry wanted to meet F. Lee Bailey, but Bailey was busy preparing his defense of heiress-turned-bank-robber Patty Hearst and never made it to the peak. Terry recognized Joe Newman, a carpet salesman from El Paso who'd supposedly removed a gold bar from a cave in Victorio Peak in 1973, the same bar that Bailey had taken to the White House. Newman had been affiliated with the Bailey group but now represented the interests of the Mescalero Apaches. The mysterious Bailey group was said to consist of former White Sands employees, most of whom had chosen not to attend. Terry had heard a rumor they'd hired a psychic to pinpoint the location of the gold, but he couldn't spot anyone who looked especially clairvoyant. For one thing, a clairvoyant would have worn warmer clothes.

Also absent was Doc's second wife, Violet Boles Noss Yancey. No one in the family had ever spoken of her to Terry; he'd learned of her existence from a newspaper article. She'd signed a contract with Norman Scott and given him one of Doc's maps, but planned to stay in Ft. Worth for the duration of Goldfinder.

Terry eavesdropped on Tony Jolley, who was telling a skeptical reporter more or less where he and Doc had buried forty-nine gold bars the night before Doc's death. Jolley reminded Terry of a fisherman who purposely remained vague about where exactly he'd caught the big one.

The only person Terry hesitated to approach was Leonard Fiege, who looked unbearably tense, as if his whole life depended on the success of this search.

Babe, in contrast, seemed entirely at ease. She'd set up lawn chairs and was now regaling listeners with poems she'd written in the 1930s about the WPA. Her recital was interrupted when Lambert Dolphin scrambled down from Soldier's Hole to confer with Norman Scott.

Scott raised his megaphone. "The existence of a tunnel at the so-called Soldier's Hole site has now been ascertained. Digging in said area will presently commence."

"They won't find nothing," Babe said. "The army carted off all that gold years ago."

In November of 1958, twenty-one years to the month after Doc Noss first found his way inside Victorio Peak, Fiege and three Air Force enlisted men located an entrance of their own. Like Doc, they used deer hunting as a pretext for their explorations, and, like Doc, they made a discovery that changed their lives.

In a sworn statement to the U.S. Secret Service, Fiege described how he had spotted a crevice halfway up the mountain and decided to look around, crawling on his belly through a series of short tunnels that led into a cavern filled with dusty stacks of gold bars. A foul smell in the air made him sick, so he crawled back outside where he was soon joined by the other men, Tom Berlett, Ken Prather, and Milt Wessel. He then reentered the treasure cave with Berlett. Each handled the gold bars, but according to their sworn testimony, neither removed any gold. Instead, they collapsed the roof and walls of the tunnel to protect their find from other treasure hunters.

Eager to establish a valid claim to the treasure, the four men consulted Lieutenant Colonel Sigmund Gasiewicz, the judge advocate at Holloman Air Force Base. Gasiewicz and two other Air Force lawyers were impressed enough by their story to join them in a partnership they named the Seven Heirs. For the next two years, the Seven Heirs sought official permission to recover the treasure. When the commanding general of White Sands Missile Range denied their request, they appealed to the Secretary of the Treasury and the Secretary of the Army.

Finally, in July of 1961, the Secret Service advised a representative of the U.S. Bureau of the Mint that the project should be allowed to go forward "as discreetly and cautiously as possible." The U.S. Mint wrote a letter recommending that any metal recovered be assayed at the Phelps-Dodge Refining Corporation and stored at the new Federal Reserve Branch Bank in El Paso.

In August of 1961, accompanied by fourteen military policemen and a Secret Service agent, Fiege returned to the peak. At first he couldn't locate the original entrance, and the Secret Service agent grew increasingly skeptical. After four frantic days, Fiege found the entrance and requested heavy equipment to get past the caved-in rocks and dirt. The Secret Service agent asked him to submit to a lie detector test.

In September, after Fiege passed the lie detector test, the army returned to the peak with a bulldozer, timber for shoring, compressed air motors, digging machinery, and electric generators. The Secretary of the Army classified the excavation Top Secret.

The secret, however, proved difficult to keep. A trio of curious ranchers stumbled upon the operation after five weeks. From the rim of the basin, they saw soldiers at work on the peak and heard what sounded like a caterpillar motor. When they approached more closely, they saw generators, Jeeps, radios, mining wedges, shoring, and cables. The officer in charge, Captain Orby Swanner, ran them off, but not before they wrote down the license numbers of some of the military vehicles.

As soon as the ranchers told Babe Noss what was going on, she called Oscar Jordan at the state land office and told him that the army was trying to jump her claim. Jordan promised to investigate. His memo regarding Babe's call includes a startling bit of background:

> Sometime last summer Colonel Sigmund I. Gasiewicz, Staff Judge Advocate at Holloman, had called me and said that some military personnel had found a large number of gold bars and that he had one in his possession.

Gasiewicz later denied ever having seen a gold bar from Victorio Peak.

In a subsequent land office memo, Jordan summarized the army's response to his inquiries. "Colonel Jaffe was not too cooperative…. He attempted to assure me that there was no operation, that it was all a myth." Colonel Jaffe insisted that Victorio Peak could not be inspected because "it was a closed area and under the surveillance of the army to exclude trespassers. The army is making tests there and carrying on necessary activities on the Range related to the military mission."

On November 6, 1961, a meeting was held at White Sands to discuss the allegations. One of Babe's attorneys described it as follows: "The amenities were barely over when Jaffe bluntly announced his position on the Noss treasure discovery—'a fake and a myth.'" The commander of White Sands insisted that no excavation had been conducted. After being shown sworn statements made by the four witnesses and photographs of the excavation equipment, the general modified his position: "If there was digging going on out there, it was not with my knowledge. And you can be sure it will be stopped immediately if it's still going on."

Soon after this meeting, another of Babe's attorneys wrote a letter to the commander pointing out the weakness of the army's position.

> Lt. Col. Jaffe assured me…that the Noss claim and the whole affair was "a fake and a myth." The trouble is that he gave exactly the same assurances…with respect to the operations which had been conducted on the premises when evidence in our possession shows beyond question that the operations were not a myth and that he knew that they weren't.

The army's credibility had suffered a serious blow.

For the next year and a half, Babe and the state land office separately pressured the army to permit a thorough search of Victorio Peak. The Gaddis Mining Company of Colorado offered to conduct an excavation under the auspices of the State Museum of New Mexico. Gaddis deposited $250,000 in an escrow account as earnest money. In exchange for 40% of Babe's interest in the treasure, Gaddis agreed to pay her $800 down and $800 a month until the treasure was recovered or the project was abandoned. Gaddis also convinced Babe to sign a waiver relinquishing "all rights, claims, or demands which she may or could have against the United States or the Secretary of Defense, by reason of its alleged unlawful taking and withholding of her personal property." In July of 1963, the army agreed to give the state museum and Gaddis Mining Company sixty days to work at Victorio Peak. Though Babe was a technical advisor for the project, she was not allowed on site.

Engineer Les Smith headed the operation, which included a seismic survey and "forty-five days [of] drilling twenty-four hours a day." The failure to intersect a passageway to the cavern led to a tunneling effort. The Gaddis tunnel ultimately reached a length of 218 feet, but it missed its target of

Soldier's Hole. The 1963 Report of the Museum of New Mexico suggests that the compass readings were inaccurate due to the heavy iron content of the diorite dike. Though the museum asked for an additional ninety days to complete its study, the army denied the request. In fact, the request itself was deemed "classified" and removed from the White Sands public files.

The army continued to receive requests from Babe Noss, Violet Yancey, and other claimants to reopen the investigation of the peak. During the first six months of 1971 alone, the Department of the Army received more than fifty congressional inquiries about the treasure. No one was more troubled by the army's refusal to permit a thorough search than Leonard Fiege. He had staked his professional and personal credibility on the story of the gold— and lost.

Soldier's Hole was unearthed after a few hours of digging. Reporters crowded around. Cameras rolled. The first person to explore the hole was one of Scott's assistants. Two military policemen patted him down and searched his pockets before permitting him to crawl into the hole. He spent fifteen minutes underground before resurfacing and submitting to another search. The army insisted that there was no gold in the mountain, but they weren't going to let anyone steal it either.

Scott's assistant told reporters that he had been inside that same cave twice before, in 1974 and 1975. He declined to explain the circumstances of those entries, but said now that the interior was different. "The blasting done by the army since then has changed everything inside Victorio Peak. There were three caves I was in before and all are now bulldozed shut by the army— dynamited shut and sealed by iron doors."

The next person inside added that a lot of work had been done in the Dome Room, an area the Gaddis Mining Company excavation had reached in 1963. "There's a campsite in there with a tea kettle, five sticks of dynamite, and some old rotted fuse. There's even a pair of red corduroy pants."

The accounts of what was inside quickly took on a life of their own. Descriptions circulated of pieces of army uniforms, army digging tools, and a box labeled "U.S. Army—Dynamite." The cave had been shored with timbers, as in a mining operation, and on one cavern wall was painted the name "Orby Swanner."

When Leonard Fiege crawled into Soldier's Hole, he didn't stay down there long. After returning to the surface and submitting to the standard search, he despondently answered questions from reporters. He described how he had found gold bars in the cavern the first time he entered it. "Now it's entirely different. There are timbers in there now. It's all shored up."

In the "Sixty Minutes" interview, Dan Rather asked him about the gold: "Is it a fantasy?"

"No," Fiege answered with visible anguish. "I physically held it in my hands. I know it was there."

Meanwhile, a few miles north of the peak, Lambert Dolphin probed for voids at a site called Bloody Hands, where members of the Bailey group claimed gold was cached. A reporter and an MP drove over from the peak and informed Dolphin that no gold had been found in Soldier's Hole.

"I never expected much from Soldier's Hole," Dolphin said. "But if my readings are accurate, I found a cave under Vicky Peak the size of a football field."

Despite the obvious fact that his right arm was wrapped in a plaster cast and supported by a sling, Norman Scott began his briefing on the fifth day of Operation Goldfinder with the usual phrase: "This morning's activity will encompass the following—"

"What about your arm?" a reporter asked.

Scott ruefully explained that yesterday afternoon he'd slipped while exploring a tunnel and torn a tendon. Though he praised the army's handling of the situation—they'd helicoptered him to Las Cruces, had his arm treated by an orthopedist, and flown him back to the peak within three hours—his pinched expression suggested the arm was giving him pain. Or perhaps the source of pain lay elsewhere. His briefings no longer attracted a large audience. Only half the reporters had bothered to make today's pre-dawn drive to the peak, and many of them evidently preferred to chat with Babe Noss.

While Scott answered a question about the status of Bloody Hands, Terry Delonas circulated among the reporters. As far as he was concerned, Bloody Hands had been a waste of time. The site took its name from the five red handprints painted with ocher on a rock wall near a spring a few miles north of Victorio Peak. The Bailey group believed that these handprints, as well as the series of diamond and cross shapes painted nearby, were not just ancient graffiti but markers indicating the presence of treasure. Though ground-penetrating radar failed to disclose any significant voids, Scott's crew had dug a hole four feet deep and three feet wide. While the crew was discussing whether to bulldoze a tree out of the way, the state archeologist had arrived and spotted two arrowhead flakes. Declaring that the flakes constituted "evidence of early man," he'd shut down the site.

The Bailey group's spokesman summed up the situation. "The official reason we did not produce gold in eleven hours or less is that the army has filled in openings on the peak and screwed up the face of the mountain."

Terry was talking to an El Paso reporter when he felt a heavy hand on his shoulder. He was wrenched around by a man he vaguely recognized, a range rider named Dayberry who, according to Babe, bore a grudge against the Noss family. Range riders were civilian employees who patrolled White Sands Missile Range by horseback or Jeep and acted as policeman, game warden, and sometimes judge and jury. To bolster his authority, Dayberry had dragged along a military police sergeant.

"What are you doing here?" Dayberry demanded.

"I'm a reporter with KENW of Portales," Terry said, indicating his press pass.

"You related to her?" Dayberry jerked a thumb at Babe, who was holding court a dozen yards away.

"She's my grandmother," Terry said.

"Arrest him," Dayberry advised the MP.

Terry waved at David Daar, who was hovering near Babe, then shouted his name. Daar shuffled over and introduced himself as the family's attorney.

"Do you think the 'Sixty Minutes' crew might be interested in filming the arrest of Babe Noss's grandson?" Terry asked. "Don't forget to tell them he has a legitimate press pass."

"Wait a minute," the MP said. "Let me get the base on the radio."

While the question of what to do moved up the chain of command, Terry wondered if jail could be worse than Clovis. He'd come home after a two-year church mission in New York because the Busy Bee Diner faced bankruptcy. His father hadn't wanted to raise prices, and the inflation of the early

'70s had consumed his profit. Nights, Terry managed the restaurant; days, he worked at a local bank. In his spare time, he squeezed in a few business administration classes at Eastern New Mexico State. The only thing he'd miss in jail was his Dodge van, which he'd carpeted and paneled himself.

A decision was passed down from the commanding general to the judge advocate to the head of security to the chief of the military police to the MP sergeant, who lowered his radio and conferred with Dayberry for a moment before delivering the verdict. "Here's the deal," the MP said. "You have to leave the range."

"No!" Terry said. "Get the camera crew."

"But," the MP said. "There's a very important *but*, so wait a minute. *But* you can come back tomorrow as long as you register as a member of the Noss claimant group."

"Do I have to be one of her three entrants?" Terry asked. "She only gets three and my mother wants to come out."

"You don't give up, do you?" the MP said. "Well, we're not exactly over-crowded. Just let the reporters think up their own questions. Okay?"

Terry agreed.

By the final day of Operation Goldfinder, a frantic effort was underway to excavate the original Noss shaft. Norman Scott and Lambert Dolphin had become convinced that Doc's story was basically true and that underneath the rocks and rubble lay a sizable cavern. Babe had told them that the debris went down thirty feet, and Dolphin's ground-penetrating radar readings had indicated twenty-nine.

The plug of rocks and dirt was being removed by a frenzied bucket brigade. The men used a jackhammer to shatter rock that couldn't be removed by hand. Scott announced that they were lowering the floor of the shaft a foot an hour, but he estimated that at least twenty feet of rubble remained. He'd already asked the army for an extension, but the request had been denied.

The only crew left filming was the one from KENW. Scott told them: "We should have attacked the Noss shaft when we first came. It was a goof, perhaps, but an honest one."

In the saddle area below the top of the peak, Babe played hostess to the reporters and claimants who hadn't gone home. The mood, despite the bitter wind, was festive. Operation Goldfinder had been reduced to the diehards.

A few days earlier, after finding nothing substantial at Bloody Hands, Geronimo Peak, or Bat Cave, Scott had realized that all the ground-penetrating radar data supported Doc's original story. None of the other stories had been corroborated. Scott asked Babe for help, promising to concentrate on Doc's shaft for the duration of Goldfinder. She agreed to let him see Doc's maps. She also brought out an old scrapbook full of pictures of Doc and herself at the peak, and now she was proudly showing the pictures to the last of the hangers-on.

By day's end it would become clear that the work to uncover the original Noss passage would take more than an afternoon. Excavation would cease and Scott's men would concentrate the remainder of their efforts on cleaning up the peak and re-sealing the openings.

At the press conference following Goldfinder, Scott would summarize what had been accomplished. "Our purpose was to prove or disprove the existence of gold in *precise* locations. Unfortunately and regrettably, the claimants and their sources were misinformed. We found no gold in the *exact spots* identified by these claimants." When asked what might be inside the Noss cavern, Scott would reply: "That's still a mystery. The real dilemma in the whole picture. And it won't be solved until someone is willing to spend a fortune excavating the blocked shaft and crevices." In conclusion he would say, "It is very, very difficult to put legends to rest. Everybody wants to find gold, including yours truly. It was a short experience that we enjoyed. And the dust baths we got were very refreshing."

Lambert Dolphin would publish his findings in the scholarly journal *Geophysics*. In his view, the series of caves and tunnels disclosed by ground-penetrating radar seemed to conform very closely with maps Doc had made based on his own explorations. Dolphin would conclude: "In view of the...so-far-proven consistency of the original Noss story, a further exploration of the peak should be undertaken."

The White Sands public information officer would have the last word at the press conference: "White Sands Military Range is now closed to further search. This exploration in conjunction with two previous efforts over the past 16 years indicates no treasure, gold or otherwise, exists in the area of

Hembrillo Basin or Victorio Peak." *The New York Times*, however, would conclude otherwise: "Scott's failure will probably serve only to enhance the Noss legend, since Dolphin's ground-penetrating radar device indicated the presence of a cavern far down inside the limestone mountain, just about where Doc Noss said it was."

All this would happen after Goldfinder. At the moment, though, there was still the possibility of a breakthrough. Scott's crew could hit a tunnel and the tunnel could lead to the treasure room. In this atmosphere of hope and good will, the young reporter from KENW asked Babe what she planned to do if Scott's efforts failed. Would she quit?

"Drip, drip, drip," Babe said. "That's how those caves got made in the first place." She put down her scrapbook and announced that she was going to climb to the top of the peak. She didn't have to look at pictures. She could stand there herself.

With a military policeman on either side, she used her walking stick to hike up the loose rock to the summit. When the MPs tried to take her by the arms, she shook them off. One MP slipped and fell to a knee. The other stopped to help him up. Babe climbed on unassisted.

It was a sight that Terry would long remember, his grandmother at the top of Victorio Peak, her white bouffant quivering in the wind, her gaze unsparing as she surveyed the efforts of the crew. When she started down a few minutes later, she looked the least bit less steady. She was eighty-one years old and would never stand atop Victorio Peak again.

8

Capitol Hill

*The test of a first-rate intelligence is the ability to hold
two opposed ideas in mind at the same time and
still retain the ability to function.*
—*F. Scott Fitzgerald*

1988

He was a Clovis boy. His higher education consisted of a few classes at Eastern New Mexico State University, a few more at Santa Ana Junior College. He had no money of his own, no experience as a lobbyist, nothing that even vaguely resembled clout. His story, at best, sounded farfetched. And he needed an act of Congress.

Alone in his hotel room at the D.C. Hilton, he cradled the phone against his shoulder and listened to the soothing voice of Judy Holeman as she tried to overcome his doubts. "You're a natural," she was saying. "Polite, persistent, and your smile gives you that little-boy-lost quality people can't resist."

The sky outside his window was black. Heavy clouds hovered over the city. He grabbed the remote, sat down on the bed, and flipped through the stations with the sound off. Michael Dukakis appeared on the screen in a camouflage tank—in a commercial for Bush/Quayle. Terry had spent the day trying to set up meetings with Ted Kennedy, Sam Nunn, and several other senators, but no one wanted to schedule appointments just before the election.

"I felt like an idiot," Terry said. "Sam Nunn's assistant asked me, 'What is this regarding?' and I knew I had about three seconds to win her over, and I said, 'Well…' and things went down hill from there."

"Was Norman any help?"

"He asked the receptionist for a date. Would you call that help?"

Terry let the television settle on an encampment of tents. He was lucky not to be camping out himself. Craig Harrison had used his position at the Irvine Hilton to swing this free room. If Craig were a maitre d' in DC, Terry thought, he'd soon be offered a cabinet post. The TV tents turned into an episode of M*A*S*H. Klinger, clad in a pink tutu, was delivering a package to the colonel.

"You don't need Norman," Judy said. "Soon you'll be lobbying with the best of them."

"Unless we go broke."

Hawkeye joined Klinger in the colonel's tent. Terry wanted to identify with Hawkeye, the competent professional with the razor sharp wit, but he felt more like Klinger, the pretender in the pink tutu. He clicked off the TV.

"Remember Babe's motto," Judy said. "Winners never quit and quitters never win."

"That's a cliché. Babe had a million of them." Besides, he wanted to say, Babe never quit, but she never won, either. He'd been thinking a lot about his grandmother lately. He imagined her jeering his feeble efforts.

Judy asked if he'd seen Senator Pryor yet and he shook his head.

"Are you shaking your head?" she asked.

He admitted that he was. She advised him to work on his telephone skills. Not everyone could distinguish between a nod and a shake of the head the way she could.

Senator David Pryor, Sr. of Arkansas was the father of Terry's friend, David Pryor, Jr. Pryor, Sr. had served four terms in the House of Representatives, then preceded Bill Clinton as governor of Arkansas from 1974-79, and was currently in his eighth year as a senator. Pryor, Jr. had worked with Terry at a brokerage company in California and become fascinated with the Victorio Peak saga.

The senator was out of town, Terry told Judy, but they were getting together next week. He'd promised to reveal the secrets of successful lobbying.

"And you thought you were all alone," Judy said.

Terry lay down on the bed and gazed up at the ceiling while Judy went on with her pep talk. He had a whole team behind him, she said, and not just well-wishers but people who would do anything in their power to help. He brought out the best in people, she said. That was his gift. He chimed in now and then. Judy let him wallow in despair and then coaxed him out of it. That was her gift. The plain white ceiling could have been a blank slate. It seemed to suggest that anything was possible, even success.

The secret of successful lobbying, according to Senator Pryor, was to believe in the system. Despite its many flaws, Pryor insisted, the system worked—if you knew how to use it. You didn't have to be rich, he said. You didn't have to be slick. But you had to follow protocol. An institution as arcane, ritual-istic, and hermetic as Congress magnified the importance of protocol.

At breakfast in the Senate cafeteria, Pryor pointed out the obvious: members of Congress, though extremely busy, worked for the citizens of the United States. "We work for *you*," he said with obvious pride. "We have an obligation to listen. Especially if you're from our home state."

Pryor's number one rule of protocol: start with the home state—in this case the home of the project. No one in Congress wanted to hear about a local matter from a colleague outside the state. Terry thought of General Jones and his outrage that Terry had gone to the Pentagon first.

Pete Domenici and Jeff Bingaman represented New Mexico in the Senate; Joe Skeen represented the district that included Victorio Peak in the House. Pryor advised Terry to call on Domenici first because Domenici was the senior senator. No senior senator wanted to be scooped by a junior senator.

Pryor helped Terry compile a list of who to see and in what order he should see them. They concentrated on members of Congress who served on committees charged with oversight of the army. Les Aspin and Sam Nunn headed the list.

"You'll need to register as a lobbyist," Pryor said.

"Are you kidding?" Terry asked.

"You're seeking legislation. That means you're a lobbyist."

"Then why do I feel like an impostor?" Terry asked—though he recognized that his whole life could be viewed as preparation for this challenge.

How many years had he spent putting on suits, calling on strangers, trying to convince them of a fantastic yarn? He'd attended ministry school as a child and seriously considered becoming a pastor. Now his faith resided in his grandmother's stories and he would proselytize members of Congress.

George Bush and Dan Quayle took 54% of the popular vote, soundly defeating the Democratic ticket. Terry soon discovered that it was as difficult to schedule an appointment after an election as before.

"And what is this regarding?" Pete Domenici's secretary asked as she poured over an appointment book the size of a road atlas.

"There's a treasure buried on White Sands Missile Range," Terry said. "It belongs to my family." The secretary looked him square in the face for the first time. "I need less than ten minutes," he said. "I have a nine-minute video tape that tells the whole story."

Domenici's secretary offered him an appointment with an aide—three weeks down the line. Terry pointedly mentioned that his friend Senator Pryor had advised him to see Senator Domenici before he met with Senator Bingaman and Representative Skeen—implying that those appointments were already scheduled. The secretary consulted a smaller appointment book.

"Would next Tuesday be soon enough?" she asked. She gave him an appointment with a senior aide, whose name Terry dropped when he called on Senator Bingaman's office. He learned the names of all the aides and spoke of them as if they'd supported his cause from the beginning.

Over the next few weeks, he developed a routine. He'd fly into Washington late Friday night—a Saturday layover lowered the fare—and fly out by Tuesday evening. Sometimes Craig Harrison would comp a room for him at the Hilton; sometimes he'd stay with one of the Pryors. Pryor, Sr. had a three-story brownstone in Dupont Circle; Pryor, Jr. had a small apartment a few blocks away. Terry hated to impose, but he loved the neighborhood, and he especially enjoyed the Pryor family custom of gathering in the senator's den to watch the eleven o'clock news and review the events of the day over a bottle of wine. Terry would describe the odd characters he'd met and the mysterious workings of Congress, and the Pryors, father and son, would offer commentary and advice.

Terry had taken to breakfasting in the Senate cafeteria with the various aides who had watched the treasure tape. He'd answer their questions and urge them to show the tape to their bosses. The New Mexico contingent had been remarkably friendly—in sharp contrast to Sam Nunn's staff, who'd grudgingly sat through the video and then dismissed Terry without even a vague promise to consider the matter further.

Senator Pryor suggested that the army might already have soured Nunn on the project. The Pentagon had sent junior attorneys to brief all the members of Congress Terry called on, "to put out the fire," Senator Pryor theorized.

One evening Terry told the Pryors about Representative Jim Wright's office—the thick cloud of blue cigar smoke, the battered old desks, and the even more ancient aides. Most of the aides Terry had dealt with were young, energetic, and over-groomed, brimming with political upward mobility, but Wright's aides were dinosaurs in extinct suits, who spoke in accents that reminded Terry of Clovis.

Senator Pryor told Terry that, on the Senate floor that afternoon, a senator had asked him how Doc Noss was doing. "He wanted a copy of the treasure tape," Pryor said.

"Was he serious?" Terry asked.

"At least half serious," Pryor said. "I think he needed a break from the budget deficit."

Terry decided that he didn't mind if the treasure tape became a source of comic relief. The more members of Congress who saw it, the better his chances of obtaining legislation.

The nine-minute video—which actually ran eleven and a half minutes—opened with a shot of Victorio Peak and a quick summary of Doc and Babe's story. A succession of sepia photographs appeared on the screen: Doc on horseback in the Hembrillo Basin, Babe holding the sword, the two of them posed with their excavation crew around a windlass. A color photo of John Dean at the Watergate hearings moved the story forward, followed by footage from the "Sixty Minutes" segment devoted to Operation Goldfinder. Subsequent clips showed family members recounting various episodes of the story; then several eyewitnesses testified as to where and when they had seen Doc Noss in possession of gold bars. The video concluded with the results of Lambert Dolphin's ground-penetrating radar survey and Norman Scott's endorsement of the Noss family claim. The video was dramatic, persuasive, and brief, omitting embarrassing details and glossing over the story's contradictions and inconsistencies. In putting it together, Terry had emphasized those elements that seemed to add to the story's legitimacy: John Dean and the Watergate connection, Dan Rather and the "Sixty Minutes" connection, the science of ground-penetrating radar, and Lambert Dolphin's Ph.D.

A week later, back in his hotel room, Terry sat down on the bed, removed his shoes and socks, and inspected his ankles for KS spots. KS, or Kaposi's Sarcoma, was one of the most common early indicators of AIDS. It usually manifested itself in the form of purple spots that appeared when abnormal cell growth clogged the tiny blood vessels near the surface of the skin. Terry checked his ankles every night; no freckle, no stray hair escaped his notice. A KS spot would probably look like an innocent bruise, but it would never heal. He had first heard about KS in 1986 at a dinner party with several gay students from Santa Ana Community College. "Raymond has the purple spots," someone said. Terry didn't know Raymond, but months later, when he learned of Raymond's death, he remembered the purple spots. "Once the spots appear," a dinner party expert had claimed, "you've got a hundred days."

All the talk of a virus killing gay men had convinced Terry to go in for a test, more for reassurance than anything else. He'd done nothing unsafe, he thought. At the Orange County Health Clinic, after the counselor in the corduroy sports coat delivered the bad news, Terry had walked as far as the waiting room and collapsed in one of the cracked orange chairs while an overhead monitor broadcast information about Acquired Immune Deficiency Syndrome, Human Immunodeficiency Virus, and Kaposi's Sarcoma—information he could no longer ignore. The habit of compulsively checking his ankles had begun that night.

Since then Terry had experimented with everything from oxygenation therapy to Mother's Health Food Kitchen. He'd tried nutritional supplements and mega-doses of Vitamin C. No symptom of AIDS had yet appeared. His ankles—again tonight—looked fine. Eventually, though, a spot would show up. Sometimes he almost looked forward to finding it and knowing for certain.

He hung up his suit and changed into jeans and a T-shirt, laid out the meager dinner he'd brought back to the room. On his bad nights—and despite the apparent progress of the lobbying effort, this was a bad night—he thought of Babe and the double-edged legacy she'd left him. In 1979, a few weeks before she died, she'd flown to a Caribbean health spa with all four of her children and their spouses. Her eldest son, Terry's uncle Harold, had hit the jackpot speculating on oil and gas leases, and had volunteered to pay expenses. Terry's aunt Henrietta was dying of cancer, and Harold hoped the spa doctors might come up with a miracle cure. If not, the trip would bring the family together for a last reunion.

Terry had been living in Santa Fe at the time, operating a successful mail order business that sold car wax to American Automobile Association members throughout the Southwest. When his mother and aunt returned from the trip, they drove from Clovis to Santa Fe to break the news of Babe's death. The spa, they said, had served up remedies for everyone's ailments: sea weed soup, tea made from Chinese roots, rubdowns with special creams and lotions. Henrietta's skin color had turned from a ghastly green to a healthy peach. Babe's arthritic knees had responded so well to a treatment with magnets that on the last day she danced a little jig of appreciation for the head doctor. While dancing, she tripped over a low concrete ledge, fell down, and broke her hip. The doctor summoned a Coast Guard plane to fly her to a hospital in Nassau. He sent along his son, who was also a doctor, to monitor her care. The small plane had no room for other passengers.

Just before Babe was loaded on board, she took off the charm necklace that Terry had given her for her seventieth birthday. The charm was a miniature gold bar.

"I want Terry to have this," she told Dorothy and Letha. "He'll know what to do."

Babe had died in surgery. By the time the family arrived, the hospital had already cremated her remains. Dorothy suspected malpractice and Letha suspected foul play.

Listening to the story in his Santa Fe studio, Terry had covered his mouth with both hands. Letha dumped out her purse on the kitchen counter in search of the gold bar necklace; then Dorothy dumped out *her* purse. Their hysteria kept Terry from breaking down. After the necklace was finally found, Letha asked Terry if she could bring Babe inside. The ashes, she explained, were in the car.

Babe's death devastated Terry. She haunted him, not as a ghost moaning and clanking chains, but as a tightness in his abdomen, a voice in his head, a recurring presence in his dreams. One Saturday morning he slept late and dreamed of winning a major award—he didn't know if it was an Oscar or a Nobel Prize, but he was giving an incredibly eloquent acceptance speech, thanking everyone who had helped him, thanking people he hadn't even met yet, when suddenly he realized that one person deserved all the credit, one person was responsible for his accomplishments, and as he told the cheering audience about his grandmother, her indomitable spirit, her extraordinary strength of will, he felt a sense of well-being unlike anything he'd ever experienced. He woke up with tears in his eyes and decided to sell his business and move to California. Babe's last words had worked on him like a spell. "Terry will know what to do." That parting shot had become his inspiration and his curse. Whenever he found himself stumbling along, groping for direction, he imagined her jabbing a blunt finger into his chest and ordering him to shape up.

He washed down the last bite of pasta salad with a swig of tepid carrot juice and then picked up the telephone to call Judy. This morning in the Senate cafeteria, one of Lloyd Bentsen's aides had asked him which senator he worked for. Judy would enjoy hearing that he could pass for a senate aide. She'd also appreciate the advice that David Pryor, Jr. had given him. Pryor, Jr. worked for the public relations firm of Hill & Knowlton, and that afternoon he'd staged a mock-interview with Terry, posing questions about the project and evaluating Terry's answers. The key to dealing with the press, Pryor had said, was *spin control*. Terry had never heard the term before, but evidently it was something he needed to master.

He remembered doing pretend-interviews with his brother Jim when they were kids. They'd corrected each other's grammar and accent in an attempt to eradicate all traces of Clovis. Jim had left home for good at seventeen. Terry had left and come back, left and come back.

A week after testing HIV positive, he'd flown to Houston to visit Jim and his wife and their newborn daughter. He remembered turning away when Jim offered the baby. He'd been afraid to touch her, afraid to communicate his disease. No one had understood why he wouldn't hold the baby.

9

Rad Tech Delonas

If you want to send a message, use Western Union.
—Cecil B. DeMille

1984

Rising between Interstate 5 and the Pacific Ocean, the twin domes of the San Onofre Nuclear Generation Station created a spectacle only the most jaded commuter could ignore, especially at sunset, especially in spring, the Southern California inversion layer filtering the last up-slanting rays of sunlight into purgatorial shades of burnt gold and blood orange.

In the netherworld of Containment Unit Two, it could have been any hour, any season. The thick concrete walls of the 170-foot dome banished all natural light and amplified the roar of turbines, the rattle of ventilators, the thud of pumps. Water and steam shrieked through the maze of pipes and ducts surrounding the nuclear reactor. Despite the deafening noise, radiation technician Terry Delonas worked slowly and carefully, cleaning up the gallon of radioactive water that had spilled on the concrete floor. Unlike the other rad techs, who tended to flaunt their recklessness, Terry put his faith in procedure, in this case methodically spreading paper towels over the puddle. When most of the water was soaked up, he placed the used paper towels in a yellow plastic bag held by a crew member called Loon. A small wet patch remained, so Terry repeated the process, laying down fresh paper with meticulous care.

The toe of the crew chief's boot nudged Terry's shoulder. Hurry it up, the crew chief signaled with a tap of the wrist. Terry nodded, but didn't hurry. He'd discovered that the less he hurried, the sooner he finished the job.

Loon impatiently drummed his gloved fingers against a pipe marked with a red "X." The "X" indicated a radioactive hot spot, but Loon was a former Navy SEAL and held the dangers of radiation in contempt. Everyone alive is radioactive, he liked to point out, as if the commonness of radioactivity proved that it was safe. Unfortunately, as Terry had deduced from the training sessions, no dose of radiation was too small to be dangerous. He did everything he could to minimize the risk. Two years of working at San Onofre would finance two years of devoting himself full time to Victorio Peak.

He checked his dosimeter. The small yellow boxes that detected radioactive gas raised no alarm. As far as he was concerned, the worst part of the job was not the abstract threat of radiation but the immediate discomfort of the heat. Decked out in paper suit, canvas suit, and rubber suit, cloth slippers, canvas slippers, and rubber boots, three pairs of gloves, hard hat, and black neoprene respirator, he monitored his temperature more often than he monitored his radiation level. Any appreciable exertion could bring on nausea, dizziness, and intense headache.

He was almost done when a radioactive gas alarm went off. The large red light inside the small yellow box began to blink. A siren added its wail to the general din. Terry's first impulse was to evacuate the area, but the crew chief, who'd been in a hurry before, now motioned Terry to keep working. A gas leak meant that a report would have to be filed, and the crew chief didn't want to file a report on an unfinished job. Terry gingerly deposited the last few paper towels in the plastic bag. The year was 1984. Terry was thirty-six years old. His hopes of returning to Victorio Peak rose and fell as often as the tide.

His plan had seemed simple when he'd moved to California. He'd write a screenplay about Doc and Babe that would be made into a hit movie. The publicity from the film would force the army to permit a search. After enrolling in a screenwriting class at Santa Ana Junior College, he'd sifted through the wealth of family photographs, newspaper clippings, diaries, letters, minutes of meetings, and trial transcripts that Babe had accumulated. He'd intended to identify the indisputable facts and put them together like the pieces of a jigsaw puzzle to form a clear picture of the truth. To his surprise and disappointment, very few facts had proven indisputable. The truth was not like a jigsaw puzzle. It was more like a crowded room where everyone shouted at once.

The airlock between Containment and the Rad Waste Building possessed all the charm of a concrete bunker—although it didn't seem to bother the other rad techs, most of whom were ex-Navy men accustomed to a certain degree of sensory deprivation. Their response to the bleak surroundings was to tell bad jokes and employ dumb nicknames. They'd dubbed Terry "Klondike" because he was looking for gold. Only the crew chief, Caldwell, was called by his real name.

As soon as Caldwell closed the thick door to Containment, the noise level diminished to a tolerable roar.

"Klondike is unclear on the concept," Loon said. "Quick in, quick out, keeps a man healthy, wealthy, and alive."

Terry's forehead throbbed. Wearing a triple suit was like standing in a barrel of sweat. Caldwell ignored Loon's comment and pointed to the opposite door, which led to the Radiation Waste building. He made a point of being the last person to leave each room.

The current version of Terry's screenplay began with a fly-over shot of the Hembrillo Basin at sunset, the camera gradually zooming in on the top of the peak, where Babe paced back and forth. The camera would catch the clothesline tied to her ankle and follow it down inside the mountain to Doc, arduously climbing up with a black bar clutched to his chest. A rock protruding into the narrow shaft knocked against the bar. An exposed corner caught the faint light and gleamed with an unmistakable glitter.

When Doc reached the surface and collapsed in exhaustion, Babe picked up the black bar and noticed the trace of golden color.

"Why, look here, Doc," she said.

Doc took his knife and scraped off a sliver of black. Fading sunlight glinted off the yellow metal underneath. "Babe, if this is gold, and all those bars down below, we can call John D. Rockefeller a tramp."

Terry had imagined the John D. Rockefeller scene so often and so vividly that it had almost written itself. The second scene, a flashback to the day Doc and Babe had met, presented more of a challenge. Terry didn't know how they'd met, though he'd heard plenty of Babe's stories about her early years.

Babe had been born in Saffordsville, Kansas in 1895, the daughter of a state circuit judge. She'd married young and had four children. After the crash of 1929, her husband Roy had gone to Oklahoma City to look for work while she'd stayed behind in Toncawah, Oklahoma, because their oldest child, Letha, had contracted malaria and typhoid fever. "Either one'll kill you," Babe had explained to Terry, "and Letha caught both." As soon as Letha recovered, Babe and the children moved to Oklahoma City, where Roy had landed a job delivering butter. That was the good news. The bad news was that he'd taken up with another woman.

"Roy Beckwith was not a bad person," Babe once said. "But he had a bad weakness, and that was the opposite sex. The chance to step into all those city houses with all that butter was too much for a farm boy like him."

She found work as an elevator operator—and the flashback would begin with the doors of her elevator opening and a gaunt man stepping in. The camera focused on the flapping heels of the man's dusty shoes. As the elevator descended to the lobby, the man started to cry.

"Why can't I get a job?" he asked Babe. "I'm a hard worker, and I've got a wife and four kids, all hungry."

"I've got four kids, too," Babe said, crying with him.

Terry had heard this story many times. "If only I'd given something to that poor soul," Babe always said. She carried sorrowful memories of the Depression. "You'll never understand how awful it was. Grown men worked all day long for half a buck."

In the scene Terry had constructed, Babe slipped the destitute man a quarter and hurried out of the building, relieved, despite her sympathy, to put distance between herself and his suffering. The sound of a piano drew her to a saloon, where she sat next to the piano player and requested an obscure and difficult song. When he shook his head, she bumped him off the bench and played the song herself. Terry had seen his grandmother pull this stunt in a pizza parlor. He had no idea if she'd done it the day she met Doc, but he imagined her rollicking honky-tonk luring Doc from the bar and up to the piano to see who had taken charge. Naturally, she added a few flourishes for his benefit.

Doc was a handsome man, dressed in black from his boots to his cowboy hat, with a neat string tie that somehow emphasized his strong physical presence. Babe, Terry had to admit, was not conventionally beautiful, but her buoyancy, her exuberance came through when she played the piano. In the early drafts of the scene, they'd told each other their life stories, but now the conversation was minimal.

"You look awful prosperous," Babe said, ever direct.

"I'm a foot doctor," Doc said.

"I could use some attention on my feet," Babe said.

The flashback ended there, and the scene returned to Victorio Peak without depicting Doc and Babe's picaresque passage to New Mexico. They'd gotten married in Sayre, Oklahoma in October of 1933, and like so many couples caught in the Dust Bowl during the Great Depression, they'd headed west. In Wellington, Texas, Doc was arrested for practicing medicine without a license. They posted bail and left town. In Roswell, New Mexico, Doc was arrested for brandishing a gun at a waitress. He served four months in state prison. Eventually, he and Babe opened a foot clinic in Hot Springs, New Mexico, a spa town that attracted Easterners seeking cures for various ailments.

The Rad Waste building was blessedly quiet until Terry's geiger counter began clicking when he held it near his head.

"Klondike's hot," Loon said.

Terry had no reason to panic. The radiation was probably confined to his hard hat. Nevertheless, the clicking agitated him. Loon deposited the bag of used paper towels in one of the yellow barrels that lined the long hallway. Caldwell reported to the health physics tech stationed next to the barrel: "Irradiated compressor water from Unit Two. Moderate waste. Gas detected." Procedure dictated that crew members remove their soggy triple suits one item at a time, disposing of hard hats in one barrel, respirators in another, plodding down the hallway in a slow-motion striptease while the health physics techs looked on in their cool surgical whites.

"Take it off," Loon said, imitating a Scandinavian actress in a once-popular shaving cream commercial. "Take it all off."

Terry tuned out the jokes, which tended to get raunchier as the layers of the triple suit were discarded. He refused to think of this as humiliating.

His screenplay jumped forward with a series of old-fashioned photographs a la *Butch Cassidy and the Sundance Kid*: Doc hanging an "Out of Town" sign on the door of the foot clinic, he and Babe loading crates of provisions into the step van, changing a tire on the drive to the Hembrillo Basin, hiking to the top of the peak with lanterns and ropes, Doc descending into the opening, Babe standing watch at the top, and then a brief scene when Doc finally emerged, panting in exhaustion. "Maybe we should hire some help," Babe said, and Doc responded, "Who do you trust?"

Terry wanted to show the hardships that Doc and Babe had overcome in the days before steel-belted radials and four-wheel drive, air conditioning, and trail mix. The ungraded dirt road ended miles short of the peak. Doc and Babe spent hours patching punctured tires. Doc had to string cans of sardines and tomatoes to his belt for nourishment while underground. As Terry deposited his rubber gloves in a yellow rad waste barrel, he could almost hear the soundtrack—Bob Wills and the Texas Playboys swinging through "San Antonio Rose."

The music would stop abruptly when Doc and Babe arrived at the peak with Serafín Sedillo, a skinny teenager from Rincon, New Mexico, whom Doc had hired to help haul out the gold. According to the report compiled twenty-five years later by the State Museum of New Mexico, Sedillo made only a single trip to the treasure room with Doc. They'd entered the mountain early one afternoon through the crevice at the top and descended a series of tight passages and narrow shafts to a vast cave that contained not only stacks of gold bars, but also the armor, chests of jewelry, fresh water stream, and human skeletons.

The skeletons always aroused Terry's skepticism, but at least Doc wasn't the only person who claimed to have seen them. Sedillo had corroborated Doc's story, which was one reason Terry wanted him in the scene when the audience finally got a view of the treasure room.

At two o'clock in the afternoon, sunlight filtered into the room through an old entrance barricaded with timbers and dirt. Terry pictured Doc and Sedillo lit by dust-speckled rays of sunshine as they explored the murky cavern in silence. Doc selected two gold bars and put one in each pocket of his camping vest. Sedillo took only one small bar.

"I thought you said you were strong," Doc said.

Sedillo shrugged. When Doc turned around, Sedillo slipped two of the smallest bars into his pants pockets.

On the long climb out, the soundtrack amplified their labored breathing.

At the top, dazzled by the fading daylight, Doc dropped his bars in front of Babe and hunched over to catch his breath. Sedillo dropped the single bar tucked under his arm. Doc borrowed Babe's rifle and pumped a shell into the chamber.

"Forgetting something?" Doc said.

Reluctantly, Sedillo pulled a bar from one pocket, then the other.

"I told you we could trust him," Babe said.

The insistent click of the geiger counter compelled Terry's attention. He'd stripped all the way to his paper suit, most of which had disintegrated from the profusion of sweat, yet he was still clicking. Traces of radioactive gas had evidently collected in his eyebrows and hair.

"Party of one to the Silkwood Room," Loon said. His smile wasn't meant to be malicious, Terry knew, but he did not like the man. He understood, though, the urge to combat the realities of this work by concentrating on anything but the work itself. While the other techs embraced nicknames and bravado, Terry focused on Victorio Peak.

The screenplay had problems he didn't know how to fix. The Gold Reserve Act of 1934 was not the stuff of Hollywood movies. The roots of the law went back to the Trading with the Enemy Act of 1917, which was amended just before the end of World War I to give the President the power to "investigate, regulate, or prohibit…any hoarding…of gold…by any person within the United States."

On March 6, 1933, two days after Franklin Roosevelt took office, he used the Trading with the Enemy Act to close every bank in the country, even though that act had expired more than a decade earlier. On March 9, 1933, after less than an hour of debate, Congress passed the Emergency Banking Act, which authorized the Secretary of the Treasury to compel everyone in the United States to surrender all gold coin, gold bullion, and gold certificates in exchange for paper money. The only exceptions were rare coins, gold coins with a total value of less than one hundred dollars, and gold used in industry and the arts. A second law passed on April 5, 1933 required not just individuals but banks to turn over their gold to the Federal Reserve Bank. By May 1, 1933, virtually all the gold in the United States was held by the federal government. Failure to turn in gold was punishable by up to ten years in jail and $10,000 in fines. The Gold Reserve Act of 1934 completed the takeover by requiring the Federal Reserve Bank to surrender its gold to the Department of the Treasury. The act called for forfeiture of any gold held in violation of the act, along with civil penalties of twice the value of the gold involved in the violation. The Gold Reserve Act remained in effect until 1974, and as F. Lee Bailey discovered during his negotiations with the Nixon administration, the government routinely seized gold without compensating the owner.

Doc and Babe violated the Gold Act when they failed to report their discovery promptly. Ignorant of the law and suspicious of the government, they feared being put in jail and having their gold confiscated. Finding a mountain full of cocaine or bootleg whisky would have placed them in a similar predicament. From 1933 to 1974, gold was a controlled substance which couldn't be sold legally—not that Doc and Babe didn't try.

In July of 1939, Babe wrote a letter to the Denver Mint, asking what she and her husband should do if they stumbled across any gold bars. Could they sell the bars to the U.S. Mint or would the government claim the treasure? The government's response only exacerbated their suspicions. A U.S. treasury agent showed up at the house in Hot Springs and spoke to Babe's teen-aged son Harold. Terry had read the official report of this interview in Doc's Freedom of Information Act file. The scene that most interested Terry was the one that must have followed, when Doc and Babe came home.

"A G-man dropped in," Harold said. "Drove all the way from Albuquerque."

"What'd he want?" Doc grunted.

"Said Mama had written a letter."

Doc glared at Babe.

"I wrote to the Denver Mint back in July," Babe said, instantly apologetic. "I didn't tell them we had gold. I just asked what if we found some."

"I wrote down the important stuff," Harold said, lifting a sheet of notebook paper. "According to something called the Gold Act, 'the finding of any gold by any person should be reported promptly to the Treasury Department, together with a statement as to the circumstances under which it was found, in order that specific instructions may be given.'"

"Does that mean they'd pay us for the gold?" Babe asked.

Doc pointed his index finger at Babe and cocked his thumb. "You done bad," he said. His hand curled into a fist, but Terry couldn't decide what to do with that fist, whether Doc slammed it against the wall or swung it at Babe or unclenched it to take a swig from his whisky flask. Babe had often referred to the ensuing fight as one of the worst of their marriage, but she hadn't elaborated on Doc's part in it. She'd never criticized Doc in front of Terry, yet Terry still harbored doubts about Doc's character—both as a movie hero and as a man.

Under the stinging spray of the shower, Terry felt his headache at first intensify and then ease. The high pressure torrent of water hurt, but it was a relief to be out of the suit, and the heat on his tired muscles felt good even while it burned his skin. Above him, the health techs directing the spray yelled back and forth over the rush of water. They were arguing the relative merits of futons and water beds. It occurred to Terry that in a movie ominous music would be playing on the soundtrack instead of this inane conversation, but he understood that the health techs were practicing an advanced form of tact—granting him the illusion of privacy while he stood naked before them.

In the darkness of Victorio Peak, Doc hunkered down next to the mining engineer he'd hired. By the gloomy greenish light of carbide lamps, they peered at the narrow opening they hoped to widen.

"Easy on the dynamite," Doc said.

"Trust me," the mining engineer said. "Nothing can go wrong."

On the word *wrong,* Terry pictured a jittery, hand-held camera zooming through the bottleneck and hurtling down the zigzagging walkways to the bottom of the shaft where a shadowy figure hid in the darkness. According to the report of the State Museum of New Mexico, Las Cruces grocery clerk Ben Samaniego had "followed Doc Noss to see where he got his gold" and sneaked down to the treasure room. As best Terry could piece the story together, Samaniego was bringing up a suit of Spanish armor when he overheard Doc and the mining engineer arguing about the dynamite. Terry imagined Samaniego crawling out of the shaft while Doc, Babe, and the mining engineer gathered around the plunger a hundred yards below. Though Terry didn't know how the real explosion had been detonated, every dynamite scene in every TV western he'd watched as a kid had featured either a plunger or a slow-burning fuse. Terry preferred the finality of the plunger.

"You positive we're back far enough?" Babe asked.

"It's a controlled charge," the mining engineer said. "Simple, easy, quick."

"The surer he sounds, the worrier I get," Doc muttered to Babe. "A hair too much dynamite could blow this mountain to bits."

"If you want the land office to inspect your claim…" The mining engineer flourished his hand at the plunger.

"The land office is our chance to be legitimate," Babe said.

Doc stepped aside and Babe replaced him at the plunger. She flexed her fingers as if she were about to play the piano.

"Let her rip," the mining engineer said.

Babe pressed the plunger home and the top of the mountain exploded in slow-motion, a torrent of rocks raining down on them as Babe gaped, Doc staggered backwards, and the mining engineer covered his head. Inside the mountain, walkways collapsed. Outside, Ben Samaniego sprawled across the Spanish armor, his twitching foot the only sign of life. The skeletons in the treasure room grinned.

The skeleton magic-markered on the door of the Decon room was riddled with red X's. Terry acknowledged it with a half-hearted salute and sat cross-legged on the concrete floor. His surgical whites, though made of soft cotton, chafed his tender skin. He knew from seeing others in this position how raw and blotchy he must look. He felt like a kid kept after school. What had he done wrong? How could he set things right? "Still Waiting to Decontaminate," the caption underneath the skeleton said. Terry leaned his back against the wall. There was no chair in the Decon room, no magazines—nothing to focus on but concrete.

Two years after the disastrous dynamite blast, on December 4, 1941, a group of enthusiastic treasure hunters gathered at the entrance to the Upper Noss Shaft, which was being dug to replace Doc's original route to the treasure room.

"The second meeting of the Cheyenne Mining Company is hereby called to order," Doc said. "Work is proceeding on schedule in the shaft. It's going to take some time, money, and labor yet, but I'd say that within a couple weeks we could have it ready to open. We need between six and seven thousand feet of lumber to finish timbering the shaft to comply with mining laws. I've got a few out-of-town gentlemen visiting Sunday who are interested in buying into the venture. I'm willing to sell off one of my percentage points to finance this thing. Anybody else willing?"

"I'll put up one of mine," Babe promptly said.

A few more volunteers chimed in.

"We've been offered a fair amount of money for this property," Doc continued. "Thirty-five thousand dollars for our talc claim, thirty-two thousand for the silver, and a hundred fifty thousand for the treasure. Who thinks we should consider these offers?"

"Not me," Babe said.

Everybody in the group agreed.

Terry had read the detailed minutes of the meeting compiled by the secretary of the Cheyenne Mining Company, a family friend, Merle Horzmann. It curdled his stomach to contemplate his grandmother's misguided expectations on that brisk afternoon in late fall. She and Doc had struggled for two bitter years after the explosion to regain access to the treasure, and success must have seemed tantalizingly close. Three days later, on the Sunday Doc was to make his pitch to the out-of-town gentlemen, Japanese bombers attacked Pearl Harbor. The United States Army annexed Victorio Peak and the surrounding desert soon after, and the Cheyenne Mining Company suspended operations for the duration of the war.

Seventy miles north of the peak, at a site code-named Trinity, the first atomic bomb mushroomed into the sky on July 16, 1945, at 5:30 a.m., rattling houses as far away as Doc and Babe's place in Hot Springs. The end of the war launched a legal battle between the U.S. Army and the State of New Mexico over the vast tract of land that included Victorio Peak. This dispute, which lasted eight years, provided Doc and Babe the opportunity to resume treasure hunting. As long as the issue of jurisdiction remained unsettled, they could conduct operations whenever finances permitted. In February of 1946, they finally arranged to have their claim assessed by an inspector from the state land office, consulting engineer Gordon Herkenhoff.

"This working consists of a shaft approximately 6 feet by 6 feet square, timbered to a depth of approximately 60 feet," Herkenhoff wrote in his report.

The shaft is reported to be 186 feet deep, with no timber beyond the 60-foot mark. I could not gain entrance to the shaft for lack of equipment to go beyond the timbered section. Dr. Noss claims that beyond the 186-foot depth, there is an incline downward at 45 degrees for 72 feet, which is now plugged by the cave-in. Beyond that there is supposed to be another incline upward at about 30 degrees for some short distance (40 feet, as I remember it) where entrance is gained to a cave some 2700 feet long, which contains many evidences that the cave was occupied as living quarters by a large group of humans for many years.

Herkenhoff's report described Doc as "a likable man who knew and was known by everybody." The report also noted that Doc had "surrounded himself with a group of real tough cowpuncher types from the Clovis area who were well armed and looked quite mean."

Based on Herkenhoff's report, the state land office granted Doc's claim, and Herkenhoff himself considered investing in the operation—until one night when Doc got riotously drunk and presented Herkenhoff with a bar that he insisted was gold even though it seemed obvious to Herkenhoff that the bar was brass.

The image of Doc haranguing Herkenhoff affected Terry like a nightmare, repellent yet fascinating. Babe had admitted to Terry that Doc had rigged up a few phony gold bars. She'd defended him on the grounds that he himself had been swindled too many times. People would promise to buy a gold bar, but once Doc handed it over, they'd refuse to pay. Doc couldn't complain to the police; the entire transaction was illegal. So Doc started selling fake gold bars, and if he got paid, he'd replace them with the real thing.

Terry hesitated to include this material in the screenplay because he didn't want the audience to lose faith in Doc. If Doc was viewed as a bad guy, then Babe might be seen as a fool—or an accomplice. Better to treat them both as heroes pitted against a hostile world.

In the year and a half between March 1938, when the first blackened bar was revealed as gold, and December 1939, when the mining engineer's dynamite charge collapsed the passageway to the treasure, Doc hauled from the depths of Victorio Peak an amount of gold bars Babe estimated at near two hundred, most of which he buried in the nearby desert for safekeeping. He never confided to Babe exactly where the bars were buried, but now and then he'd dig up a few and try to sell them. Babe had told Terry that in the fall of 1939, not long after the G-man's visit, Doc had put aside his misgivings and taken five gold bars to the Denver Mint, where the staff drilled holes in the bars, valued them at $20.67 per troy ounce, and issued Doc a hold certificate for $97,000, redeemable as soon as legal ownership was established. Unfortunately, in order to establish legal ownership, Doc and Babe needed to have the state land office inspect their claim, which obligated them to provide safe access, which was why they'd hired a mining engineer.

The explosion that followed only intensified Doc's paranoia. He never attempted to redeem the hold certificate for fear of being prosecuted. In a story full of frustrating twists, one of the worst involved this certificate. After Doc's death, the footlocker where he'd kept it disappeared, and when the family contacted the Denver Mint, they were informed that the mint identified receipts by number only, not by name.

Terry had grown up haunted by Babe's litany of deals gone sour: the Denver Mint fiasco, a series of bad bargains in Mexico, the Phoenix banker who stopped payment on a check for $60,000 and absconded with three bars of gold. He shouldn't have been surprised that the years of frustration and failure had strained his grandparents' marriage beyond the limit, but Babe had never even hinted at any serious discord between them. Terry remembered the sick feeling in his gut when he'd first read about Doc's second wife in an article in the *Albuquerque Journal.* What upset him most was not that Doc had left Babe for another woman, but that Babe had kept such a secret.

In retrospect, the clues he'd missed as a child appeared obvious. Whenever visitors pushed conversation in a direction Babe hadn't liked—toward the subject of Violet Boles, for instance—Babe quickly preempted all questions: "I ain't no Catholic, and you ain't no priest, and this ain't confession."

Terry's Aunt Letha blamed Doc's desertion on Merle Horzmann, secretary of the Cheyenne Mining Company and supposed family friend. Long after Doc's murder, Merle had been killed in a head-on collision when a vehicle packed with teenagers strayed across the double-yellow lines of Interstate 10. Babe and Letha had attended the funeral in Lordsburg, New Mexico, and afterwards Merle's husband had given them permission to go by the house and get the Cheyenne Mining Company files. Flipping through the files on the drive back to Clovis, Babe had found a series of letters Merle had written to the New Mexico state police in the early 1940s, letters so bizarre that even after Terry read them for himself he could hardly believe they existed.

The first letter, addressed to Captain Roy Vermillion, told of "lurid things" done by a group called the "Guerilla or Gorilla Gang," led by a man known as "the Dr." or "Doc." The second letter attempted to implicate Doc in one of New Mexico's most notorious unsolved cases, the disappearance of the Lorius party in 1936.

> In the June issue of the Finger Print and Identification Magazine from Chicago, there is a picture and the finger prints of Enrico Sapietri, alias Enrico Sampietro...whose age was 36 in 1937, which would check with my information; height 5'11 1/2"; weight 200; hair coarse wavy brown; eyes BLUE; complexion fair; neat dresser; occupation, engraver (his own statement); nativity, claims Milan, Italy. Middle finger left hand stiff and cannot be bent at joints. Man is wanted by U.S. Secret Service, Treasury Department for counterfeit notes.
>
> If you have not already done so, it might be wise to compare the fingerprints of M.E. Noss with these. His age is the same, and I have heard him declare that in 1937 he weighed 200 pounds, and it may also account for his reason for never doing any work in which he would have to use his fingers. I have also seen him dress so he looked just like this picture does, and I understand there is a way to change the color of the eyes, and at that time he could have had wavy hair, though now it is straight, but coarse, and he keeps it dyed...

As incredible as Merle's letters were, the response of the police was even more amazing—and more chilling, as far as Terry was concerned. "Your file regarding 'Doc Noss' has been received, and may prove of great value in this case," wrote Tom Summers, the Chief of the New Mexico State Police. "We have an investigator on the case and have hopes of being able to assist the Department of Justice in taking the Doctor out of circulation. Sorry to say we were unable to identify Noss as Enrico Sapietri. The finger prints of the two subjects are not the same.... In the event there should develop anything of interest in this case, you will be promptly advised."

Doc had long believed that someone was informing the police of his activities. They seemed to know his plans before he did and harassed him at every opportunity. His prime suspect, perhaps not surprisingly, was the person closest to him, but he never confronted Babe with his suspicions, and she had no way to repair the rupture between them. Eventually, the loss of trust led Doc to leave her.

The principal flaw in Letha's explanation was that Merle Horzmann wrote most of her letters in 1941, and Doc didn't run off with Violet Boles until 1947. Nevertheless, despite this chronological deficiency, Letha insisted on blaming Merle for Doc and Babe's breakup. The alternative would have been to acknowledge Doc's drinking problem, his temper, Babe's intractable will. Letha preferred to cast Merle as the villain, to treat Doc's "fling" as a temporary aberration. In the end, according to Letha, Doc regained his senses and reconciled with Babe. Terry couldn't deny that he found comfort in Letha's version of family history. It reinforced the theme of all the stories he'd grown up with, the theme of Doc and Babe's abiding love.

Instead of wasting valuable screen time on Merle Horzmann, Terry would simply show the day in 1947 when Roscoe Parr brought Violet Boles to the peak and introduced her as the daughter of a wealthy Arkansas mine owner. When dainty Violet led the way up the mountain to the Upper Noss shaft, prancing over the rocks in her tight skirt and cowboy boots, Doc ogled her from behind until Babe whacked him across the nose with her floppy hat.

Doc married Violet Boles on August 8, 1947. He gave his age as forty-two, though he was probably fifty-three at the time. Violet was thirty-six, "bone skinny," according to Letha's disparaging description, "dark headed and black eyed." The legitimacy of the marriage was contested after Doc's death on the grounds that Doc and Babe never legally divorced. Terry chose to avoid the issue and keep the focus of the movie on Babe, who, if the family stories were accurate, feared that Doc had discovered another way into Victorio Peak and somehow gotten trapped inside. She spent days tramping the peak and the surrounding desert, but located no clues to Doc's disappearance.

Months later, she took a job selling Washington National insurance. One day she called on a prospective customer named Ed Stahl. Terry had heard the Ed Stahl story over and over as a child, without ever pondering the implications of Doc's absence. The story had the ring of a folk tale, its details embellished with each retelling. Ed Stahl had closed the living room window, perched on the edge of the couch, and announced to Babe that in fact he needed some damn good insurance. Then, lowering his voice, he confided that Doc Noss's claim expired that night, and he, Ed Stahl, planned to jump Doc's claim.

"I guess you do need insurance," Babe told him.

"Sign me up," Ed said.

Terry had never asked how it was that Ed Stahl failed to notice Babe's last name, but as soon as he signed the forms, she snatched her copies, bustled to the car, and headed for Santa Fe. When the land office opened the following day, she was first in line. The clerk refused to allow her to renew the claim in Doc's name because Doc wasn't present to sign, so she renewed it in her name only. Then she drove to the peak and posted copies of the new claim papers in the tobacco cans that marked the boundaries of the Noss site.

Early the next morning, Ed Stahl tracked her down at her house in Hatch. It was barely light, the blinds were drawn, and evidently he didn't recognize her at first as his insurance agent.

"You Mrs. Noss?" he asked.

"Mm-hmm," she said, afraid her voice would rouse his memory.

"You just renew the claim on Victorio Peak?"

"Mm-hmm."

"How'd you know it was due to expire? You must keep mighty good track."

"Nah, you told me," she said, and snapped open the blinds.

After Stahl overcame his consternation, he asked if he could be her partner. "I'm an expert treasure hunter," he said.

"What experience you got?" she asked.

Stahl gritted his teeth to help him think better. "Well, I don't really have much experience, but I do have a heap of desire."

Babe burst into good-hearted laughter and held out her hand. "If desire makes an expert, I'm the world's leading authority."

Terry regretted the story's farfetched coincidences, but he appreciated its cinematic quality. Besides, there was no disputing that on January 10, 1949, Babe had indeed renewed the claim, setting in motion the series of events that would culminate in Doc's death at the hands of Texas oil man Charley Ryan.

Ryan owned a small company in Alice, Texas, that sold and repaired oil field equipment. In November of 1948, Doc had answered Ryan's ad for a truck driver and field man. Doc's dilapidated truck proved no match for the washboard roads of the oil fields, so Ryan advanced him enough cash to buy a new truck, under an agreement that Ryan would hold title until Doc paid him back. Ryan also agreed to cover $200 worth of checks Doc had bounced in Bishop, Texas. Doc and Violet moved into Ryan's remodeled garage, and Doc entertained Ryan with stories of vast treasure buried deep inside a pyramid-shaped mountain in southern New Mexico.

After Babe had renewed the claim, Doc's old partner Roscoe Parr telephoned Doc with the news that Babe now held exclusive rights to the entire treasure. Doc's suspicions of Babe seemed confirmed. He promised to sell Ryan fifty-one bars of gold stashed in the vicinity of Victorio Peak if Ryan would finance a trip to New Mexico. Ryan agreed.

Meanwhile, Babe resumed full-scale operations at the peak. She hired a bulldozer operator to put in seventeen miles of graded road and a mining crew to dig what would become the Ova Noss Intercept hole. When Doc and Ryan arrived in Las Cruces, along with their wives and a few of Ryan's oil business associates, Babe endured a double shock: her long-lost husband was alive, and married to another woman.

Doc and Ryan filed lead and copper claims on several sites in the Hembrillo Basin and hired a crew of their own to work just a mile from Victorio Peak. Occasionally, Doc and Babe would catch a glimpse of each other in the distance, but for weeks they avoided meeting face to face. Terry envisioned their reunion as a Hollywood classic. He took a few liberties with the facts, but only to capture what he felt to be the essence of the truth.

Sunset at the peak. Babe's crew piled into a truck and drove off toward Hot Springs. Doc stepped out from behind a stand of cottonwoods and began the long, slow climb to the top of the mountain. At the entrance to the Ova Noss Intercept, he stopped to catch his breath and survey the progress of Babe's work. The wind, which often picked up at sunset, whistled in his ears. Behind him, in the shadow of an overhanging rock, Babe sat on a ledge with a shotgun across her lap.

"Turn around, Doc, and let me get a good look at you," she said.

He hooked his thumbs through his belt loops and regarded her with an expression best described as bittersweet. "I was thinking how much this mountain has changed," he said. "The spring over by the cottonwoods dried up."

"Not dried up," she said. "Just moved underground."

"Maybe," he said. An uncomfortable silence stretched between them. "Appears you're doing a fine job here. You'll probably hit pay dirt any day now."

"Half of it's yours, Doc."

He glared at her. "I heard from Roscoe how you cut me out of the claim."

"Cut you out?" She peered at him with childlike incomprehension. "You weren't here to sign."

"'Course I wasn't here. Not with you tipping the cops on every move I wanted to make."

Her face seemed to lose its shape. She tried to push herself up from the ledge but couldn't find the strength.

"You all right, Babe?"

"I never tipped nobody." Distractedly, she gestured at the newly dug shaft leading down into the mountain. "I did all this for you."

"Sure you did," he said.

She stood up and propped the shotgun on the ledge. He took her elbow and escorted her to the edge of the shaft.

"Push me in if you don't believe me," she said.

They stood side by side, barely brushing at the hips. "I've made mistakes," he finally said. She covered his mouth with her hand. The soundtrack echoed the rollicking honky-tonk Babe played the first time they met. "Charley Ryan means to cheat me," Doc said. "I overheard a conversation. But don't worry, I got a plan."

Terry must have heard that line, or a more grammatical variation, in a hundred movies. *I got a plan.* The scene would always fade as soon as the hero began to whisper the specifics. Terry loved the old movie clichés. Their predictability was so reassuring. The hero would encounter enormous obstacles, yet the plan would succeed. Sometimes, half seriously, Terry expected his own life to achieve such celluloid perfection. Doc and Babe, he assumed, must have harbored similar delusions.

On March 4, 1949, a few days after their reconciliation, Babe's son Marvin Beckwith flew to the peak in a Piper Cub piloted by Curtis Noble. The ostensible purpose of the flight was to notify the crew at the peak that the bulldozer operator, Jack Woods, had gotten stuck in Hatch waiting for a part needed to repair the bulldozer. Terry believed that the real purpose of the flight was to fly gold bars from the peak to a landing strip near Hatch, with an eventual destination in Mexico. Doc wanted to remove the gold in three quick loads before Charley Ryan could steal it from him. Unfortunately, the plane developed a mechanical problem; Marvin and Curtis had to wait several hours for the necessary part to arrive; and instead of making the first flight in the morning, they didn't reach the peak till early afternoon. The wind had picked up by then, and the plane hit an unexpected downdraft. It crashed in the basin a few hundred yards east of the peak. The impact knocked Marvin Beckwith unconscious and broke Curtis Noble's neck.

Doc was the first person to reach the wreckage. He loaded Curtis and Marvin on an old mattress in the back of his pickup, covered them with blankets, and drove to Hatch. Curtis Noble died en route. An ambulance rushed Marvin, still unconscious, to William Beaumont Hospital in El Paso. Doc delivered Curtis Noble's corpse to the Hatch mortuary.

Meanwhile, in Hot Springs, Babe was driving home from the market when a siren sounded behind her. The flash of a cherry-top filled her rearview. As soon as she pulled over, a local policeman huffed up to the car. "I'm afraid your son Marvin was killed in a plane crash out at the peak."

Babe sped to the diner where Letha worked as a waitress. Lunch was long over and Letha was at the beauty parlor having her hair done. From her perspective sitting under the dryer, she saw Babe rush in, wildly flailing her arms. When Babe lifted the dryer and screamed that Marvin was dead, Letha rushed outside, hair curlers still in place. She ran halfway down the block before Babe drove up beside her and pushed open the passenger-side door.

Cut to Doc in a phone booth at the Valley Auto Company gas station in Hatch. "Come on, Babe," he said, listening to her line ring and ring. Frustrated, he dialed his stepdaughter Dorothy and found her at home feeding her baby, one-year-old Terry Delonas. "Your brother Marvin's been hurt," Doc told Dorothy. "But he'll survive." The baby fussed in the background— Terry's cameo. "Let Babe know I wanted to go to the hospital. Let her know I got real important business to settle. And let her know not to worry if she hears bad things about me. A good knife holds its edge."

At that moment, Babe and Letha raced by the gas station on their way to the mortuary, but they didn't see Doc, and he didn't see them.

The mortician was preparing Curtis Noble for an open-casket funeral when Babe and Letha arrived. "Marvin!" Babe said, dropping heavily to her knees. She stood up with difficulty as the mortician explained the situation. Letha, limp with relief, patted her hair and felt the unexpected metallic presence of curlers, which she distractedly removed and handed to Babe.

Emerging from the phone booth, Doc noticed a familiar figure at the gas pumps, a lanky cowboy who nodded and tipped his hat. "How's that sweet Letha doing, Doctor Noss?"

"She's married," Doc answered gruffly. "What's your name again?"

The cowboy, a twenty-seven-year-old army vet bound for a rodeo in Gallup, New Mexico, introduced himself as Tony Jolley.

"You staying the night?" Doc asked. "I might have a little job to do."

Oblivious to the gray walls of the Decon room, Terry envisioned a close-up of Babe and Letha driving to the hospital in El Paso, each staring straight ahead, and then a tracking shot of the car alone on the highway as daylight faded from the desert sky—and Doc rapped on the door of Tony Jolley's cabin. Without a word spoken between them, Tony Jolley grabbed his cowboy hat and climbed into Doc's pickup. As they headed east out of Hatch, the sunset at their backs, Doc reached across Jolley to open the glove compartment. A Colt .38 revolver and a silver flask lay across a stack of maps. Doc handed Jolley the flask.

By the time they reached their destination, the flask lay empty on the seat between them. The truck's headlights revealed a Western-style windmill beside a muddy watering hole.

"There's a shovel in the back," Doc said.

By the light of a kerosene lamp and a crescent moon, Doc paced off seven steps from the base of the windmill toward a prickly pear cactus. "Dig here." He watched intently as Jolley turned over the first few shovelfuls of dirt, then grabbed the shovel, dug the hole a foot deep, and struck metal. The vibration sent a shiver through his arms and chest. He unearthed a gold bar and let Jolley heft it.

"Where are we?" Jolley said.

"New Mexico," Doc said. "And it's your turn to dig."

Fade to the army doctor at William Beaumont Hospital lightly resting his hand on the small of Babe's back, attempting to usher her out of the waiting room. Letha trailed behind, her hair a spectacular mess.

"Believe me, Mrs. Noss, your son is going to be fine," the doctor said. "His worst injury is a broken leg."

"Then why's he in a coma?" Babe asked, shaking free of the doctor's hand.

"*Coma* is not the term I would use."

"He's still out, isn't he?"

"He suffered quite a shock."

"He rode forty miles on a mattress next to a cadaver," Babe said. "You'd be shocked, too." She hurried into the room before the doctor could stop her, laid her head on Marvin's chest, and listened to his heartbeat. When she looked up at the doctor and Letha, they leaned towards her expectantly. "Ain't a coma," she said. "Just sleep. Let's go find a hotel before the sun catches up with us."

According to Tony Jolley's sworn declaration, he and Doc drove from the windmill at what he subsequently learned was the Bruton ranch to a spot in the Hembrillo Basin near the old Henderson ranch, where they reburied the gold bars in a series of shallow holes. Then they took a break to eat a can of beans and some crackers, and Doc explained that he was moving the gold to keep his partner from double-crossing him. Jolley didn't ask for details. He estimated that over the course of the night he and Doc moved 110 gold bars among various locations. It was nearly daylight when Doc dropped him off at the motel cabin.

Terry had reconstructed the crucial events of the following afternoon from the transcripts of Charley Ryan's murder trial. Between one-thirty and two o'clock on Saturday, March 5, 1949, Doc's Hembrillo Basin crew pulled up at Charley Ryan's house in the company Jeep. They found Doc's blue pickup truck with "Ryan Tool Company" stenciled on the door parked out front facing the wrong way.

Willard Blake, the foreman of the crew, testified that Ryan and two of his associates marched out of the house with Doc. Ryan's wife lingered in the doorway. Ryan approached Blake and demanded to know what he was doing with the Jeep. Blake explained that Doc had given him permission to borrow it because Blake's own vehicle had broken a spring. Blake then gave the time book to one of Ryan's cronies, Jack Lawrence, who went inside to figure up the crew's pay for the week.

When Doc started for his truck, Ryan drew a gun—a Smith and Wesson .38—cocked it, and motioned Doc back into the house. Blake waited outside. Even from the sidewalk, he could hear Ryan's voice and Doc's raised in argument.

Terry could only guess what they were yelling at each other. "I told you I didn't steal your Jeep," he imagined Doc saying.

"No, but you sure as hell stole my gold," Ryan might have responded.

"If you pay me, I'll give it to you."

Terry pictured Ryan vehemently gesturing with his gun hand as he talked. "I'm giving you one last chance to tell me where you hid the gold."

Doc looked down as if to consider the matter and then charged Ryan, knocking him backwards into the living room window, which cracked but didn't shatter. Willard Blake prudently climbed into the Jeep. Doc dashed outside and Ryan followed. From the edge of the porch, Ryan fired a single shot from his .38 and Doc fell between the curb and the truck. Ryan strode toward him. "Get up from there," Ryan shouted.

Ryan's wife came out on the porch. "Shoot the son of a bitch," she screamed.

Ryan fired one more shot. Doc crumpled over the front fender of the pickup.

Willard Blake and the rest of the crew jumped out of the Jeep and ran, without their pay, for several blocks.

After a full day and night of sleep, Babe and Letha ventured from their hotel room in search of food. They stopped at the front desk to drop off their key.

"Are you Mrs. Noss?" the desk clerk asked. "I'm afraid I've got bad news. Your husband's been killed, ma'am."

"It wasn't my husband," Babe said with a bright smile. "It was my son. And he wasn't killed. He just broke his leg."

The desk clerk handed her the newspaper. "Mine Foreman Slain at Hatch," the headline read. Letha peered over Babe's shoulder.

Hatch, March 5 (AP) - M.E. Noss of Hatch was shot to death today. Charley Ryan surrendered voluntarily to Dona Ana County officers.

Sheriff A.L. Apodaca received the following account of the shooting.
Noss, labor foreman for Ryan's mining company, and Ryan engaged in a loud

argument over their business about 3:00 p.m.

Noss hit Ryan and knocked him into a window. Then Noss ran outside toward a pickup truck owned by the mining company. Just as he reached the truck, two shots were fired.

One of the bullets hit Noss in the right cheek just below the eye and lodged at the base of the brain below Noss' left ear.

No charges have been filed.

To exit the Decon room, all Terry needed to do was step into a decontamination booth and shut the door. A geiger counter would automatically monitor him from head to foot. If radiation had dropped to an acceptable level, the green light would flash and the exit door would click open. What could be simpler? Yet Terry hesitated. He had a superstition. Some rad techs tried to leave every five minutes, but Terry believed that each try used up a little luck. He knew it was irrational, but he hated to be turned back. He preferred to wait till he was sure.

Three days after Doc's death, Merle Horzmann, as administrator of Doc's estate and secretary of the Cheyenne Mining Company, filed a petition claiming that Doc died with no will and that Babe, as his widow, was sole heir. Merle sent a letter to Violet seeking "all documents, jewelry, trinkets, suitcases and their contents, trunks and their contents, bullion or other metals, regardless of where they came from, and all money, or anything whatsoever belonging to him [Doc] at the time of his death on March 5, 1949, as may have come to the Cheyenne Mining Company under an original agreement made and entered into in Las Cruces, New Mexico, on June 14, 1941 in the office of Benson Newell."

"Let me assure you that we have no intention to harm you in the least," the letter concluded. "It will be most helpful to yourself if you comply with this request."

Violet countered with a motion of her own claiming that *she* was Doc's widow and that a will had been left. The motion described Doc's estate as having "a value of almost fabulous proportions." Violet's lawyer, Melvin Reuckhaus, insisted that Violet held rights to all "documents, maps, and directions."

As the treasure of Victorio Peak became front page news, the Secret Service released to the press an FBI memo detailing Doc's criminal record. The

Santa Fe New Mexican ran a long article based on the memo.

> Identification of the late Dr. Milton Ernest Noss as an ex-convict today dampened nationwide interest in a treasure hunt in southern New Mexico which he set off. His FBI record notes that he has operated in the "confidence racket, old gold brick and gold mine swindle and buried treasure swindle."
>
> The quest he left behind is being carried out by Mrs. Ova Noss, his former wife, in Hembrillo Canyon of northern Dona Ana County.
>
> Noss, who was recently shot and killed at Hatch, claimed to have discovered a golden treasure and a mine there. He told of bars of gold bullion stacked like cordwood and a rich vein of ore. He said a cave-in prevented his removing the ore.
>
> Warden Howell Gage disclosed today that a Dr. M.E. Noss had done time in the state penitentiary here. He was sent up from Roswell in 1935, having been committed to [serve] from six to nine months for "insulting while armed"....
>
> The FBI report also shows:
>
> That the convict was arrested at Wellington, Texas, in 1934, charged with theft and practicing medicine without a license, and jumped bond.
>
> That he was arrested in Albuquerque in 1944 and charged with impersonating a federal officer. (The disposition of this case is not shown.)

Secret Service agent James Hirst told the Associated Press that a bar he'd taken from Doc's personal effects was "definitely not gold."

A few days later, though, the Secret Service officially denied having taken *any* of Doc's personal effects. Babe and Merle suspected the Secret Service of trying to cover their tracks. The inventory of Doc's personal property that Merle filed with the court accused the Secret Service of having seized Doc's trunk, his strong box, and fifty-four bars of gold. Though Babe had not seen the contents of the trunk for years, she believed that it contained a jeweled crown, gold coins, maps, and receipts from the Denver Mint.

According to the sworn statement of bulldozer operator Jack Woods, a Secret Service agent [James Hirst] had driven out to the peak shortly after Doc's death and asked Woods "to do a little grading" at a site near the peak "to see if we could uncover gold bars that had been put there quite awhile back in the presence of a Jack Lawrence and another man [Ryan's associates]." Wood bulldozed the site, but no gold bars were unearthed.

> Jim Hirst...asked me if I would stop in to see him in his office in the Federal

Building in Albuquerque, which I did. He asked me to tell him all I knew about the Doc Noss death and the buried treasure and I asked him if he thought there was anything to the story. He said that they had been after Doc Noss for peddling gold for years and that the gold had to be coming from some place and he believed there was something to the story.

As far as Terry was concerned, the frenzied maneuvering that followed Doc's death revealed the strong degree of certainty people felt that the treasure existed. No one, not even the Secret Service, would have expended so much effort on a phantom treasure.

When Charley Ryan's trial convened in Las Cruces on May 26, 1949, spectators crowded into the courtroom, eager to glean a clue to the current whereabouts of Doc's gold. Babe and Letha commandeered the front row, where they shouted advice to the special prosecutor, Melvin Reuckhaus, who, despite the potential conflict of interest, also represented Violet Boles Noss, demurely seated a few rows behind Babe and Letha. In another potential conflict of interest, Ryan's defense attorney, Benson Newell, had represented Doc in several matters, including the formation of the Cheyenne Mining Company.

The first prospective juror set the tone of the trial when he testified that anyone who plugged Doc Noss deserved a medal. Judge William T. Scoggins fixed the juror with a fierce glare. "Despite your obvious prejudice against the deceased, you will make your decision on the basis of the evidence you hear before this court and not based on your pre-conceived ideas, will you not?" Neither side challenged the juror.

After a brief opening statement, the prosecution managed to establish that Charley Ryan fired the shot that killed Doc Noss. Then the prosecution rested. No attempt was made to present a motive for the killing. Gold was never mentioned.

The defense called the reverend of Ryan's church and the vice president of Ryan's bank to extol his sterling character. Ryan himself testified that Doc had convinced him to invest in a lead mine. "I was the only honest man he had ever found," Ryan said. After arriving in Hatch, Ryan began talking to fellow Masons and was aghast to learn that Doc had a bad reputation. On the day of the killing, Doc asked to borrow $350, and Ryan refused. "If you don't let me have this $350, I will kill you," Ryan woodenly quoted Doc as having said. When Ryan refused, Doc hit him and ran outside yelling, "I will kill every last one of you sons of bitches."

Under questioning, Ryan explained that Doc wanted the $350 to pay for an assay of metal reputed to be gold.

"I said, 'No, Doc, I told you before I came up here that I didn't want any part of the gold because I have found out from Mr. Walters that it is against the law to have more than two ounces of gold in your possession at any time. Therefore, I don't want any part of it.'"

"Why did you shoot him?" the defense attorney asked.

"I was afraid of him. He had already hit me in the house. He is quite a bit bigger than me. He had bragged about how many people he had killed. I didn't want to kill him, but I was trying to protect my family, my home life, my associates."

During cross-examination, the prosecution accused Ryan of changing his testimony since the preliminary hearing.

"I read the statement over, and the little lady made quite a few mistakes," Ryan said.

Special prosecutor Reuckhaus asked Ryan to repeat exactly what he had said to Doc when they went back into the house.

"'I have found out from good reliable citizens here that you are no good, you have robbed these people and cheated them. We are through. We are going back to Texas. I am going to have the sheriff arrest you and send you to the penitentiary. That is where you belong.'"

When the special prosecutor asked him why he fired the second shot, Ryan testified, "I thought he had fell down there to make me believe I had hit him, then he would jump up and go around and get his gun. I hollered at him. After the first shot, I hollered again." Ryan insisted that he had never fired a gun before in his life. "I was lucky to hit him, but I think it was an act of God."

After Ryan's pious performance, a succession of witnesses denounced Doc as a gun-toting con man.

"Was Doc's reputation good or bad?" the defense attorney asked each witness.

Lulu Fincher's response was typical. "Bad—with emphasis on the bad."

When the defense rested, the prosecution declined to present any further evidence. Not a single witness was called to defend Doc's character. No counter-argument was offered. The jury deliberated for less than two hours before finding Ryan not guilty on all counts.

Neither Babe nor Letha cried at the verdict. Terry pictured their grim exit from the courtroom as he himself rose to his feet. The movie couldn't end at the trial, he decided. It would have to end at Victorio Peak.

Despite occasional interference from the army, Babe and her crew, the Hardly Able Mining Company, continued to work intermittently at the peak until 1955, when the army won its lawsuit against the state of New Mexico and evicted Babe for the last time.

As Terry entered the decontamination booth, he permitted himself a shallow sigh of satisfaction. If traffic was light, he'd be less than an hour late. A quick meeting with Ralph Monroe would leave him time to race home and scribble down these new ideas. If he could just finish the screenplay, a retired press agent friend had promised to get a Disney executive to read it.

The geiger counter in the decontamination booth reached Terry's thick eyebrows and clicked. The red light flashed. The door to the outside world refused to budge. Terry stepped back into the Decon room. His screenplay would remain unfinished, but the story of Doc and Babe would play on in his imagination, forever possessed of the flickering enchantment of an old movie.

10

In for a Nickel,
in for a Dime

*For some people there's a day
when they have to come out with the great Yes
or the great No.*
—C. P. Cavafy

June 1993—David Schweidel

The second call came when Boz and I were in Colorado. We'd brought our laptops to a ramshackle house in Telluride. We wrote mornings and hiked afternoons. Our plan was to hack out an outline and sample chapter. The hikes gave us time to talk strategy. In the three weeks since meeting Terry, I'd read hundreds of pages about the Noss family saga, the history of gold in the Southwest, and the treasure hunt now in progress. Sorting out the story was like wrestling an octopus. The challenge was to grasp all the tentacles at once.

When Boz called Terry to clear up a few questions, Terry trumped us with news of a major development. I remember Boz mouthing the words for my benefit: *major development.* Seemed a tunnel-finding expert had come to the peak and located an enormous cavern. A tunnel-finding expert from the Department of Defense. With a Ph.D. in Physics. How this expert located the cavern, Terry didn't happen to mention. Boz and I could stay in Telluride and write, or go to Las Cruces and get the scoop.

· · ·

Boz drove; I jotted down ideas for organizing the book. The problem with chronological order, we agreed, was too many facts too soon. Coronado's quest for the Seven Cities of Gold? The exploits of Chief Victorio? Better to create interest first. Give the reader a framework to hold together all the details. The key, we decided, was to focus on Terry. Present the details, whenever possible, from *his* perspective. For Terry, the details went beyond facts; they had emotional content.

What about us? Should a pair of intrepid reporters be in the story? We saw no reason to insinuate ourselves.

Both of us liked the idea of starting in the middle. It worked for *The Iliad*, Boz said. Chapter One would show Terry at the Pentagon; Chapter Two, Terry as a kid. We'd move back and forth, from Terry's efforts to win an Act of Congress to past events, like Goldfinder and Doc's murder. We split the book into two parts, each consisting of seven chapters. The ending, by necessity, remained hazy. It would depend on when discovery was made and what, exactly, was discovered.

The best way to tell the story, we assumed, was like a novel, presenting crucial events in scenes narrated from the point of view of a participant, usually Terry. We chose this approach because we wanted to convey not only the facts—most of which were in dispute—but also the *experience* of plunging into a treasure hunt.

Ten hours after leaving Telluride, we walked into the ONFP house in Las Cruces. It was a Sunday night, and the treasure hunting crew had put off their drive to base camp because game two of the NBA finals had gone into overtime. Phoenix vs. Chicago, Charles Barkley vs. Michael Jordan. Boz and I felt right at home. We'd been listening to the game on the radio. When Phoenix finally won, somebody called it a good omen. The plucky underdogs from out west had kept the faith and been rewarded. Terry didn't look so sure. He'd emerged from his room to cheer along with everyone else, but now the strain showed, as if he, too, carried the burden of trying to beat the perennial champs.

The major development, he told us after the crew had left, was almost too good to be true. The physicist from the Department of Defense had spent two days tramping the peak and the surrounding desert. Not only had he located all known tunnels and caves and accurately estimated their size and depth, but he'd also proclaimed the existence of a major cavern near Geronimo Peak.

How did he find the tunnels? we asked. What technology did he use?

Technology might not be the best word, Terry said. He used an L-shaped brass rod.

Our disappointment seemed to register on Terry's face. The Ph.D. from the Department of Defense was a dowser. Oh, and he'd already returned to DC, another little item Terry had neglected to mention in the phone call with Boz. Yet we couldn't hold a grudge. Terry looked worse than we felt. His eyes had a milky glaze. His nagging cough was dredging up stuff from deep in the lungs. He apologized for any confusion. The chaos level, he said, was higher than usual. The Director of Field Operations had just been let go.

The intrepid reporters pressed for more info. Long story, Terry said. He was obviously tired. We set a time for an interview, then went to Boz's, occupied for the summer by house-sitters, but out back stood a former chili-drying shed that Boz and his wife had converted into a guesthouse. Casa Schweidel, they called it, at least when I visited.

Five a.m. buzzed the alarm too soon. Boz and I drove to the peak in the dark with one of the treasure hunters, Greg Engstrom, a retired army major in his late forties who'd met Terry while serving at White Sands Missile Range. Greg talked and talked. In the universe of Victorio Peak, he played the role of Greek chorus.

The crew was down, he said. No one knew whether to trust the coat hanger or not. *Coat hanger* was Greg's term for the dowsing rod. If the coat hanger flopped, the crew would have to go back inside the mountain. Digging out the mountain took courage, Greg said. Breaking rock with no jackhammer, no dynamite. The other day three men had worked all morning to move one rock. Then they hit a bigger rock. BFR, in Gregspeak: Big Fucking Rock.

Greg had his doubts about dowsing, but he did tell a story of spraining his ankle in Taiwan. The Chinese doctor had covered the ankle with herbs. The herbs smelled horrid; the ankle healed overnight. It wasn't Western science, but it worked, Greg said. Then he launched into his story about high tech and low tech. We'd heard it before, on our previous visit, how high tech and low tech beat the Russians in Afghanistan. When the rebels had needed weapons, the U.S. sent in Stinger missiles. To carry the missiles into the mountains: Tennessee mules. No spare parts, no breakdowns. High tech and low tech. That's what we need, Greg said, to find this treasure.

He told his stories well, but they suffered in the retelling. He tended to use the same words, same inflections. The drive did not fly by. We stopped now and then; I'd jump out, open a cattle gate, and close it behind us. As soon as the sun cleared the rim of the mountains, the light took on a dullness I associated with extreme heat. Even the dust seemed thicker this time around. Greg was extolling the virtues of one of his inventions—the special jacket for crosswalk guards or his magnetized map of the United States—when we came upon a car stuck in the sand.

The car belonged to another treasure hunter, Mike Levine, who was down on his knees digging sand away from the left rear tire, digging by hand, but the sand was especially fine after several months without rain, and it kept filling back in. One moment I was standing tall, hands clean, jeans blue, the next I was down in the dirt on my knees. It's a moment I've looked back on since, that switch from clean to dirty, from bystander to participant. Eventually, after twenty minutes of digging and wheel-spinning and bracing with pieces of wood, we pushed Mike's car free. I have to admit, though, that before the last try, the futility of our efforts seemed to affect the likelihood of treasure in Victorio Peak. The logic was idiotic but persuasive: *If I'm on my knees scooping sand with both hands, how can there be any gold?* The fallacy, no doubt, had a flip-side: when work went well and the desert performed its magic, discovery seemed imminent. What a burden, though, to be a member of the crew, if the presence or absence of treasure depended on how you felt.

Boz and I spent less than 72 hours in the Victorio Peak universe. One episode stood out. Wednesday morning, Boz and I went to the ONFP house to interview Terry. By then, he'd been diagnosed with bronchitis. His brother Jim was flying in from Houston to handle negotiations with a man named Marketic, who claimed to know the whereabouts of a cache of gold bars and was willing to sell his information for half the take. Terry felt too rundown to haggle. I'd give away the ranch, he said. Not that we have a ranch.

Brother Jim arrived just as Terry and Boz and I were headed to lunch. Most of the crew were at the house. Terry had called them in from the peak the night before. Everyone was standing around the living room, debating the pros and cons of cutting a deal, when Marketic and his posse made their entrance. Fancy cowboy hats, flashy boots, belt buckles that sparkled. The star was Marketic's daughter, Miss USA of 1992. Among the orbiting treasure hunters, she exerted quite a pull.

Terry, though, heaved a raspy sigh. Welcome to meeting number five thousand, he said to Boz and me. And they're all exactly like this.

On the drive back to Telluride, we talked about Terry's weariness. He'd answered our questions all morning and half the afternoon, with wit and energy. His attention never flagged. Yet in that moment when he'd turned to us and sighed, we'd sensed his fatigue, his frailty.

Our route took us north to Albuquerque, then west on I-40, traveling toward sunset. This was Georgia O'Keefe country. The rugged mountains turned pink; the sky, a delicate peach. The tender colors softened the harsh landscape. As my mind drifted from nature to art, the usual road-trip reflections, I had the unexpected thought that Terry might commit suicide. The thought lingered as the light slowly faded.

How do you think the story will end? I asked after a while.

Boz shrugged. A little more highway rolled by. I just want to see Terry walk into that big cavern, he said. Even if he finds *nada*. I just want to see him walk in there.

After dark, we stopped at a bar on Highway 666, somewhere north of Gallup. The other customers were all young men, all Navajo, all drinking Budweiser. Another basketball game was on TV, but we didn't feel right at home. No one looked at us. No one spoke, except when we ordered our Buds. The sound on the TV was broken or off. Boz went in search of the men's room. The ice box hummed. When Boz came back, he gave me a look that I assumed had to do with the men's room. I ducked out the back door. The yard was dark except for a bare bulb inside a stall that locked from the outside. Chickens clucked in the darkness. I left the door to the stall open for fear that someone would lock me in.

An hour down the road I mentioned the door. I said it might be a metaphor, for getting locked inside the story.

Did you leave it open? Boz asked.

Did you?

The last part of the drive, Boz talked about getting back to his family, the virtues of marriage and parenthood. You'd make a good dad, he said.

By the end of the week, we'd completed a sample chapter and outline. Boz sent the packet to his agent, who sent it on to his editor. A month and a half later, home in my Oakland apartment, I got the third call.

Boz, I should mention, loathes the telephone. He often sounds like he's breaking bad news. He'd heard from his agent, he said. His editor had found our proposal impressive but preferred to wait on any advance. The prospects for our book, according to the publisher, depended on the outcome of the treasure hunt. If Terry and company struck gold, so might the book. If they struck out, the book's likely value would drop. Waiting might make sense for the publisher, but did it make sense for us? Boz was working on a new novel; I was working only on *this*. No advance meant no security. If I left my job to spend time at the peak, there was no money-back guarantee. Yes, we could wait for discovery, then try to rush a book into print, but the quality would suffer, and besides, the story went beyond treasure, and maybe I *had* gotten locked inside.

One thing for sure, whenever I mentioned the story, people wanted to hear more. Everyone asked different questions. What were the treasure hunters like? Had the army stolen the gold? The story was like an ink-blot test. It took many forms: mystery, techno-thriller, soap opera, folk tale. Some people brought up Kafka; others, the Knights Templar.

Where did the gold come from? That was the question that nagged me the most. I'd been doing research at the Bancroft Library, tracking down references to treasure in the Southwest. If a fortune lay buried in Victorio Peak, there should be clues to its origins in the historical record. I took the grain-of-truth approach. Doc had found *something*, but was it worth the time to write a book?

What do you want to do? Boz asked, his phone-voice low and mournful.

I didn't know. If our success depended on the truth of Doc's story, we were no better off than Terry.

Instead of quitting my job, I wangled a two-month leave of absence, un-paid. In September, with the treasure hunters on the verge of what Terry called *the last big push*, I packed a suitcase and moved into Casa Schweidel.

PART III

(Overleaf) Doc and Babe and the Cheyenne Mining Company, 1941.

11

DC to LC

When you set out for Ithaka
pray that your road's a long one
—C. P. Cavafy

1989-1992

Briefcase in hand, Congressional ID badge pinned to the lapel of his dark blue suit, Terry Delonas strode the labyrinthine corridors of the Capitol Building as if he knew his way around, and in fact he did find the hearing room half an hour before his meeting with Alma Moore, the chief counsel of the House Armed Services Committee. He'd left himself extra time because the chance of getting hopelessly lost seemed higher with no one else along. Though he missed Bill Casselman's polished presence, the phlegmatic calm of Ralph Monroe, even Norman Scott's tenacity, he relished the prospect of meeting with the chief counsel alone. The give and take of face-to-face negotiations was a talent he'd discovered over the past few months. He kept things simple, he put his faith in the system, and his low key sincerity seemed to win people's trust.

The empty room was smaller than he expected from having seen it on TV, shorter than a conventional courtroom but wider. Seals representing each branch of the military hung from the walls, along with a copy of the Constitution. He sat down at a conference table, popped open his briefcase, and removed the latest set of photographs of illegal excavations conducted at Victorio Peak.

• • •

After his first meeting at White Sands Missile Range, in April of 1988, he had received a call at the Las Cruces Hilton.

"Well, you caught us," the caller said.

"Who's this?" Terry had asked.

"This is Bill. One of the guys who dug the tunnel you showed General Jones today. We didn't mean to jump your claim. We had no idea the Noss family was still in the hunt."

Terry let Bill talk. Ten people were involved in the operation, Bill said. Most worked at the base, four as military policemen. "We've accomplished a lot. Taken Babe's shaft down and to the west. There's cool air coming from somewhere down there. It could be a cavern. I think we're pretty damn close."

"Pretty damn close," Terry said, employing the tone his therapist used when she wanted to draw him out.

"The point is, we'd like to throw in with you, if you're willing. At least talk to us. Let us show you what we've done."

On his next trip to Las Cruces, he'd met with the group at a dimly lit restaurant. They brought photos far more revealing than the ones Norman Scott had acquired, including pictures taken inside the shaft that showed the remains of a windlass Babe had used back in 1955 and the new thirty-foot tunnel the group had dug. Bill Childers turned out to be an Equipment Specialist for Test and Evaluation Command at the base; his wife, a secretary to the Deputy Commander. Childers had become interested in Victorio Peak during Operation Goldfinder. After getting assigned to White Sands in 1986, he'd called Lambert Dolphin and posed as a graduate student writing a paper about the peak. Dolphin had answered all his questions, even offering his best guess as to where the treasure lay. Childers and his group had simply followed Dolphin's directions.

"Another few weeks and we'd have found it," Childers said. "Give us a chance and we'll finish the job."

"If we hired you," Terry said, "we could be held responsible for what you've done. Which, technically, was illegal. Our whole project would be compromised."

"Maybe on an unofficial basis?"

"I can't do anything that might mess up our relationship with the army," Terry said. He thanked Childers and the others for talking to him.

"We envy you," Childers said. "We really do."

Terry left with the photos and later gave copies to General Jones, who had investigated no further, and in fact never acknowledged that any illegal digging had occurred.

The chief counsel of the House Armed Services Committee would view the matter with more concern.

Alma Moore was a good listener. In Terry's limited experience, most people in Washington were *quick* listeners: they listened until they determined whether you were friend or foe, weak or powerful, solid citizen or crackpot. As soon as they made their assessment, they moved on. Alma Moore, in contrast, had the patience to hear you out. She asked questions. She caught nuances. She was an unimposing figure, a matronly woman in her mid-fifties wearing a conservative blue suit and cream-colored blouse with a minimum of ruffles, but when she spoke, her words commanded attention.

"If the army is ripping us off," she said after Terry showed her the photos, "we'll have them for lunch."

She marched over to the framed copy of the Constitution and jabbed her finger at Article 1, Section 9. "No Money shall be drawn from the Treasury, but in Consequence of Appropriation made by Law," she recited. "Congress appropriates the money—doesn't anybody get it?"

Terry attributed her outrage to the Iran-Contra scandal. Congress had voted to suspend aid to the Nicaraguan contras, but the executive branch, in the person of Lieutenant Colonel Oliver North, had bankrolled the contras anyway, siphoning the proceeds from secret arms sales to Iran in flagrant violation of the law. Alma Moore seemed to suspect that the army might regard the Victorio Peak treasure as a potential source of funds unrestricted by the mandates of Congress. Terry chose not to mention that he had met with the diggers and that they appeared to have pursued the treasure entirely on their own. Instead, he presented the portion of the truth that best supported his case. "The general insists he knew nothing about it."

"Somebody had to know," Alma Moore said.

"What we're trying to figure out is why the army has gone to such great lengths to keep us off the peak," Terry said. "They claim there's nothing there, but the pictures tell a different story."

Alma Moore promised to help Terry uncover the truth, and he left the meeting convinced that he'd gained an important ally.

On March 16, 1989, the chair of the House Armed Services Committee, Les Aspin, wrote Terry an encouraging letter:

> I just wanted to let you know I am doing everything I can to open White Sands Missile Range to your expedition. As you know, the U.S. Army claims that the U.S. Congress will have to pass legislation providing you access to Victorio Peak. I am not satisfied with the Army's claim and I am looking for ways to have the Army reconsider. In the meantime, please stay in touch....

A few days later, Alma Moore summoned a senior Pentagon attorney to meet with Terry and Bill Casselman. She wasted little time on pleasantries. "What does the army think it's doing?"

"There's no mystery," the Pentagon attorney said in the most reasonable of tones. "A civilian wishes to conduct a search on a U.S. Army base. The base requires direct compensation for all expenses incurred. Appropriate legislation must therefore be obtained."

"Why?" Alma Moore asked.

"That's the law," the attorney said.

"Les Aspin doesn't think so."

"The army does."

Alma Moore paused as if to consider the value of further conversation, then pointed to the door. "Thank you," she said. "You're dismissed."

"Pardon me?" the attorney said.

"Good-bye," Alma Moore said. She turned to Terry as if the attorney were already gone. "If they won't let us do this the easy way, we'll just have to do it the hard way." The strategy she outlined was to order the army to draft the provision and attach it to the military appropriations bill, which would become law by the end of the year. "If the army writes it," she said, "they can't oppose it. In fact, everyone will assume it has their full support."

Afterwards, Bill Casselman called the meeting a turning point. Terry didn't argue, but in his mind the turning point had come earlier, when Alma Moore delivered her impassioned speech in front of the Constitution. The story would become part of his pitch to potential investors, how he'd finally found someone on the inside who believed in their cause, someone with clout, someone who wouldn't quit.

A commercial for Orange County's largest car lot played on the big-screen TV set up at the far end of the Irvine Hilton's Presidential Suite, which Craig Harrison had finagled free of charge for the evening's festivities. "Unsolved Mysteries" was premiering its Victorio Peak episode, and a few dozen friends and investors had gathered to celebrate. Terry, surrounded by a circle of well-wishers, hoped the show wouldn't flop. He caught a glimpse of Craig replenishing the supply of hors d'ouvres at the buffet table, and for a second Craig's face seemed shadowed with a similar worry. Then Craig must have realized he was being watched; he flashed Terry his sunniest smile. With his long blond hair and surfer build, he looked like he'd stepped out of a Beach Boys song.

"I remember Robert Stack from 'The Untouchables,'" someone near Terry was saying.

Robert Stack hosted "Unsolved Mysteries." The show had a pulp nonfiction format, and Stack's portentous tone turned every story into melodrama, not that the saga of Doc and Babe needed much help in that direction. Terry had been leery of tabloid television when the producer of the show approached him, but he'd decided that the sleaze factor was outweighed by the chance to rouse public interest in the peak and thereby pressure the army to permit a search. Now, though, moments before the broadcast, he worried that a cheesy production might jeopardize congressional support. "We don't like having just murders and missing-person stories," the producer had told him. His mother used to say that people judged you by the company you kept. She'd disapproved of "The Untouchables."

Terry, despite his misgivings, smiled brightly. "Robert Stack starred in *Airplane*," he said. "I think he has a sense of humor."

The shooting of the segment had gone surprisingly well. The governor of New Mexico, Garrey Carruthers, had agreed at the last minute to appear on camera. The director and his crew were hundreds of miles away at Carlsbad Caverns filming a reenactment of Doc and Babe's discovery of the treasure, so Terry had volunteered to take a freelance crew to Santa Fe and conduct the interview. "This is a solvable mystery," Governor Carruthers had said. "Let's do it."

Despite the governor's endorsement, Terry had been plagued by fears that the show would somehow discredit the project, grossly misrepresenting the facts or committing a substantial legal or political blunder. Unwilling to let the worst happen, he'd shown up at the first editing session uninvited, knocking on the door of a Coalinga sound studio at six a.m. "We don't tolerate crashers," the editor, John Cosgrove, had said. Terry had promised not to say a word, and Cosgrove had let him in. When questions arose during the session—was the gold discovered in '37 or '38? Who planted the dynamite?—the scriptwriter would hesitate and Terry would whisper the answer in his ear. Cosgrove soon bypassed the scriptwriter and questioned Terry directly. The session went so well that Terry had been formally invited to the second edit, where a stand-in for Robert Stack had read the final script while the film footage was cut to match.

So Terry had a fair idea what to expect from the premiere, yet when the lights dimmed and Craig turned up the volume on the big-screen TV, he flinched. What if Alma Moore or Les Aspin saw the show and found it ridiculous? Then Robert Stack appeared in a trench coat and everyone cheered.

Twenty-one million people watched the Victorio Peak episode of "Unsolved Mysteries." The boisterous crowd in the Presidential Suite clapped and whooped at the final line: "But maybe, just maybe, they'll find the greatest treasure the modern world has ever known." Terry was surprised that the investors he considered most sophisticated were among the most enthusiastic, though one pronounced the show "high camp." Alex Alonso quibbled with the camera work, Ralph Monroe found the program "not entirely frivolous," and Judy Holeman lavished particular praise on the interview with Governor Carruthers.

The only harsh criticism came from Terry's aunt Letha. "The guy who played Doc walked hunkered over like a bear. And Mama was much more dignified than the woman who played her. They picked the horriblest people to represent us."

Craig offered his review after everyone else had left: "Masterpiece Theater it wasn't."

"A little trashy," Terry agreed, "but the suite was first class."

Craig flicked off the lights and closed the door behind them with a barely perceptible click. Terry started for the elevators.

"Wait," Craig said.

The two of them stood alone in the carpeted hallway, which seemed to emit a faint electric hum. When Craig put his hand on Terry's arm and pursed his lips like a little boy trying to look serious, Terry had the terrible intuition that Craig was dying—the oxygenation therapy had failed and he'd developed full blown AIDS. As Craig gazed appraisingly into his eyes, Terry braced himself for the confession.

"You okay?" Craig asked.

"Me?" Terry said. "I'm fine."

"You look like shit," Craig said. "Pardon my French."

Terry found himself unable to speak. He patted his face as if in search of a stray crumb.

"You let this TV show take you up and down like a roller coaster," Craig went on. "You need to catch your breath."

"I'm fine," Terry repeated. "Besides, the show's over."

"Not 'The Terry Delonas Show,'" Craig said. "This week Terry goes to Washington. Next week Terry goes *mano a mano* with General Jones."

"I can't stop now," Terry said.

"Why not?" Craig asked. "Why not get off the roller coaster for a while?"

"I don't have time," Terry said.

"You're such a drama addict," Craig said.

"That's not fair," Terry said.

"But maybe, just maybe,"—Craig imitated Robert Stack's stern baritone—"the drama addict can take a day off now and then."

Terry bowed his head as if in acceptance of Craig's judgment and they started down the hall.

"So how's *your* health?" Terry asked.

"Tip-top," Craig said.

Terry put his arm around Craig's shoulders. His heartbeat began to slow down. False alarm.

·   ·   ·

The morning after the broadcast of "Unsolved Mysteries," Terry was sitting in his cubicle at American Savings and Loan when Bill Casselman called with the news that the Department of the Army had approved the petition. In practice, approval meant little—Terry still needed an act of Congress— but the timing of the approval permitted him to believe that the broadcast had convinced the army to relent. It was a cheery thought on a day when depression threatened to overwhelm him. He felt hungover, not from last night's one glass of champagne, but from the aftershock of his premonition, which, though mistaken, lingered in his mind like a bad dream. He couldn't shake the idea that Craig was dying.

Craig refused to consult a conventional doctor. He believed that the oxygenation therapy had cured him—and Terry too. The two of them had driven down to Tijuana for the first "miracle shot." Per the doctor's instructions, they'd fasted on fruit juices for three weeks prior to the visit. The doctor, newly arrived from England, had administered blood tests and then injected them with a secret formula designed to quadruple the amount of oxygen in their blood and thereby "burn up" the virus. After several months of blood tests and shots, the doctor had declared them cured. Terry regarded the diagnosis as a long shot at best. He'd continued to see his personal physician and pursued other, less exotic treatments. Craig, on the other hand, had quit seeing doctors altogether. He'd proclaimed his health excellent, and that was that.

Terry took his fifth and sixth Ibuprofen of the morning. Though he tried to keep his private life separate from the project and from his job, sometimes the barriers he erected seemed as flimsy and artificial as the partitions around his desk. He could have walked over to Judy's cubicle and talked to her about Craig, but instead he went to work on the savings and loan brochure he was supposed to be writing, only to abandon it a few minutes later and pull out the yellow legal pad with his "To Do" list for the project.

The legislative effort was gathering momentum. Representatives Joe Skeen and Marvin Leath had officially asked Les Aspin to add language to the upcoming appropriations bill that would provide for the army's reimbursement. The Secretary of the Army's general counsel had received letters from Representatives Skeen and Leath and Senator Jeff Bingaman requesting that the army draft legislation "to permit the White Sands Missile Range to be directly reimbursed for expenses incurred in allowing a private entity access to the range." Alma Moore had assured Terry that the army would comply. No opposition appeared likely to arise in Congress.

General Jones presented the biggest obstacle to the success of the project, Terry decided as he doodled on the legal pad. Jones's staff had drawn up a list of prospective charges for the first three months of the search that totaled a staggering $479,000. Jones continued to insist that all work be contracted through the base at rates that Terry regarded as exorbitant. The environmental assessment was the most egregious example. The base wanted to charge $200,000. An outside contractor would do the job for $40,000. Jones, however, refused to budge.

The man was a mule, Terry thought. It occurred to him, as his pen hovered over the notepad, that Craig Harrison practiced his own brand of mulishness. He refused to face unpleasant possibilities. Terry vaguely remembered a joke of Babe's about a mule and a hickory switch. First, the punch line went, you had to get the mule's attention.

June 8, 1989. Army Materiel Headquarters, Alexandria, Virginia. A telecommunications satellite connected the conference room in Alexandria to a conference room at White Sands Missile Range. The purpose of this satellite link-up, paid for by ONFP at a cost of $10,000, was to involve representatives from Congress and the Pentagon in negotiations with General Jones.

Unfortunately, only Gordon Hobbs from the Department of the Army and Congressional aide Bruce Donisthorpe had joined Terry and his support team of Norman Scott, Bill Casselman, and financier Ed Carpenter. They were no match for Jones, whose imposing figure now appeared on the video screen. Decked out in combat boots and camouflage fatigues, he looked more than capable of dispatching a gaggle of bureaucrats in conservative suits from two thousand miles away.

True to his military roots, Jones began the satellite conference with a preemptive strike, refusing to deal directly with Terry on the grounds that another claimant might sue him for showing favoritism. Jones would deal only with someone who represented *all* the claimants, which left Norman Scott to do the talking for Terry's contingent, or, as Scott termed it, *contingency*. When Scott mentioned that the license agreement was being negotiated in the name of ONFP, Jones responded with obvious derision: "That ain't the smart way to go." Scott suggested that the issue was unimportant since the rightful owner of any treasure found would be adjudicated in court, but Jones was not swayed. "I will not deal individually with the Ova Noss Foundation or any other individual claimant," he said.

Terry felt compelled to respond. "We've already spent a great deal of money inviting the other known claimants to come forward."

When Bill Casselman attempted to elaborate ONFP's position, Jones cut him off: "We have nothing to discuss, sir. I will not discuss the issue with you."

The rest of the meeting consisted of Jones and Scott debating the costs of the project.

"I cannot, unfortunately, because the government won't let me, charge anybody beyond their actual costs," Jones said with a grin. "If I could make a profit, I'd be in good shape. But neither, Norman, will I eat a penny." Jones said that if he spent twenty-five cents mailing Scott a letter, Scott would be charged for it based on the standard rate. "All you get charged for, Norman, is what you use. The rate comes out of the Department of Defense manual. We can't change the rate." Jones's point soon became abundantly clear. He would charge the project for every cost the base incurred. The rate was fixed and beyond his control. "Understand," he said, "there ain't no free lunch."

Scott eventually won the concession that ONFP could hire private contractors to perform certain services, including the environmental assessment. The only other positive development occurred when Ed Carpenter interrupted the haggling to declare that once the license agreement was signed, money would be no problem. Terry appreciated Carpenter's guarantee. Otherwise, he regarded the satellite conference as a $10,000 mistake. A communications satellite, he lamented, was no substitute for communication. High technology did not automatically provide a solution. Sometimes it simply made failure more expensive.

Representatives Joe Skeen and Marvin Leath introduced the military appropriations bill, with Terry's provision attached, in the House of Representatives on July 11, 1989. The Office of the General Counsel of the Department of the Army began formal negotiation of the license agreement soon after. The army's initial proposal apportioned fifty percent of the treasure to the army. Terry balked. "The army has insisted for more than thirty-five years that this treasure doesn't exist—now you want half of it? Does that mean we can go to the press and release a statement that the army now admits there *is* a treasure?" The army's negotiator asked Terry what percentage he thought the army should receive. "How about zero?" Terry asked. Eventually, the army agreed.

Negotiations with General Jones remained stalled. In an August meeting at White Sands Missile Range, Terry lost his patience. He was trying to convince Jones to reduce or eliminate several charges, when Jones surprised him with a new $80,000 charge for a communication hook-up between Victorio Peak and military police headquarters. With Norman Scott, Bill Casselman, Ralph Monroe, a pair of Pentagon attorneys, and Jones's senior staff looking on, Terry raised his hands in surrender. "It's never going to happen, is it? We're never going to get to the peak." He stood up and turned to leave the conference room, but General Jones intercepted him at the door. Then Jones did something entirely unexpected. He put his arm around Terry's shoulders and gently guided him back to his place at the table.

"We'll work these differences out," Jones said.

Terry sat back down. Discussion resumed. There was no sudden breakthrough, no swelling of sentimental music in the background, but the general's uncharacteristic show of kindness left Terry stunned. It was as if the general had momentarily dropped a mask; as if his cantankerous wrangling were part of an act, a game he enjoyed so much he wouldn't let his opponent quit. The episode revived Terry's hope. He would keep playing the game till he won.

On November 6, 1989, President George Bush, the elder, signed the Department of Defense Authorization Act. Section 2821—tucked away on page 399 under "Miscellaneous Provisions"—authorized the Secretary of the Army to "issue a revocable license to the Ova Noss Family Partnership...to conduct a search for treasure trove in the Victorio Peak region of White Sands Missile Range." Subparagraph (b) required ONFP to reimburse the army for all costs and specified that "reimbursement for such costs shall be credited to the Department of the Army appropriation from which the costs were paid."

The Clovis boy had done it. With the help of an unlikely assortment of volunteers and paid professionals, he'd won passage of an act of Congress. Yet despite the magnitude of the achievement, no one threw a party to celebrate. There was too much work to do. A week after the bill went into law, Terry quit his job at American Savings and Loan. Judy quit her job six weeks later.

The next order of business was to finalize the license agreement, but disputes arose over everything from the actual name of the peak (Victoria or Victorio?) to the definition of *artifact* (did the term include jewelry?) to the size of the area ONFP would be permitted to search. One provision declared the agreement to be "revocable at the convenience of the government." Another required ONFP to keep $200,000 in an account controlled by White Sands Missile Range. The base would simply withdraw whatever amount ONFP was deemed to owe, and ONFP would immediately replenish the account. Ralph Monroe characterized the arrangement as a violation of standard accounting procedure and an invitation to larceny. The army took four weeks to revise the license, then gave ONFP two days to respond. Ralph warned Terry not to be stampeded into signing a bad agreement.

Fundraising, too, presented unexpected problems. Ed Carpenter had given Terry an oral commitment to bankroll the project once the license agreement was signed, but Terry continually needed money to pay Bill Casselman and Norman Scott, as well as the cost of flights, phone calls, etc. A consortium of Oklahoma businessmen, after two years of weighing the options, decided not to invest, citing the unfavorable language of the license agreement and "the inability to 'see all the cards' or put our finger on the entire, ever-changing story."

The act of Congress was just another stop on a long road.

In January of 1990, the army granted ONFP ten days at the peak to do preliminary fieldwork for the environmental assessment. Terry barely managed to rush through a deal with a 25-year-old Los Angeles millionaire to pay for the operation. The young tycoon presented General Jones with a check for $54,877, and everyone got busy. Norman Scott served as field director. EcoPlan of Albuquerque, New Mexico shot aerial photographs of the peak, studied the flora and fauna in the vicinity, and put together a detailed topographical map. Human Resources, Inc. of Las Cruces provided archeological support. Lambert Dolphin confirmed the findings of his 1977 ground-penetrating radar survey. Retired airman Tom Berlett pointed out the spot where he and Leonard Fiege had crawled through a narrow opening into a cave filled with stacks of gold bars. Terry solicited bids from subcontractors for road repair, drilling, tunneling, and site restoration. All accessible fissures were explored and mapped. General Jones assigned six MPs to guard the ONFP crew. The MPs prohibited Alex Alonso from videotaping —until Terry informed a reporter, and the local news accused the army of interfering with the project. After Terry endured a screaming session in Jones's office, Alex was permitted to videotape, but only with an army photographer at his elbow monitoring every camera angle—"for security reasons."

ONFP paid dearly for the ten-day stint at the peak. The base's un-itemized bill totaled more than $125,000. When Terry demanded an explanation, the base's financial officer attributed the unexpectedly high support costs to, among other things, "increased involvement of our command and legal staff," "discussion of communication requirement," and "photography support." The rate for each of the six MPs exceeded $50 an hour. Price gouging, Ralph called it. Terry called it revenge. General Jones hadn't appreciated the videotaping flap. He'd consulted his lawyers ("increased involvement of our command and legal staff"), screamed at Terry ("discussion of communication requirement"), and assigned a man to tail Alex ("photography support").

Terry settled the bill but protested the exorbitant rates. The army operated under a three-tiered rate system: the rate charged to the army itself, the rate charged to other government agencies, and the rate charged to civilian contractors. At the satellite conference, General Jones had quoted support costs at the second rate, which had seemed astronomical then, but which would have been a bargain compared to the civilian rate. The base's financial officer pointed out that Terry was a civilian. Terry pointed out that no other civilian contractor had been required to obtain an act of Congress.

Nevertheless, the base continued to charge ONFP at the highest rate when Lambert Dolphin returned to the peak in May of 1990 for a final ground-penetrating radar survey. Dolphin had developed a new system twenty times more powerful than the one he'd used during Goldfinder. He gathered data at more than a hundred sites, not just above ground but inside the peak in the accessible tunnels and fissures. His findings established the location of a large cavern approximately 200 feet below the Gaddis tunnel dug in 1963.

Meanwhile, negotiation of the license agreement dragged on. The problem, Terry came to realize, was the same in Washington as it was in New Mexico. The army had no incentive to compromise. He needed the army; the army didn't need him. He could accept their terms and pay their rate—or quit.

By the time the license agreement was finally signed, on April 4, 1991, General Jones had been replaced by General Hite as commander of White Sands Missile Range, Norman Scott had left the project, and the declining Southern California economy had discouraged several potential investors, including Ed Carpenter.

By the time the actual search began, on July 20, 1992, two and a half years had passed since the signing of the act of Congress, General Hite had been replaced by General Wharton, and Terry's first symptom of AIDS had appeared, a purple lesion the size of a dime on his left calf.

12

The Only Cure Is Gold

*The white man suffers a disease of the heart,
and the only cure is gold.*
—Hernán Cortez

1539

Before Francisco Vasquez de Coronado and his army of conquistadors ventured north into the unknown region the Spaniards had named *Nueva Mexico*, Coronado dispatched a scouting party led by a Franciscan friar, Marcos de Niza, and guided by a former slave, Esteban the Moor. The friar and the former slave set out from Compostela on foot with a small contingent of soldiers, priests, and Indians. Friar Marcos wore a plain gray robe made of Zaragosa cloth. Esteban the Moor wore a dazzling patchwork of brightly colored pieces of cloth stitched together like a quilt and decorated with feathers and bells so that he jingled when he walked. These two unlikely pioneers differed as much in temperament as they did in fashion, but they shared a similar faith in the unlimited wonder of the New World.

Friar Marcos had served with Francisco Pizarro, the conqueror of Peru, and Pizarro's stories of vast riches still haunted the friar's dreams. After Pizarro had captured Atahualpa, the ruler of the Incas, in his palace in the Andes, Atahualpa had attempted to buy back his freedom. "I will cover this floor with gold," Atahualpa had promised, "if you will let me go." Pizarro had shuddered in astonishment at the prospect of so much gold, but Atahualpa had misinterpreted the reaction and raised his offer. "I will fill this room with gold as high as you can reach, and if that is not enough, I will fill the next room with silver." Pizarro used his sword to scratch a line nearly nine feet above the floor, and Atahualpa sent word to the far reaches of the Incan empire. Soon, from the Temples of the Sun in Cuzco and Quito, porters began to arrive carrying heavy loads of finely wrought gold plates, gold vases, and gold figurines. Spanish treasury officials valued the take at 40,000 to 60,000 *castellanos* (the equivalent of $600,000 to $900,000) each day for more than eight weeks. Just before the glittering pile reached the line on the wall, Pizarro ordered that a metal collar be placed around Atahualpa's neck and slowly tightened until the Incan ruler strangled to death. All the gold, no matter how artful its form, was then melted down and shipped back to Spain. Thousands of Incans were converted to Christianity. Though Friar Marcos had missed the Peruvian conquest, Pizarro's stories of fabulous treasure had inspired the friar to hope that his efforts in New Mexico would produce a comparable bonanza for God and country.

Esteban the Moor had amassed no fortune in the New World, but his experiences were as fabulous as any conquistador's. In 1528, two years after Pizarro landed in Peru, an expedition set sail from Cuba with the intention of colonizing Florida. A series of terrible storms left four survivors shipwrecked on the coast of what is now Texas, three Spaniards and a Moor, the first aliens to enter the vast interior of the American Southwest. As they traveled across Texas, they encountered many natives, some of whom believed that these strange-looking visitors possessed miraculous powers, including the power to heal. Esteban became a kind of medicine man, gathering amulets, feathers, and scraps of cloth from the natives he met. One of the Spaniards, Alvar Nuñez Cabeza de Vaca, afterwards wrote a chronicle of the journey, in which, casting himself in the role of healer, he told of breathing into the mouth of a sick Indian and reciting prayers in Latin. When the Indian's health fortuitously improved, the "superstitious natives" presented gifts.

> Among the articles that were given to us, Andres Dorantes received a bell of copper, thick and large.... They told him that they had gotten it from others, their neighbors, and we asked them whence these had obtained it. They said that it had been brought from the direction of the north, where there was much copper, and that it was highly esteemed.

Cabeza de Vaca also reported receiving jewels.

> To me they gave five emeralds made into arrow-heads, that they use at their cel-
> ebrations and dances. They appeared to me very precious. I asked them whence
> they had got these; and they said that they were brought from some lofty moun-
> tains that stand toward the north, where there were populous towns and very
> large houses, and that they purchased them in exchange for bunches of plumes
> and feathers of parrots.

After nearly two years, Esteban and the Spaniards, along with an entourage
of native followers, crossed the Rio Grande and traveled south into Mexico,
eventually reaching a Spanish settlement. Cabeza de Vaca returned to Spain
and wrote his chronicle, which became a sensation. Esteban preferred to
remain in the New World. When asked to serve as guide to Friar Marcos, he
readily agreed to return to the land of his unforgettable odyssey.

Accounts of the journey of the friar and the former slave probably contain
as much legend as fact. Some historians speculate that the two men clashed,
perhaps because Friar Marcos envied Esteban's wealth of experience, perhaps because Esteban resented the friar's authority. For whatever reason,
Esteban took several Indians and traveled ahead. To communicate with the
friar, Esteban, who could neither read nor write, occasionally would send
back one of the Indians with a cross to indicate that all was well. The farther
north they traveled, the larger the crosses grew. One day an Indian staggered
into the camp of Friar Marcos carrying a cross almost as large as a man. Friar
Marcos hurried to the outskirts of the Zuni pueblo of Hawikuh, where he
was met by the last of Esteban's Indian escorts, who reported that the Zunis
had killed Esteban and hacked his body to pieces. The motive for the slaying
was never determined. Friar Marcos prudently decided not to advance any
closer to the pueblo, but he did observe it from a distance. "It appears to be
a very beautiful city," he wrote in his journal. "The houses are all of stone,
with their stories and terraces, as it seemed to me from a hill from whence I
could view it." From the friar's perspective, the walls of the city glittered in
the clear desert air, and one of the friar's Indian guides told him that this
pueblo was the least opulent of the seven cities of gold the friar so eagerly
sought. Friar Marcos returned to Compostela "with more fear than food,"
and reported to Coronado that he had located the first of the seven fabled
cities.

Coronado rode out of Compostela with three hundred gentleman sol-diers, seven hundred Indians, and a platoon of friars. The *caballeros* wore shining armor and sat astride magnificent horses outfitted with leather har-nesses and silver stirrups. The foot soldiers carried crossbows, swords, and shields. The Indians sported war paint and feathers. A herd of cattle, sheep, goats, and pigs trotted behind the cannons.

Two months later, on April 22, 1540, Coronado reached Culiacán and decided that traveling with such a large force was too slow. He pushed on with twenty-five foot soldiers, a few Indians, and Friar Marcos.

By the time the expedition reached Hawikuh, provisions had grown scarce, tempers short, and animals thin. The dazzling city that Friar Marcos had described in such glowing terms proved to be nothing more than a pueblo of mud and rock. The historian of the expedition described it as "a little, crowded village, looking as if it had been crumpled together." Coronado wrote to the Viceroy that Friar Marcos "had not told the truth in a single thing that he has said, for everything is the very opposite of what he related except the name of the cities."

Coronado seized Hawikuh, but the military victory provided little glory. What he and his men craved was not war but the spoils of war. They kept asking the Indians where to find the seven cities of gold, and finally an Indian called *Bigotes* (Whiskers) told them of *Tiguex*, a faraway province with immense herds of wooly, humpbacked cattle roaming vast plains of golden grass. Bigotes led the Spaniards north along the Rio Grande, where they spent the winter of 1540, commandeering whatever they needed from the Tewas, their involuntary hosts. When the Tewas protested too vehe-mently, the Spaniards responded by destroying a few villages.

The Indians of the Southwest seemed to learn quickly that the best way to handle the Spaniards was to tell them about a distant treasure, the more distant the better. Certainly, the Spaniards tended to hear what they wanted to hear. In the spring of 1541, an Indian called the Turk spoke of Quivira, a kingdom far to the east ruled by an emperor who slept under a tree deco-rated with bells made of the finest gold. The Turk described gold ships float-ing down a river six miles wide, with fish the size of horses swimming near the banks. The Turk led the Spaniards all the way to what is now central Kansas, where Coronado discovered the grass houses of the Wichita and a chief who wore a copper plate around his neck, but not a single city of gold, in fact no gold whatsoever. He executed the Turk and then turned back toward Mexico. Three priests who asked to stay in Kansas were never heard from again.

Why did Coronado believe so strongly that he would find seven cities of gold in New Mexico? The story of the seven cities predates the discovery of the New World. Supposedly, when the Moors invaded Spain, seven bishops fled with the treasures of the Catholic church and sailed west to build seven magnificent cities. A map from 1482 places the cities on the nonexistent island of Antilia, drawn in near the Cape Verde islands off the coast of North Africa. After the voyage of Columbus, the cities simply migrated a few thousand miles farther west.

Despite the mythical origins of the tale of the seven cities of gold, Coronado did have ample precedent to believe that New Mexico would yield enormous riches. Spanish mining operations in Peru, Panama, Honduras, Costa Rica, Nicaragua, and Hispaniola had already doubled the amount of gold being mined in the world. Hispaniola alone was shipping more than forty tons of pure gold a year back to Spain.

Of all the Spanish enterprises, though, none exercised a stronger hold on Coronado's imagination than the conquest of Mexico. When Hernán Cortez burned his ships on the shores of Vera Cruz in 1519, the Aztec capital of Tenochtitlan held close to 300,000 inhabitants. Tenochtitlan's markets overflowed with gold, silver, jade, turquoise, chocolate, vanilla, copper, tobacco, and slaves. The ruler of the Aztecs, Montezuma, traveled in a feather-covered carriage carried by noblemen, and if he deigned to walk, the noblemen swept his path clean and spread fine cloth over it so that his feet never touched the ground. Young maidens offered him hundreds of freshly-prepared dishes at each meal.

One day a messenger approached Montezuma with portentous news. "I come to advise you that a great mountain has been seen on the waters, moving from one part to the other, without touching the rocks." The great mountain was Cortez's galleon. The year 1519 was called One Reed in the Aztec's cyclical calendar, the year that the god Quetzalcoatl was prophesied to return to Mexico from over the great waters to the east. If Cortez had arrived at a certain Bethlehem stable twelve days after a miraculous birth, the coincidence would have been no greater. He fit the description of an Aztec god about as well as he fit the description of a wise man. He had a beard. He wore a cross. He even bore gifts of a sort: horses, cannon, vicious war dogs.

Not surprisingly, Cortez was treated with extreme deference by the first Aztecs he encountered. He gave them his helmet and ordered them to return it filled with gold dust. Montezuma sent Cortez dozens of gold figurines and a silver disk the size of a wagon wheel, as well as the helmet filled with gold dust and gold nuggets. "It was this gift which cost Montezuma his head," Cortez's lieutenant Torquemada later wrote.

Montezuma regarded Cortez with an uneasy mixture of awe and suspicion. This mysterious stranger might be the second coming of Quetzalcoatl or he might be an evil impostor. Montezuma tried to address both possibilities. Along with the lavish gifts, he sent his most powerful sorcerers to cast spells on the Spaniards.

When Cortez and his men entered Tenochtitlan, they found ornate palaces, massive towers, sumptuous temples, and lavish floating gardens. "To many of us," one soldier wrote, "it seemed doubtful whether we were asleep or awake…for never yet did man see, hear, or dream of anything equal to the spectacle which appeared to our eyes on this day." The Spaniards soon discovered that the Aztecs' enchanted dream also had its nightmarish aspects, including the *tzompantli*, skull racks displaying severed human heads. The Aztecs sacrificed thousands of people every year. The priests would lay the victim on a stone slab at the summit of the temple, cut open the chest, rip out the still-beating heart, and burn it in the Eagle Vase as an offering to the gods.

After Cortez and a small contingent of soldiers arrived at Montezuma's palace, Montezuma proudly ushered them into the chapel. Historian H. H. Bancroft describes the scene:

> Withdrawing a tasseled curtain, he [Montezuma] displayed the images [of the Aztec gods], glittering with ornaments of gold and precious stones, which at first drew the attention of the beholders from the hideous form and features. Before them stood the stone of sacrifice, still reeking with gore, and around lay the instruments for securing the human victim and for tearing open the breast. On one altar could be seen three hearts, and on the other five, offered to the idols, and even now warm and palpitating with life. The interior walls were so smeared with

human blood as to obscure their original color, and to emit a fetid odor which made the Spaniards glad to reach the open air again.

Cortez asked permission to build an altar of his own. Montezuma reluctantly consented. While looking for a place to put the altar, one of Cortez's men noticed a freshly plastered portion of wall that seemed to conceal a doorway. Cortez ordered the plaster removed. Again, Bancroft supplies a description.

> Aladdin entering the cave could not have been more surprised than the Spaniards were on stepping into the chamber there revealed. The interior fairly blazed with treasures; bars of gold were there, nuggets large and small, figures, implements, and jewelry of the same metal; and then the silver....

Montezuma permitted Cortez and his men to take everything except the images of the gods themselves. Eventually, though, the Aztecs rebelled against the acquisitive Spaniards and drove them from Tenochtitlan on the bloody night known as *La Noche Triste*. Cortez, who had forged alliances with the Tlaxcalans, the Aztecs' traditional enemies, reconquered Tenochtitlan after a long siege, but the profusion of gold that he and his soldiers remembered was nowhere to be found. "When finally the royal officials gave their report," Bancroft writes, "it appeared that the total gold collected from the captives and sacking parties, and smelted into bars, amounted to one hundred and thirty thousand *castellanos*...altogether far below the expectation of even the most moderate among the fortune-hunters."

Cortez promised to protect the surviving Aztec leaders in exchange for the missing gold, but when they refused to divulge its whereabouts, he ordered them tortured, their feet slowly roasted over a low fire. Though many of the victims named possible hiding places, only a small amount of gold was recovered. Some Spaniards believed that the gold had been spirited north and stockpiled in a cave.

Is it possible that Aztec gold was hauled from Tenochtitlan to Victorio Peak, a journey of more than two thousand miles? The Aztec traders, the *pochteca*, had certainly traveled as far north as Victorio Peak to trade for turquoise with the Pueblo Indians, but to convey a cargo of heavy gold bars such a distance would have required a sizable operation, and no evidence of such an operation exists in the historical or archeological record.

Nevertheless, the Aztecs and their fantastic world of jaguar skins, eagle feathers, skull racks, and human sacrifices stretched the limits of the Spanish imagination. The vast hoard of gold and silver Cortez discovered in Mexico raised the expectations of Coronado and his cohorts. They set out for New Mexico determined to equal, if not surpass, the achievements of Cortez. *New Mexico*. The name itself was an act of sympathetic magic, an attempt to conjure the wealth and wonder of Mexico in the uncharted region to the north. When Coronado returned from his two-year search with no plunder to speak of, he regarded the expedition as a failure, even though he had begun the epic enterprise of extending Spain's dominion over the Southwest. He had also begun an enduring New Mexico tradition, the quest for phantom treasure. His legacy of unimaginable riches lurking somewhere in the heart of the desert would tantalize generations of future fortune hunters.

"The white man suffers a disease of the heart, and the only cure is gold," Cortez once told Montezuma. Despite the allure of finding such a cure in New Mexico, no Spaniard journeyed there for more than forty years following Coronado's grand failure. The chief deterrent was lack of support from the King of Spain. No private citizen could afford to transport a small army across the treacherous expanse of desert against the opposition of hostile natives. In 1573, the King issued a set of royal ordinances outlawing the use of violence against the natives and proclaiming that no Spaniard would be allowed to undertake discovery and settlement of new lands without the King's personal authorization. Mexico itself continued to provide abundant riches for the Spaniards to exploit. Gradually, though, with the discovery of massive silver deposits in Zacatecas, Durango, Chihuahua, San Luis Potosí, and Nueva León, Spanish settlements moved farther and farther north, and the wilds of New Mexico began to seem more accessible. The arrival of a few copies of Cabeza de Vaca's book sparked a renewed interest in the land to the north.

In 1581, despite the royal ordinances, Spanish merchant Antonio de Espejo launched an unauthorized expedition to the Rio Grande to search for a rumored lake of gold. He didn't find it. According to his journals, when he asked the Indians about the region Coronado had explored, "They told us that there was gold in that country, and that the people were clothed and wore bracelets and earrings of gold." The Indians insisted that Coronado had stopped just short of the gold country, perhaps because he'd run out of water. Espejo decided to travel west rather than east, and found "rich mines" near present-day Prescott, Arizona. "I found them, and with my own hands I extracted ore from them, said by those who know to be very rich and to contain much silver." (The Spanish word *mina*, often translated as *mine*, also means *vein* or *deposit*, an ambiguity which makes the early Spanish accounts easy to misinterpret.)

In 1590, the lieutenant governor of Nuevo Leon, Gaspar Castaño de Sosa, took more than a hundred settlers north to New Mexico without the King's approval. When he met a band of Indians hauling a load of rock laced with gleaming metal, he confiscated the rock and assayed a portion of it, slipping a silver mug into the assay pot, so that the assay produced a small silver ingot. Eventually, the Viceroy of New Spain sent fifty soldiers after the group and Castaño de Sosa was brought back to Mexico in iron fetters.

In 1593, Captain Francisco Leyva de Bonilla led a small force all the way to Kansas, where he quarreled with his second in command and was overrun by Apaches.

None of these unauthorized expeditions returned with any gold. Of course it's conceivable that the discovery of gold could have been kept secret. An unknown explorer could have stumbled upon a major mining operation or even the seven cities of gold. However, no reference to such a discovery has survived in any soldier's diary or priest's journal, much less in any official record. To suppress news of gold secreted back into Mexico or shipped to Spain would have required a conspiracy of monumental proportions.

In 1598, the King of Spain appointed Juan Oñate to begin the settlement of New Mexico. Oñate's father was one of the founders of Zacatecas. His wife was the granddaughter of Cortez and great granddaughter of Montezuma. Oñate conducted his followers to the junction of the Chama River and the Rio Grande, not far from present-day Santa Fe. The son of a silver baron, he brought along heavy mining and smelting tools, and soon after setting up camp, he launched an extensive search for deposits of precious metal.

Oñate's first letter to the Viceroy referred to "the great wealth which the mines have begun to reveal and the great number of them in this land, whence proceed the royal fifths and profits." (The royal fifth was the twenty-percent share of all mining proceeds that went directly to the treasury of Spain.) Oñate was not the most reliable witness, however. His letter also mentioned the abundance of pearls and the proximity to China and the South Sea.

In Oñate's "Account of the Discovery of Mines" written in 1599, he describes a visit to a mine where an Indian gave him a gift of fine ore. "The said mountains are without doubt the richest in all New Spain, for the witness [Oñate] has been in almost all the mines of New Spain, and he has seen that this country has the same qualities, especially the rich mines of San Andres."

Oñate terrorized the natives. In retaliation for an attack, he captured the Indians of Acoma pueblo and sentenced each man to have one foot cut off and to serve twenty years as a slave. The cruelty of Oñate and the leaders who succeeded him would one day spur the Pueblo Indians to revolt.

Though Oñate failed to strike it rich in the mining business, the route he established between Mexico and New Mexico would become famous first as the El Camino Real and then as the Santa Fe Trail, and a fortune in gold and silver would be transported on it. The most dangerous portion of the route crossed the ninety-mile stretch of desert known as the Jornada del Muerto. A *jornada* is a brief journey, the distance traveled in a day. *Muerto* means dead person or dead man. The best translation might be Dead Man's Trail, but the Jornada has also been referred to as the March of Death, the Journey of the Dead, and Scalp Alley. Travelers learned to fear the Jornada not only because of the scarcity of water but also because of the fierceness of the Apaches in the region. At the heart of the Jornada, only a few miles from the route traveled by countless caravans, stands Victorio Peak.

Caravan service between Mexico City and Santa Fe began in 1609. A caravan consisted of four groups of eight wagons, each group escorted by a company of a dozen soldiers. The wagons, when fully loaded, weighed nearly four thousand pounds and required a team of eight mules. The wagon wheels were made of iron. Caravans usually tried to speed through the Jornada as quickly as possible, traveling at night if the moon was near full, but the passage took three days, and the names of the campsites offer a glimpse of what the passage was like: Perillo, named for a little dog who trotted into camp with muddy feet when the thirsty caravaners had grown desperate for water; Aleman, named for the legendary massacre of a party of German merchants; Laguna del Muerto and Ojo del Muerto (Dead Man's Lake and

Dead Man's Spring), named for the likely consequences of a chance encounter with the Apaches.

By 1630, the Spaniards operated twenty-five missions in New Mexico, with sixty thousand Indian converts scattered among ninety pueblos. The decision to convert was often made under duress. As the El Camino Real brought more and more Spaniards to New Mexico, the pressure on the Pueblo Indians to submit to Spanish authority increased. In 1680, the Pueblos rose up against the Spaniards and drove them from New Mexico, not to return till 1692.

There is a theory, more popular among treasure hunters than among historians, that during the twelve years of the Spaniards' absence, the Indians scuttled all mines and hid the traces. After the Spaniards reconquered New Mexico, the Indians refused to divulge the location of these mines because gold and other precious metals incited the Spaniards to commit acts of horrific brutality.

Josiah Gregg, who traveled throughout the Southwest in the early 1800s, subscribes to this theory in *Commerce of the Prairies:*

> Tradition speaks of numerous and productive mines having been in operation in New Mexico before the expulsion of the Spaniards in 1680; but that the Indians, seeing that the cupidity of the conquerors had been the cause of their former cruel oppressions, determined to conceal all the mines by filling them up, and obliterating as much as possible every trace of them.
>
> …that many valuable mines *were* once wrought in this province, not only tradition but authenticated records and existing relics sufficiently prove. In every quarter of the territory there are still to be seen vestiges of ancient excavations, and in some places, ruins of considerable towns evidently reared for mining purposes.

Whether or not extensive mining operations were conducted in New Mexico before 1680, the Southwest provided fertile ground for tales of lost treasure: El Chato's deathbed confession, the Lost Adam's Mine, the Lost Dutchman Mine, and the Lost Padre Mine, also known as the Padre Larue Mine, which, according to Doc Noss, was a source of the Victorio Peak treasure.

The many versions of the Larue legend agree that near the end of the eighteenth century a French priest named Larue was assigned to a poor mission in Mexico. Folklorist Arthur Campa places the mission just north of Durango. Several years of drought left the Indians under Padre Larue's charge near starvation. Church officials responded to Larue's repeated requests for help with the advice to trust in God. One day an old soldier who had been serving in New Mexico arrived at the mission. The soldier had fallen ill on his journey, and Padre Larue tried to nurse him back to health. When the soldier's condition worsened, he confided to the priest that he had found a substantial vein of gold up north. He had planned to raise money in Mexico City to finance a mining operation, but now he realized that he would soon die. Padre Larue listened carefully to the soldier's deathbed directions, and after the soldier's death and a further year of drought, Padre Larue led his congregation of Indians north to the site the soldier had described, not far from present-day Las Cruces.

The vein, of course, proved rich. Every month Larue would send someone into the town of Mesilla to buy provisions, but otherwise the group avoided all contact with outsiders. Eventually, church officials in Mexico City noticed the disappearance of Larue's entire mission. A priest named Maximiliano was dispatched to investigate. Maximiliano pursued the trail of clues and rumors north to Mesilla, where he happened to see a pair of Indians paying for a wagonload of supplies with a bag of gold dust. The Indians refused to answer Maximiliano's questions, but he shadowed them back to their camp and then returned a few days later with Spanish troops.

In some versions of the story, the soldiers slaughtered Padre Larue and his followers. In other versions, the camp was deserted. Either way, all traces of the mine and the gold had been concealed, to remain a mystery forever, or at least until the day Doc Noss descended into Victorio Peak.

In the late 1930s, Doc claimed to have unearthed an ancient parchment map with Padre Larue's name on it. Babe's daughter Letha still remembers the map vividly, the leathery texture of the parchment, the fancy black lettering. A word map, she calls it, written in Castilian Spanish. She describes how Doc took the map to four professors at New Mexico State, asking each of them to translate a different section. Doc supposedly stored the map in the notorious footlocker that disappeared after his death. His second wife, Violet Boles Yancey, kept a photostatic copy of the map in a safe deposit box in Fort Worth.

In New Mexico, the truth could be as improbable as any folktale. In 1828, a Mexican mule herder followed some strays into the Ortiz mountains south of Santa Fe and spotted a glittering rock that reminded him of the gold-bearing ore he'd seen as a boy in Sonora. His wild notion turned out to be correct. The gold mine established at *El Placer* would earn $60,000 to $80,000 a year in the 1830s. Major gold strikes would be made in six different mining districts within a seventy-five mile radius of Victorio Peak. Not surprisingly, the presence of precious metals soon attracted the attention of the United States.

In 1822, the year after Mexico gained its independence from Spain, seventy men with pack animals and a few wagons carried $9,000 worth of goods from Missouri to Chihuahua via the Santa Fe Trail. In 1846, according to historian Max Moorhead, caravans comprised of 750 men and 363 wagons transported approximately a million dollars worth of goods along the same route. "Once the bulky bales of dry goods were sold [in Chihuahua]," Moorhead explains, "the traders were encumbered [on the return trip] by little more than a compact cargo of coin, silver bars, and gold dust."

This cargo was packed on mules in "sacks made of fresh rawhide, which shrank on drying and, pressing the contents tightly, eliminated all friction. A pair of these packages, containing between $1,000 and $2,000, constituted a normal load for a single mule." Moorhead points out, "Mules cost more than oxen, but they lasted longer, traveled faster, and seldom had to be shod. Their major weakness was that they were more easily stampeded, especially during Indian attacks."

As traffic increased along the Santa Fe Trail, such attacks became more frequent, particularly in the Jornada del Muerto. The government of Mexico responded in 1835 with an official policy of extermination, paying a hundred pesos (roughly $100) for each adult male Indian killed. A scalp constituted acceptable proof. The policy was soon augmented to include a fifty peso bounty for the scalp of an Indian woman and a twenty-five peso bounty for the scalp of an Indian child.

Although traders complained bitterly about financial losses inflicted by Apache raids, stolen gold was seldom reported. No trader wanted to acknowledge how much gold the caravans were smuggling.

In 1846, the U.S. Army seized power in New Mexico. Stephen Watts

Kearney and his forces marched into town after town, rounded up the local people, and addressed them in the public square.

> I have come amongst you by orders of my government, to take possession of your country and extend over it the laws of the United States…. Those who remain peaceably at home, attending to their crops, and their herds, shall be protected by me in their property, their persons and their religion; and not a pepper, not an onion shall be disturbed or taken by my troops without pay, or by the consent of the owner. But listen! He who promises to be quiet and is found in arms against me, I will hang!

Surrounded by soldiers, few citizens protested. In less than two years, the treaty of Guadalupe-Hidalgo would be signed and New Mexico would become a territory of the United States. The following year the California gold rush would begin, and gold fever would forever change the face of New Mexico.

The Apaches would not welcome this change, but in 1846 the U.S. Army's peaceful overtures compared favorably with Mexico's policy of total extermination. The Apache chief Mangas Colorado (Red Sleeves) met with U.S. Army officials to discuss the possibility of trading mules for supplies. (Not surprisingly, the Apaches acquired a lot of mules.) Lieutenant William Emory described the scene:

> A large number of Indians had collected about us, all differently dressed, and some in the most fantastical style…. Several wore beautiful helmets, decked with black feathers, which, with the short skirt, waist belt, bare legs and buskings, gave them the look of pictures of antique Greek warriors….

Historians suspect that among the Apaches accompanying Mangas Colorado that day was a young warrior named Victorio. Years later, Victorio would lead his band of Warm Springs Apaches against the U.S. Cavalry, winning a particularly fierce battle defending the mountain that became known as Victorio Peak.

13

Fantastic Start

If a thing is worth doing, it is worth doing badly.
—*G. K. Chesterton*

July 1992

The caravan departed from ONFP headquarters at six in the morning, a shiny ribbon of four-wheel drive vehicles streaming down Missouri Street to Telshor Avenue. Many of the vehicles had been washed the evening before in preparation for this trek across the desert—not because anyone failed to comprehend the dusty nature of the drive, but because the volunteer crew of amateur treasure hunters believed they were making history and wanted to look their best. The heavy rains of the past several days had given way to brilliant blue sky. The air was suffused with the scent of creosote. The temperature, already in the low eighties, would rise to one hundred five. They drove in tandem the few blocks down Telshor, hung a left on Lohman, then merged onto the freeway, Interstate 25, where they proceeded north, a parade of burnished optimism, the sun now high enough to peek over the Organ Mountains, bright enough to turn each car window into a sheet of light. With this simple anointment, the journey began.

Alex Alonso rode shotgun in the lead vehicle, a maroon Blazer. He would have preferred to drive, but Jerry Cheatham had slipped behind the wheel. Jerry was a retired air traffic controller, fifty-eight years old, a burly back-slapper with a booming bass voice and a passion for jokes. Jerry was also the son of Letha Guthrie, grandson of Babe Noss, cousin of Terry Delonas.

Perhaps as a consequence of this blood tie, Terry had appointed him Director of Field Operations. Alex himself had been appointed Director of Video Documentation and DataCam Exploration. The project might be short on cash, but it was rich in titles.

The volunteers in the back seat maintained a respectful silence. Alex flicked on the radio and tried half a dozen stations before turning it off. Years ago, when Alex donated office space to the project, Terry guaranteed that his life would be ruined. The slow-moving convoy brought to mind that prophecy.

"We want Exit 32," he said, glancing at a passing mile marker. "Just twenty-seven miles to go."

A few minutes later, Jerry roused himself to speak. "What do you call a lawyer buried up to his neck in sand?"

"An unfinished job?" Alex couldn't resist beating Jerry to the punch line. His punishment came when Jerry settled in behind a creeping big rig. Alex tried to drum up a conversation, but no one had much to say, as if there were no point in talking until they reached the mountain.

Alex pressed his foot down on an imaginary accelerator and daydreamed about the DataCam. It was his own invention, a remote-control camera that might soon provide the first glimpse of the treasure. All they had to do was drill a hole into the right cave and lower the camera down the hole. Alex pictured himself viewing video footage on the DataCam's computer screen. A touch of the keyboard would enable him to rotate the camera three-hundred sixty degrees. The 200-watt lamps would illuminate even the farthest reaches of the cave. On the screen, Alex imagined, a dark shape would appear. He'd zoom in for a close-up. Rows and rows of dusty gold bars—he'd see them before anyone else. Of course, he reminded himself as the Blazer puttered along, the first step was to drill into the cave—and ONFP didn't have a drill rig yet. The big discovery might not happen for many days.

At Exit 32, the caravan turned onto a dirt road and headed east across the desert toward the San Andres Mountains. The Blazer raised a cloud of dust that coated the Bronco behind it, whose dust covered the next in line, until the air was so thick that the drivers in the rear had to continue forward largely on faith. The distance between vehicles remained slight, however, because the road forked often and no one wanted to get lost in the desert in the middle of July.

Alex thought of the money ONFP had spent on road repairs, thousands of dollars to remove rocks, fill in holes, blade the road smooth—all wasted. The brutal rains of the past week had returned the road to its former state, a desert trail pocked with deep ruts, sharp rocks, jarring washboard, and patches of thick mud. A jackrabbit darted across the road and disappeared among the creosote and yucca. The long fingers of the ocotillo rocked in the wind as if counting intruders.

Jerry slowed down when the road reached the Hill ranch. Dick Hill, now eighty-five years old, had complained about vehicles arrogantly racing across his land during Operation Goldfinder. The road passed right by the Hill ranch house. Jerry poked along at five miles an hour, and the other vehicles followed, bumper to bumper behind the Blazer. Terry had emphasized to the crew that he wanted a good relationship with Hill. He wanted this expedition to be marked by courtesy rather than arrogance, which was why he'd agreed to pay Hill for use of the road, even though the law didn't require it.

They drove among Hill's white-faced cattle for three miles, advancing slowly, honking at the lumbering creatures that eyed the caravan with indifference and moved from the road without haste. Around a muddy bend, the road disappeared—engulfed by a brown lake. Jerry braked hard and the Blazer fishtailed, sliding sideways to a stop near the water's edge. He and Alex sat for a moment in silence. No lake was supposed to be here. It stretched the full width of the road and beyond the sandy shoulders a dozen yards in either direction. Its length was more difficult to determine because they couldn't see an end to it—a mammoth puddle that swallowed the road and reflected the sky.

Alex jumped out of the Blazer. "This is a mirage, right?"

Jerry lowered his window and said something about the desert rains—"monsoons," the locals called them. Alex scrambled onto the hood of the Blazer and peered at the lake. He still couldn't see the end of it, so he climbed higher, onto the Blazer's quivering roof. Dust from the convoy behind them swept forward and settled over the lake, floating momentarily on its tranquil surface, the invisible skin of this remarkable body of water.

"It goes a long ways," Alex said. "But I doubt it's very deep."

"I don't know," Jerry said. He still had both hands on the steering wheel.

"Don't worry, captain," Alex said. "We won't sink." He jumped from the roof to the hood, then down to the soft sand, falling forward, landing on all fours, jerking back his left hand so that he tumbled onto his side and against the front tire. His hand had landed an inch from a small but gnarly cactus, its tight concentric swirl of thorns a festive shade of pink. "Almost bad luck there," he muttered.

The Great Lake of the Upper Chihuahua Desert proved to be less than two feet in depth. As Jerry drove along at a turtle's pace, cracking jokes about quicksand, it occurred to Alex that they might have underestimated the desert. The hard part was supposed to be over. All they had to do now was recover the treasure. Listening to the water splash against the Blazer's side panels, he wondered if they were in for a rude surprise.

At the boundary of White Sands Missile Range—the old HEL site, staging area for Goldfinder—the convoy stopped and waited in the gathering heat for the military police. An hour later—an hour late—a squad of three MPs arrived and led the way on the twisting climb into the San Andres. At the rim of the Hembrillo Basin, when the MPs stopped to unlock the iron gate blocking the road, Alex jumped out of the Blazer and jogged over to the edge of the rim. The volunteers followed. As the other vehicles in the caravan pulled up, most of the crew hiked over to have a look.

Victorio Peak rose before them like an ancient lump of clay, slumped on one side, somber, mysterious, possessed of a battered dignity. The roads gouged into its face reminded Alex of hieroglyphics, a cryptic message from the past. He felt almost as if he were dreaming, returning to a place he never fully remembered when awake. The sun cast long shadows across the floor of the basin, glinted off the aluminum targets the army used to test its anti-aircraft weapons. The fallen darts, drones, and tow cables lent the otherwise pristine desert a surreal quality that Alex had indeed forgotten. He found it easy to believe that epic events had once occurred here. He found it easy to believe that epic events would occur here again.

One of the volunteers let out a whoop. Another howled like a coyote. Alex wished that Terry were standing with them now. Terry would have appreciated this moment.

ONFP headquarters, as the crew liked to call it, was a modest ranch-style house with a two-car garage in a quiet Las Cruces neighborhood, furnished with lawn chairs in the living room, mattresses on the bedroom floors, and peak memorabilia everywhere: newspaper clippings on the walls, old photographs lining the shelves, inspirational mottos posted at eye level, maps of New Mexico, the Hembrillo Basin, and Victorio Peak, even a color poster of gold bars recovered from another lost treasure, the sunken Spanish galleon *Atocha*. A large Plexiglas case prominently displayed a detailed scale model of the peak. The carpet was cheap shag and the furniture was obviously scavenged, but the motif was pure Disney—the able but slightly goofy detectives pitch in to solve a whopper of a case.

The back room of the house served as the office. File cabinets overflowed with papers, as did both desks and the top of the copy machine. At nine-thirty in the morning on the first day of the search, Terry was sitting in his pajamas at the smaller desk, where he'd cleared space for his legal pad, a cup of coffee, a plate of toast, and several bottles of pills. Judy Holeman was talking to an investor on one telephone, the other line was ringing, but the house seemed blissfully quiet to Terry. With the crew gone, there were no sleeping bodies to step over, no crowd milling outside the bathroom, no TV yapping in the background. He sipped his weak coffee and tried to savor the relative calm.

"I'm sorry," Judy said. "He's not available at the moment. May I help you?"

Judy was a telephone virtuoso and Terry hated the instrument, but now and then she'd put through a call from a reporter or anyone else he needed to talk to, like Les Smith, who'd promised to get back to him about acquiring a drill rig.

Terry jotted down a note on his legal pad. *Things to stress. High tech search. Team of dedicated volunteers. Spirit of cooperation.* Most reporters seemed to accept whatever spin he put on the story. He managed another bite of toast and then swallowed his last large pill with a swig of coffee. The AIDS medication left him nauseated and exhausted, the purple lesions from the Kaposi's Sarcoma now covered his left leg up to the knee, but otherwise his health was reasonably good, whatever that meant. Some days he felt terribly unlucky, other days he felt extraordinarily blessed.

In August of 1990, a few days after discovering the first lesion, he'd gathered his closest friends and broken the news. Judy knew, Alex knew, Craig knew. Most people, he'd chosen not to tell. He hoped his illness would not affect the project. His role in the actual search would be minor. He lacked the skills to lead the field operation. Once the treasure was found, he planned to step back in, and oversee the inevitable legal battle. Barring disaster, he estimated that recovery of the treasure would require three to six months. There was no reason his health should have deteriorated significantly by then. Besides trying every drug recommended by the American Medical Association and oxygenation in Tijuana, he'd found a doctor in Venice Beach who specialized in alternative approaches. Dr. Guggenheim, Swiss, with a Henry Kissinger accent, always scheduled Terry for the day's last appointment to allow time to talk about the project. So far, Terry's T-cell count remained high.

"Why don't you go back to bed?" Judy asked, covering the phone's mouthpiece.

"Can't sleep." Terry didn't attempt to describe his agitation. His mind had been racing since the moment he woke up. The Ova Noss Family Partnership was finally getting the chance to conduct a full search of Victorio Peak.

"They should be there by now," Judy said when she hung up.

It didn't surprise him that she'd guessed his thoughts. "I should have gone."

"You should have stayed in Newport Beach."

"And miss all this fun?" He raised his coffee mug and toasted her across an abyss of stacked papers. His desire for the project to run smoothly without him was matched by his desire to be indispensable. And so he'd shuffled out to the office in his pajamas to see what he could do. "Maybe I'll just sit here and rest my eyes," he said. Before he fell asleep, he heard Judy close the blinds.

At the base of the peak, crew members yawned and stretched, slapped on sunscreen and checked their metal detectors while the ranking MP reviewed the ground rules in a loud monotone: "Do not go off in separate directions. Keep us informed of your whereabouts at all times. This is for your safety." Each member of the crew had signed a waiver releasing the army from all liability for any "injury, pain or suffering, disfigurement or death" sustained during the search. The waiver ended on an ominous note:

It is expressly understood by the undersigned that the site of the search has been impacted by missiles and munitions and that there exist many dangers and hazards on White Sands Missile Range, due to its geography and the nature of its mission, and that these hazards and dangers include, but are not limited to, the following: Natural rough terrain, wild animals, man-made obstacles, abandoned tow cables, missile debris, dangerous tunnels, caverns and caves and unexpended projectiles and unexploded explosives, both exposed or in the subsurface.

The MP now reminded them of these hazards, reading haltingly from a well-creased copy of the waiver. The crew gazed off at the basin or up at the peak, each beholding a different share of beauty and danger, desolation or enchantment. Alex, in his role as Director of Video Documentation, walked among them taking close-ups of their faces.

Andy Pruitt was the president of a treasure-hunting club in Washington State. Roger Lane was the vice president. Harry Albright sold televisions and satellite dishes in Michigan. Patricia Heydt, the only woman in the crew, was a retired English teacher. Her husband Richard was a retired captain in the Colorado Highway Patrol. Gene Klier was a carpenter from Sea Tac, Washington. Bob Wood was the president of another Washington treasure club.

Alex zoomed in on Jerry Cheatham, who popped a stick of spearmint gum in his mouth and enthusiastically chewed for the camera. Jerry was responsible for bringing the Washington contingent into the project, and, oddly enough, vice-versa. In the fall of 1991, Jerry had been selling computer equipment in Seattle. One of his customers, Bob Wood, happened to have a treasure magazine on his desk. Jerry asked if the name Doc Noss rang a bell. "Every treasure hunter knows Doc Noss," Bob said. When Jerry said that Doc was his step-grandfather, Bob invited him to give a talk at the next meeting of his treasure club. While gathering information for the talk, Jerry called his cousin Terry and learned of the act of Congress, the environmental assessment, and the impending search. Terry sent him aerial photographs, geological cross-sections, a timeline of the crucial events in the Victorio Peak story, and Jerry ended up delivering presentations at a dozen different Washington treasure clubs. He'd raised $125,000 in investments and recruited a corps of volunteers eager to search for buried gold bars.

The treasure clubbers called themselves *metal detectorists,* a clunky appellation as far as Alex was concerned. He associated metal detecting with old codgers trudging along the beach in polyester shorts and black socks, metal detector swaying back and forth like a blind man's cane. Even so, he was grateful to have them on the team. If they found a stash of gold bars, ONFP would be inundated with investors.

After the MP finished his lecture, the archeologist addressed the crew. He had a soft voice and a quick grin, but none of the metal detectorists grinned back at him. Alex wondered if they disapproved of his long hair and scruffy beard. "I do all the digging," he said. "If you see something on the ground, you can pick it up and look at it, but don't put it in your pocket. Put it back on the ground. If you get a signal on your metal detector, mark the spot with a ribbon. You're all carrying ribbons, right? You find. I dig. Is that clear?"

Tony Jolley spoke next. The crew paid him the respect of actually listening. Jolley was one of the few people known to have profited from Doc's treasure. He and Doc had dug up, moved, and reburied 110 bars of gold in various locations within a few miles of the peak. In 1961, Jolley had returned to the area, sneaking onto the base under a full moon and removing several gold bars. He was vague about exactly how many, but quite specific about how he'd deposited the bars in a Swiss bank account, borrowed money against the deposit, and forfeited on the loan. The borrowed money had paid for the ranch in Montana that he still owned. The crew referred to him as *The Legend*.

"Why didn't you take all of it?" Alex asked with the camera rolling.

"I didn't want to get too greedy," Jolley said. He nodded toward the MPs. "I didn't want to get caught." Alex focused on Jolley's large, expressive hands. "But I always thought I could find a few more of the places where we buried bars. If I remember right, there's a couple not far from here."

"Let's go," one of the metal detectorists said. "Let's rock'n'roll."

"Hold your horses," Jerry said. He introduced Oren Swearingen to provide further orientation. Crew members checked their watches.

Swearingen, a freckle-faced dentist in his mid-sixties, didn't fit Alex's image of a treasure hunter, but treasure had exercised a powerful influence on his life. In 1954, while attending dental school in Dallas, he'd met Doc's ex-wife Violet Yancey and seen her copy of the map that Doc claimed to have found at the peak. The map, roughly a foot and a half wide and two feet long, included a detailed drawing of the network of caves inside the peak and several paragraphs of beautiful but indecipherable writing. Swearingen described the writing as "archaic Spanish." He said that the only part of it he could read was the dated signature: "La Rue, 1797."

Of all the explanations for the presence of gold in Victorio Peak, the legend of Padre Larue's lost mine was probably the most farfetched, but no one in the crowd questioned Swearingen's credibility. Whatever had brought them here, it wasn't a skeptical bent.

Entranced by the treasure map, Swearingen had taken the drastic step of enlisting in the Air Force and getting himself stationed at Holloman Air Force Base. The commanding general—his dental patient—arranged permission for him to go deer hunting in the Hembrillo Basin, a pretext that allowed him to make dozens of visits to the peak in the 1950s. What drew him back again and again was a cave he found. The cave ended at a large vertical shaft filled with small rocks. This shaft, he presumed, descended straight to the main cavern.

He led the crew up the road onto the peak and showed them where the opening to the cave had been. No evidence of a cave remained. "I've long suspected the army dynamited it shut," he said. "I must have crawled into that cave on thirty different occasions. Sometimes I'd sit at the edge of the shaft for hours. If there wasn't a treasure right below me, I don't know what."

The sun beat down from almost straight overhead. The line of pale clouds that had appeared on the horizon offered little promise of shade. Alex groaned when Jerry told everyone to listen up. He'd grown weary of talk. Jerry announced that this was not a dress rehearsal, advised against getting in a piss fight with a skunk, and reminded everyone that they represented Ova Noss. The treasure clubbers then followed Tony Jolley down the road and into the desert. Their metal detectors gleamed like wet tentacles, strangely menacing and futuristic, but the men themselves had already lost their polish. Sweat drenched their T-shirts, wind tousled their hair, sand settled into the wrinkles and creases of their exposed skin. Nevertheless, and at long last, the search for treasure at Victorio Peak had begun.

One MP and the archeologist drove along behind the treasure clubbers. A second MP stayed with Oren Swearingen and the Heydts, who intended to look around for signs of Oren's Cave. The third MP eyed Alex as he slung his video camera over his shoulder.

"I'm the Director of Video Documentation," Alex explained with an apologetic shrug. "I need to climb the peak and get a shot of the whole enchilada." He started up the road and didn't look back. The road traversed the northwest side of the peak, passing near several openings, which he pointed out like a tour guide, though the MP betrayed no interest. "Berlett and Fiege were Air Force guys," Alex said, as he shot a few seconds of video at the Fiege-Berlett hole. "They passed lie detector tests and the whole bit. Only Fiege said the treasure cave was up there"—Alex pointed 150 feet up the peak toward Soldier's Hole—"and Berlett said it was down here."

The MP was probably still a teenager, Alex decided, a teenager who carried a gun. In answer to Alex's direct question, he admitted that he was from Waterville, Maine.

They hiked past Soldier's Hole and up to where the road ended, a relatively flat area roughly the size of a tennis court. "This is called the saddle," Alex said. "And that's the Ova Noss Intercept hole." He indicated an opening sealed with wooden planks. "*Intercept* because Babe was trying to intercept Doc's passageway *below* where it had gotten blown up when he used too much dynamite. But that's another story."

As they scrambled to the top of the peak, dust flying, loose rocks rolling, he pretended not to notice the slack-jawed grin on the MP's face. The slight breeze at the top provided little relief from the withering heat, but the view was spectacular. Alex shot a slow 360 of the basin, beginning at the west rim where they'd driven in, and turning clockwise to the north, commenting as he went.

"See that ripple in the ground? That's the dike. It runs east-west for I don't know how many miles and cuts right through the peak. It's volcanic. And that's the battlefield where Chief Victorio fought the U.S. Army. I hate to tell you, but he kicked your guys' butt."

The MP remained silent. Alex pointed out the knob formation due north of the peak, panned all the way around to Antenna Ridge to the south, and finished by standing over the entrance to Doc's original shaft and shooting down through the rebar grate that covered it, into the darkness.

"This is where it all started," he said. "Doc climbed down from here and found the treasure."

"How much you think there is?" the MP asked, his voice high and squeaky.

"Sixteen thousand bars, the story goes."

"How much you get if you find it?"

"That's up to the boss," Alex said. "I'm just a volunteer, not an investor."

"It's gonna be tough," the MP said. "How's that guy gonna remember what rock he buried something under forty years ago? It all looks exactly the same."

The MP pronounced his judgment with no malice, which only made it harder for Alex to dismiss. Though the peak was small for a mountain, it extended over a vast area. The treasure could lie anywhere.

"Take the camera," Alex said.

"I don't think I'm supposed to," the MP said.

"Just aim and shoot."

The MP reluctantly accepted the camera and pointed it at Alex.

"Press the red button. There you go." Alex stood on top of the original Noss Shaft and looked into the camera. He wanted to congratulate Terry, but what could he say that wouldn't sound hokey?

"I think we're on," the MP said, nervously jiggling the camera.

Alex gazed down at where the metal detectorists were imperceptibly inching across the desert and signaled the MP to get a shot of them.

"You're right," Alex said. "We're on."

Each volunteer worked a nine-by-nine-foot quadrant in an area north of the peak where Tony Jolley recalled having buried twenty-four gold bars. Catclaw now covered much of the area, though Jolley remarked that in his day there had been none. The sharp thorns of the catclaw tore first at clothes and then at flesh, a mere nuisance in the beginning, but after an hour of swinging a metal detector through its tangled limbs, it became a curse, a manifestation of evil. The crew worked slowly, unable to find a rhythm, hampered by the searing heat, the relentless spikes, stickers, and needles of the desert plants, until Bob Wood called out a strike: "Bring in the archeologist! It's not gold, but it's big. Real big."

The crew passed around canteens and candy bars while the MP got on the walkie-talkie to the archeologist, who was reading a paperback in his truck parked on the road about a quarter mile away. The archeologist ambled over in no particular hurry and borrowed Bob Wood's metal detector, passing it over the spot and listening through the headphones.

"That's nothing for you guys," he said with a scowl. "Let's not waste our time."

"Aren't you going to dig it up?" Bob Wood asked.

"I don't think so," the archeologist said.

"It's your job," Bob Wood said.

The archeologist reluctantly got down on his knees and dug with a small shovel. After a few minutes, he hit metal. Eventually, he unearthed an anvil.

"See?" he said. "Nothing for you."

He let Bob Wood have his photograph taken with the anvil, then reburied it.

"What good does that do?" Bob Wood demanded.

"It's the law," the archeologist said, an answer that left the crew fuming as he walked back to the truck.

According to the Archeological Resources Protection Act of 1979, "No person may excavate, remove, damage, or otherwise alter or deface…any archeological resource located on public land…unless such activity is pursuant to a permit." The key term was "archeological resource," which was defined to "include but not be limited to: pottery, basketry, bottles, weapon projectiles, tools, structures or portions of structures, pit houses, rock paintings, rock carvings, intaglios, graves, human skeletal materials, or any portion or piece of the foregoing items." An anvil was unquestionably a tool. The maximum penalty for violating the law was a fine of not more than $20,000 and imprisonment for not more than two years.

The next time the crew made a strike, the archeologist waved the metal detector over the spot and refused to dig. No amount of protest from Jerry could convince him to change his mind.

The trip back to the highway seemed twice as long as the trip out. This time Alex drove, but he got stuck in the middle of the pack and had to crawl along, eating dust, which hung in the air much thicker now—the recent rains had kept the morning dust down.

The volunteers sat slumped against the doors in the back seat. Jerry, riding shotgun, had already fallen asleep. Alex consciously straightened his back. The smell of coconut-scented sunscreen reminded him of the beach, the ocean, the cool Pacific breeze. He thought about stopping the Blazer at the huge puddle, so they could get out and roll in the mud.

It had been a frustrating day. The metal detectorists had located nearly a hundred targets, but the archeologist had dug up only a few, the anvil and some large caliber cartridges that probably dated back to the battle between the army and Chief Victorio.

"Who needs archeologists?" one of the volunteers now asked, stirring from his lethargy. "To a guy who's as fanatical about metal detecting as I am— you've got a good signal and they won't let you dig it up? I found twenty-millimeter shell casings out there today, beat-up bullets, and I wasn't even supposed to touch them." He barely mustered the energy to shake his head in disgust. "Archeologists are all alike. They think they're too damn good for us. Four years of college, paid for by mom and dad. If they want to dig with a damn toothbrush, that's their business, but don't ruin things for us."

The longer he talked, the more sympathy Alex felt for archeologists, who, after all, did thankless and complex work. This particular archeologist might be a pain, but who could argue with the value of preserving a record of the past?

"I just wish we'd found some gold," the other volunteer said. "Gold has such a particular sound—it blows your headphones off."

It occurred to Alex that his own ears were ringing, pounding really, as if a great chaotic noise had been blaring in the background for hours. When they reached the Hill ranch, he realized that he'd missed the lake, and then he understood that it was gone, evaporated, four hundred feet of water in the morning, and by the end of the afternoon not even a drop.

It was only Day One, he told himself, an encouraging but exhausting thought.

By Day Three of the search, Judy had mastered her rap. When Terry strolled into the office with his coffee, toast, and pills, she was on the phone, as usual, praising the crew's enthusiasm and tireless work ethic. She didn't mention their grumbling about the archeologist and the MPs. Instead of saying that the metal detectorists hadn't yet located any gold bars, she said that they'd already managed to eliminate several large areas from consideration. Instead of saying that the search was inefficient, ill-equipped, and underfunded, she said that every day was a new adventure. She tried to end each call on an up note: "They could be waving their metal detectors over one of Doc's stashes right now."

Terry felt better today, clear-headed enough to confront his worries. "Listening to the crew last night," he told Judy when she hung up, "they sounded frustrated. They need direction. It's my fault—"

Judy launched into a lecture on what a great job he was doing, but a phone call from Les Smith undercut her reassurances. Smith was the engineer who'd conducted the Gaddis Mining Company's 1963 excavation of the peak. Judging from his drawn-out description of Denver's recent weather, he didn't share Terry's urgency.

"Any luck on the drill rig?" Terry finally asked.

Smith made a long story short, but not too short. Terry found himself nodding impatiently. The sort of drill rig they needed, according to Smith, did not grow on trees.

"I understand," Terry said. "Thank you so much." He cradled the phone gently on the receiver. Judy was watching him. "You think drill rigs are listed in the yellow pages?" he asked.

At two o'clock that afternoon, he received a more disturbing call. It came from Jerry Cheatham at the peak. "You're not going to believe this," Jerry said. The connection cut in and out. Static filled the line. The story emerged in short bursts. A few members of the crew had opened up the entrance to the Starlight Room, a cave near the top of the peak on the north side. A wooden hopper and old shoring timbers were stored inside the cave, which led to a narrow fissure filled with rocks and debris. The crew wanted to remove the rocks and explore the fissure. The archeologist had prohibited them from doing so on the grounds that the Starlight Room was an historical site protected by law.

"That's ridiculous." Terry felt the vein in the middle of his forehead throb.

The crew had demanded that the archeologist consult the environmental officer at the base. The environmental officer had supported the archeologist, saying that only four sites were authorized for digging. The Starlight Room was not one of them.

"Bring the crew home." Terry enunciated each word carefully, to make sure Jerry understood. "We won't tolerate these conditions."

He sat quietly in his swivel chair, staring out the window at the backyard, the mountains beyond. Judy was watching him again. When he fetched his legal pad and started writing, she took the portable phone and left him alone.

"Dear General Wharton," he began, then crossed out "Dear."

> For forty years we have been kept off Victorio Peak because the military and archeologists said that this site had no historical or archeological importance—hence, no treasure could exist there. Now we are being kept from doing necessary excavation because it is deemed by these same authorities to be an important archeological site.

The irony was almost too galling to contemplate. After insisting that the peak held nothing of value—after using it for target practice—the army had decided to "protect" it from ONFP. As far as Terry was concerned, the episode at the Starlight Room was just the latest example of the army's determination to obstruct the project. Yesterday, the archeologist had prohibited the metal detectorists from working at the site of the old Henderson Ranch. Terry wondered if General Wharton had ever read *Catch-22*.

> The Henderson Ranch, which was built with Noss family materials, was destroyed by Army missile testing. It now consists of scattered piles of sheet metal. How could a little metal detecting inflict more damage than the army's missiles?

Terry poured his anger and frustration into the letter, which gradually lost its coherence, until he knew that he would never mail it. Nevertheless, he kept writing.

His biggest complaint was not the overzealous archeologist but the rate being charged for support costs. Soon after General Wharton took command, Terry had asked him to bill ONFP at the lower government rate General Jones had quoted during the satellite conference. Wharton, after consulting with his legal officer, had declined. He had agreed, however, to renew the license agreement until May 1993 and promised not to run up ONFP's charges. A quick discovery, Terry had told himself, would render the rate problem moot. Now, faced with the army's latest restrictions, he wondered if he'd been a fool to launch the search.

The sun had just set when Judy ventured back to the office and turned on a desk lamp. Terry handed over his legal pad, then massaged his temples while she read the letter.

"We should've waited until we were ready," he said. "Things were bound to go wrong."

"We couldn't keep waiting," she said. "Everyone would have lost faith. You should hear the investors now. They're ecstatic."

"They won't be tomorrow."

The phone rang again, an Associated Press reporter calling from Albuquerque.

"I'll take it," Terry said. His reflection in the dark window looked surprisingly calm. "All work at Victorio Peak has been terminated due to restrictions imposed by the army," he told the reporter, then covered the mouthpiece. "Do I sound enigmatic?" he asked Judy. "I'm trying to sound enigmatic."

General Wharton's secretary phoned at eight-thirty the following morning to ask if the general could stop by the ONFP house for a brief visit. He had a function to attend in Las Cruces and would only be able to stay a few minutes. Evidently, his office had already received calls from reporters inquiring about the termination of the search.

General Richard W. Wharton arrived at the ONFP house at nine o'clock in full dress uniform, his chest spangled with medals and ribbons. He was fifty-four years old, a Vietnam veteran decorated with the Bronze Star, the Meritorious Service Medal, and the Army Commendation Medal. He greeted Terry with cautious reserve and declined to step inside. The crew milled around the living room, trying to sneak a peek at him. Terry, exhausted after a sleepless night, gritted his teeth to stifle a yawn.

"We want to cooperate," the general said. "We want you to get your work done. We support you."

Terry nodded politely, his hair still wet from the shower.

"You can *always* call me," the general said. "*Never* shut down again. We all have to comply with the archeology laws, but there's no reason for anyone to get jerked around." The general invited Terry to meet with his staff that afternoon to iron out the current difficulties. "If you run into any problems, give me a call," the general added as they shook hands. "I'd prefer to communicate directly, rather than through the press."

When Terry joined the crew in the living room, they gave him a round of applause.

Terry designated his brother Jim, due to fly in from Houston, to lead the ONFP delegation at the meeting. He spent the rest of the day alone in his room, the smallest in the ONFP house, a six-by-ten sanctuary with a mattress from a single bed on the floor and an apple crate that held his books and his reading light. Between fitful naps he stared at the mercifully blank walls and tried to pretend that the project didn't exist, that he was an ordinary person with an ordinary life. What would such a person think about? How would such a person fill his time? Anymore, he had no idea.

The meeting at White Sands Missile Range opened with the usual hostility. General Wharton's staff criticized ONFP for inadequate preparation. If ONFP had submitted a complete list of proposed exploration sites, the matter of which sites were off limits could have been settled in advance. Furthermore, if ONFP had been ready to drill, no one would have cared about these peripheral sites.

The ONFP contingent accused the army of bad faith. How could anyone claim to be surprised that ONFP wanted to investigate the sites where Doc and Babe and others had worked? The historical significance of those sites was surpassed by the historical significance of the present search.

The environmental officer pointed out that the army operated under exactly the same archeological constraints. "There are fifty-year-old Quonset huts we can't knock down because the law says they're historical. We all have to play by the same rules. Our hands are tied."

"We believe in the importance of history," Jim Delonas said. "But it's a matter of degree and judgment. These restrictions are ridiculous."

The recriminations continued until Jim mentioned General Wharton's visit to the ONFP house. The general's staff hadn't heard about it yet. Jim informed them that the general had asked to be called in the event of a problem. "Seems like we've got a problem now," Jim said. "Shall we call him?" The general's staff saw no reason to trouble the general. Instead, they offered a modest concession. ONFP could conduct its explorations as long as the basic structure of the mountain remained intact. The language was vague enough to satisfy both sides for a while. "The hostility didn't exactly melt," Jim told Terry later, "but maybe there was a little thaw."

．　．　．

Four members of the ONFP crew began excavating the Starlight Room with picks and shovels the next day. A backhoe would have simplified the job, but to put a backhoe in there, a bulldozer would have been needed to cut a new road, and a new road would have altered the basic structure of the mountain. The picks and shovels unearthed nothing of interest. Meanwhile, the metal detectorists resumed their search of the Hembrillo Basin.

On Day Six, Alex crawled into Soldier's Hole and discovered a plastic Pepsi bottle filled with water, a can labeled "Hydraulic Fluid Automatic Transmission February 1976," and 150 wooden planks six to eight feet long, none of which he remembered seeing when he'd explored the hole in January 1990. Terry wrote a scathing letter to Alma Moore, notifying her—and the House Armed Services Committee—of the incursion.

On Day Seven, Oren Swearingen spent an hour in Soldier's Hole and declared that it was exactly as it had been left two and a half years before. As if to prove his point, he drank the water in the Pepsi bottle.

"But the passage seems so much wider now," Alex said.

"Tight spots grow tighter in memory," Swearingen said.

Terry had to send Alma Moore a retraction.

On Day Eight, a backhoe scooped out a ton of rocks and dirt where the entrance to Oren's Cave was supposed to be. The metal detectorists covered 100,000 square feet of desert and found a horseshoe.

Day Nine was an off day. Instead of working at the peak, the crew received a briefing from the base's Explosives Ordnance Division on how to deal with unexploded missiles and ammunition ("Don't touch anything") and afterwards Terry held a press conference.

On Day Ten, Terry flew to California to consult a doctor about his leg while Les Smith supervised the drilling of the first bore hole at the peak. The drill rig, a cheap rental that could only drill straight down to a maximum depth of fifty feet, was set up in the saddle three-fourths of the way up the peak, on the northwest side near the rim. According to the ground-penetrating radar results, the treasure cave lay approximately 400 feet below, and not directly below, but nearer to the center of the mountain. In other words, the cave could only be reached with a slant rig capable of drilling eight times deeper than the rig they had. Their only hope was to drill into a passage that would lead them to the treasure room. "I'd rather be lucky than good," Jerry said. Alex stood by with the DataCam.

The first hole hit a void between 16 and 18 feet. When Alex attempted to lower the DataCam into the hole, he discovered that the diameter of the hole was too small to accommodate the torpedo-shaped casing, which measured precisely four inches wide. Smith switched from a three-inch bit to a four-inch bit to drill the second hole. Again, though, the DataCam wouldn't fit. To drill a hole four inches wide, they needed a 4.5-inch bit.

"This is a learning experience," Smith said.

Alex disagreed. "This is a pain in the ass."

Smith moved the rig to the supposed site of Oren's Cave and drilled the next hole with a 4.5-inch bit, but progress was slower with the larger bit. When lightning struck on the far side of the basin, Smith called the drilling to a halt.

On Day Eleven, Smith drilled several more holes, but the sides of the holes were soft and crumbly, and Alex hesitated to use the DataCam for fear that dust would ruin it. Rather than sleeving the holes with PVC tubing to protect the DataCam, Smith recommended waiting till they acquired a better drill rig. Heavy rains again forced the crew to quit early.

On Day Twelve, the drill rig was returned to the rental agency. The backhoe crew at Oren's Cave struggled to remove an enormous boulder while Oren stood by, confidently predicting that the entrance to his cave lay right below. Under a steady rain, the backhoe finally pushed aside the boulder to reveal only more rocks and dirt underneath.

Torrential rains kept the crew at the ONFP house on Day Thirteen.

On Day Fourteen, the metal detectorists finished searching the permitted areas. The backhoe was returned to the rental agency.

On Day Fifteen, Terry flew in from California. He gathered the crew in the living room of the ONFP house and announced the suspension of operations at the peak.

"Don't be disappointed," he told them. "We're off to a fantastic start."

14

Victorio

Why did the Apaches fight so hard?
—*Howard Bryan*

1880

Chief Victorio of the Warm Springs Apache, in April of 1880, led an attack against a U.S. Cavalry unit setting up camp at the base of Victorio Peak. Nearly a century later, Albuquerque newspaper reporter Howard Bryan attributed the clash to buried treasure.

> It was a set-piece battle, the only such battle Victorio ever fought. That was unusual, and they fought for two days. *Apaches just don't do that.* They hit and run. The battle was over a fresh-water spring. The troopers were desperate for water, and the Apaches, for some reason, wouldn't give it up. The name of the spring? Hembrillo.... And why did the Apaches fight so hard? I figure they were protecting their hiding place, their headquarters....
>
> It became convincing to me that Doc Noss found Victorio's old hideout. The swords, the Wells Fargo boxes, the trussed-up skeletons, nothing dating later than 1880. It adds up to Victorio and the fact his band was run off before they could move any of it.

The reporter interviewed a 109-year-old Albuquerque man, Max Madrid, who claimed that his godfather had been a friend of Victorio's and that Victorio had confided to the godfather about all the treasure the Apaches had stolen from soldiers and settlers over the years and buried in a mountain, concealing the hiding place with earth and timbers. The godfather had told Madrid that the treasure was probably "still up there, near a big spring." The reporter seemed to give credence to the story.

How well does the historical record support such speculation?

Three hundred years after the lure of the seven cities of gold brought the Spanish conquistadors, the discovery of gold in California brought the American forty-niners. Before the gold rush began, the population of the entire New Mexico territory, which included Arizona, was less than 55,000, most of whom were Indians living in small pueblos or roaming the desert. The few towns were controlled by Hispanic families long established in the region. Most townspeople had been citizens of Spain until 1821, then citizens of Mexico until the United States won the Mexican-American war in 1848. The 60,000 forty-niners who surged into the territory shifted the balance of power, tilting it toward the Anglos.

Mining was already a significant industry in New Mexico. The Pueblo Indians had been mining turquoise for centuries. The Spaniards had founded what would become the world's largest copper mine at Santa Rita. A Mexican mule herder's gold strike had prompted the opening of several mines in the Ortiz Mountains south of Santa Fe. After 1849, the mining industry would boom. Gold would be discovered at Pinos Altos, the Organ Mountains, Tubac, the Pyramid Mountains, Elizabethtown, the Sangre de Cristos, Hillsboro, Kingston, Grafton, Hermosa, Lake Valley, Winston, White Oaks, Nogal, and Jicarilla. More than thirty thousand pounds of pure gold would be mined within a seventy-five mile radius of Victorio Peak. The ranching business would also thrive. In 1849, a few thousand cows grazed the New Mexico desert. By 1870, the number would rise to 50,000; by 1880, 350,000. Miners and ranchers, Anglo and Hispanic alike, would often dispute among themselves over land or politics, but they agreed that their worst enemy was the Apaches.

The name *Apache* comes from a Zuni word meaning *enemy*. The Apaches had raided Indian pueblos even before the arrival of the conquistadors. They'd attacked Spanish caravans on the El Camino Real and American mule trains on the Santa Fe Trail. They stole horses, mules, cattle, sheep, rifles, bullets, and an unreported amount of gold. What they didn't take from their enemies, they took from the desert: rabbit, juniper berries, yucca flowers, pigweed. The flesh of the mescal cactus, cooked down to a sticky syrup and dried in sheets, provided sustenance on the arduous rides from one watering hole to the next. The Apaches generally traveled on horseback or muleback, in small bands, raiding as far south as the silver mines around Chihuahua. The new border between the United States and Mexico gave them a safe haven to retreat to when pursued by forces of one country or the other. In 1849, the Governor of Chihuahua doubled the bounty for an Apache scalp to 200 pesos. In practice, it didn't matter whether the dead Apache was male or female, adult or child. Bounty hunters in Chihuahua received 17,896 pesos that year. Authorities on the U.S. side of the border soon instituted a similar policy. In the burgeoning New Mexico territory, the Apaches quickly became public enemy number one, the perpetrators of every unsolved theft and murder, the most obvious obstacle to prosperity for the thousands of settlers struggling to establish themselves in the rugged desert land.

Charles Overman, special agent for the Apaches in Soccorro, New Mexico, described the prevailing conditions in 1852:

> The Jornada del Muerto is travailed with fear and trembling, and the expressions of almost every party that arrives from the lower country add to the impression that an almost total blockade is maintained on that important thoroughfare.

The governor of New Mexico, James Calhoun, voiced his outrage: "These wholesale robberies and murders are of such uninterrupted continuance that the inhabitants of this Territory are in a state bordering on despair."

The Apaches, despite the wholesale robberies attributed to them, failed to prosper. Indian Agent James M. Smith characterized the Mimbres and Mescalero Apaches as "poor, miserable and filthy."

The Indian agents of the era occupied an awkward position. They had great responsibility and almost no authority. Often, they arrived in the Southwest with little regard for the Indians under their charge, but the more they saw, the stronger their sympathy grew. This sympathy tainted them in the eyes of their superiors in Washington. They risked being accused of losing their objectivity and "going native." One of the most insightful and articulate of the Indian agents was Dr. Michael Steck, a physician from Pennsylvania who accepted the appointment as agent for the Mescalero Apaches in 1853 in order to bring his ailing wife west for the invigorating desert air. In November of 1858, when Victorio's band straggled back from a stay in Janos, Mexico, Steck portrayed them with compassion:

> They are...almost naked and actually in a starving condition. They have occasionally received rations from the Govt. of Mexico. They have suffered much from disease and many of them have died.... Scarcely a family returned but has their hair cropped short, the badge of mourning for some relative. They believe they have been poisoned, and I have but little doubt that many of them have, as reports have reached here from the citizens of Janos that many of them had been poisoned, and the symptoms as described by the Indians resemble those of poisoning by arsenic, probably administered in whiskey as that formed a part of their rations.

Victorio, it's worth noting, did not drink.

Major Van Horne of Fort Stanton paints an equally vivid picture of the Apaches' sad state: "They devour a dead mule with avidity, and eagerly eat up the leavings of dogs."

In 1858, John Butterfield's Overland Mail established twice-weekly stage-coach service between St. Louis and San Francisco. The route went through El Paso, then up the Rio Grande to Mesilla, then east to Tucson. The first Wells Fargo branch in the New Mexico territory opened in Yuma in 1859; the second, in Tucson in 1860. The accelerating settlement of the West put increasing pressure on the Apaches.

On December 4, 1860, a band of Pinos Altos gold miners "attacked and killed some of the peaceful Indians at old Ft. Webster," Dr. Steck wrote to Indian Superintendent James Collins. In general, the settlers made no distinction between marauding Indians and Indians who lived in peace on the reservations. Not surprisingly, when the settlers sought to avenge their many grievances, the peaceful Indians provided the more convenient target. The prevailing public attitude could be summed up in two not-so-contradictory slogans: "There's no such thing as a good Indian" and "The only good Indian is a dead Indian." Hate-mongering sold newspapers and won votes on election day. The Apaches had few defenders. Acts of vigilante violence against them were applauded. "Nobody was ever punished for killing an Indian," wrote Steck.

When the Confederate Army, under the leadership of Lieutenant John Baylor, marched into the Southwest, their Indian policy could be summed up in one word—extermination. Baylor wrote to one of his captains:

> The Congress of the Confederate States has passed a law declaring extermination
> of all hostile Indians. You will therefore use all means to persuade the Apaches or
> any tribe to come in for the purpose of making peace, and when you get them
> together kill all the grown Indians and take the children prisoner and sell them to
> defray the expense of killing the Indians. Buy whiskey and such other goods as
> may be necessary for the Indians.... Leave nothing undone to insure success, and
> have a sufficient number of men around to allow no Indian to escape.... I...look
> to you for success against these cursed pests who have already murdered over 100
> men in this territory.

The Apaches tormented the poorly supplied Confederate Army, which soon
abandoned the Southwest, leaving the Apaches free to roam the New Mexico
territory unimpeded by any military presence until the arrival of General
James Carleton and the California Column in August of 1861. Martial law,
also known as "Carleton Law," governed New Mexico for the next four years.

In communications with his superiors in Washington, Carleton emphasized the mineral riches of the territory under his command, the fierceness
of his enemy, and the need for more troops and weapons. Like many generals before and since, he did his best to drum up support for a massive military campaign. He would write to Postmaster General Salmon Chase:

> If I can but have troops to whip away the Apaches, so that prospectors can explore
> the country and not be in fear all the time of being murdered, you will without a
> shadow of a doubt, find that our country has mines of the precious metals, unsur-
> passed in richness, number and extent by any in the world.... The gold is pure.

He sent along a gold nugget, to be presented to President Lincoln, if such a
gift "be not improper."

Carleton enlisted the famous Kit Carson to carry out the assault on the
Apaches. His last order to Carson, dated September 27, 1862, is typically
blunt: "All Indian men of that tribe are to be killed whenever and wherever
you find them." The murder of Mangas Colorado followed soon after. Mangas
Colorado had done battle with U.S. forces for years. Kit Carson called him
"doubtless the worst Indian within our boundaries, and one who has been
the cause of more murders and of more torturing and of burning at the stake
in this country than all others together."

Judge Joseph Knapp of Mesilla, in an open letter to Carleton published in the *Santa Fe New Mexican,* recounted the story of Mangas Colorado's brutal slaying:

> But little more than two years have passed since Mangas Colorado, the most powerful of all Apache chiefs, voluntarily came into one of your posts and agreed to deliver himself and his band of Apaches to your control. He was confined in the guardhouse; that night he was aroused from his sleep, some say that a soldier threw something and hit him, and others that he was punched with a pole, and because he raised himself up to see what had disturbed his sleep, he was instantly perforated with bullets and killed. Next morning at dawn his lodge was attacked, and his wife and daughter shared the fate of husband and father. Not content with having killed a prisoner of war, without cause, your soldiers tore the scalp from his head and severed his head from his body, and after boiling the flesh, they exhibited the skull as a badge of honor, while the scalps of himself, his wife and daughter were worn as ornaments.... This black flag policy has, as might have been expected, borne its consequent fruit. It has prevented the Indians from surrendering themselves, and led them to revenge.

In the spring of 1863, Kit Carson rounded up those Apaches who hadn't been killed—about 400 Mescalero men and their families—and marched them to Bosque Redondo, a new reservation on the Pecos River in southeastern New Mexico. Bosque Redondo means *round forest,* a poor name for an area sixteen miles long and half a mile wide, featuring a few scattered trees. Carson also herded hundreds of captured Navajos to Bosque Redondo in an infamous episode in the history of the Southwest known as "The Long Walk." The Apaches and the Navajos clashed immediately.

Victorio steered clear of Bosque Redondo, despite his apparent willingness to give up the warrior life. In his negotiations with General Nelson Davis, Davis quoted him as saying: "I and my people want peace—we are tired of war—we are poor and we have little...to eat or wear—it is very cold—we want to make peace, a lasting peace."

General Carleton, meanwhile, refused to acknowledge the misery at Bosque Redondo. "The Indians on the reservation are the happiest people I have ever seen," he wrote. Carleton's policy of malignant neglect was finally challenged by Dr. Steck, who dared to advocate humane treatment of the Apaches:

> Human nature exhibits itself as well in the Indian as in the Anglo-Saxon; supply the wants of either, and the disposition to revolt is suppressed or materially weak-

ened. This was clearly shown by the Mescaleros and Gila Apaches from 1854 to 1860. Liberally supplied with goods during that period by their agents, they remained quiet and planted large breadths of corn. But for the discovery of gold mines in the immediate vicinity of their fields, which attracted a population not exactly, in disposition as well as in numbers, adapted to the best interests of the Indian, and the Texas invasion, they would at this time be at peace and comfortably situated. It may be urged that to locate and feed 12,000 Indians is an expensive method of treatment. It is susceptible of the clearest proof, however, that such a policy is not only the most philanthropic, but the most economical. It needs no prophetic eye to see that, in a few years, the Indians of New Mexico must be exterminated, unless the government interposes its benevolent hand to protect and support them.

Carleton's Bosque Redondo experiment failed to solve his Apache problem. Most of the Mescaleros escaped from the reservation as conditions worsened. Major General John Pope reported on the final exodus: "Just before winter set in, in 1865…on the third of November, during the night, every Apache who could travel arose and vanished. In the morning only the sick and the crippled were left, and within a few days they vanished also." The conflict between the Apaches and the U.S. military would only intensify in the years following the Civil War.

One of the great treasure tales of the Southwest, collected by J. Frank Dobie among others, begins in the shadow of the Civil War with the fall of Maximilian in Mexico and recounts the perilous journey of a small party of the emperor's loyalists who gathered from his palace all the gold and jewels they could carry on horseback and fled north. Riding only at night, they eventually crossed the Rio Grande, only to be attacked by a band of Confederate soldiers returning home. The soldiers slaughtered Maximilian's followers, stole their treasure, and stashed it in a nearby mountain cave. Just before the soldiers went their separate ways, they too were attacked—by Apaches who killed all but one of them. The lone survivor told the story on his deathbed and left behind a map.

The treasure is usually placed in the Guadalupe Mountains, but Doc and Babe claimed to have found in Victorio Peak letters written by Maximilian's wife Carlotta. Many supporters of the Victorio Peak project believe that Maximilian was one of the sources of the Victorio Peak treasure.

Do any facts exist to support the enduring legend? According to Percy Martin, an English historian writing in 1914, Maximilian's commander-in-chief, Marshal Bazaine, left Mexico City with 22,000 ounces of gold. Liberal troops intercepted him and confiscated the gold, but General Porfirio Diaz later returned it. Martin's account, if true, suggests that one man close to Maximilian may have managed to bring a small portion of the emperor's treasure out of Mexico. Whether anyone else did is a matter of pure conjecture. The story of the Confederate soldiers certainly has all the earmarks of a folktale: the convenient mountain cave, the decision to hide the treasure rather than divide it, the lone survivor's deathbed confession. The odds that any part of Maximilian's treasure found its way to Victorio Peak seem astronomical.

In 1869, the Governor of New Mexico, Robert Mitchell, declared all Navajo and Apaches to be outlaws and authorized the citizens of the territory to kill "every such depredators [*sic*]."

In 1870, Indian agent William Arny called the Apaches "the most savage, barbarous, and uncivilized Indians on this continent."

> Their exploits in the way of murder, robberies and torture are unparalleled in the history of any other tribe of Indians: they have robbed mails, burned Stage Coaches, have torn out, cooked and eaten the hearts of some persons, and have burned at the stake stage passengers and other prisoners who have fallen in their power; they have killed miners, and retarded the mining operations of one of the richest portions of the United States.

In 1871, the citizens of Grant County, New Mexico passed a resolution to "organize themselves into a posse and follow their stock to wherever it may be, and take it by force wherever found, even if it be at the sacrifice of every Indian man, women, and child."

Private citizens, local officials, and the federal government had reached a rare consensus: the Apaches could not be permitted to roam free. They must be captured or killed at any cost. The process was almost complete. First they had been dehumanized; then demonized; now they would be destroyed.

In 1872, the Apaches sought a permanent reservation at Cañada Alamosa. Their request was denied, at least in part because of the area's mineral riches. Instead, the Ojo Caliente reservation was established near Tularosa. The

Apaches, including Victorio, disliked Ojo Caliente, but when they ran out of food or got sick, they would come to the reservation for several days or weeks. The result was a game of tag with the reservation and the army. They'd stay at Ojo Caliente until confinement grew intolerable and then they'd go raiding.

When the commander of the district of New Mexico, Colonel Edward Hatch of the Ninth Cavalry, met with Victorio at Ojo Caliente in April 1876, he found the Apaches "extremely defiant."

> They were well armed with Springfield, Winchester or Sharps rifles and carbines, Colts and Smith and Wesson Revolvers, the women and boys with muzzle loading arms and well supplied with ammunition. They declared openly that the Government had acted in bad faith, that no meat had been issued to them for four weeks, that many of their young men were away on raids for horses and mules and it was better for them all to go than to remain and starve.

Unless reservation conditions drastically improved, Victorio argued, the Apaches would be better off making peace with Mexico and raiding in the United States. Since the Mexican-American War, Mexico had become poor and the United States rich. Hatch promised nothing.

In September of 1876, a company of soldiers and Navajo scouts attacked Ojo Caliente. Victorio and his followers escaped to the mountains. A month later, Ojo Caliente was again attacked, this time by a mob of private citizens. Many Apaches moved to the reservation at San Carlos, but it was overcrowded and undersupplied, and Victorio saw it as worse than Ojo Caliente.

The discovery of gold in Percha Canyon in 1877 sent prospectors swarming to Percha Creek and the nearby San Andres, Caballo, and Fray Cristobal Mountains. Anti-Apache sentiment grew even stronger. The Apaches were blamed for the murder of Harry Pye, who discovered the "Pye Lode" at Chloride. Pye's head was found dangling from a juniper tree, reputedly as a warning to the white man to stay away from the Apache reservation.

In September of 1877, Victorio and another Apache chief, Loco, stole horses and a large quantity of flour from the White Mountain Apaches at the San Carlos reservation and led 300 followers down to Mexico. During the next year and a half, Victorio traveled back and forth across the border, occasionally negotiating with various Indian agents for a guarantee that he and his people be allowed to live in peace at Ojo Caliente. In June of 1879, tired and out of supplies, he surrendered for the last time.

He might have spent his remaining years on the Ojo Caliente reservation if he hadn't heard there was a "paper" out against him, an indictment in Grant County charging him with horse stealing and murder. He probably never considered defending himself before a jury. The citizens of Grant County had already legalized the killing of Apaches. So, on August 21, 1879, Victorio bolted once more, pursued by Major Albert Morrow as far as the Mexican border.

The *New York Sun* reported on Victorio's exploits when he returned to the American side:

> Victorio, the leader of the Warm Spring Apaches, has, at length, turned and rent his pursuers. On Sunday last [November 9], he ambushed a company of fifty men from New Mexico, who were on his trail, and killed thirty-two of them, the other eighteen…escaping to tell the story.

Lt. Gatewood vividly described the night-time battle. "The whole top of the mountain was a fringe of fire flashes." Victorio's men were armed with "improved Winchester rifles," and plenty of ammunition. They rolled huge stones down on Gatewood and his men, who retreated. Gatewood would never forget the lull that followed:

> …the only noise was the tum-tum beaten by Victorio himself all during the fight, accompanied by his high keyed, quavering voice in a song of "good medicine." He was at this juncture holding forth to our scouts, trying to persuade them to desert and join his men, and together they would kill the last white and black soldier present. He didn't succeed.

As usual, the Apaches who remained on the reservation were punished for Victorio's acts. General Pope called the Apaches a "miserable, brutal race, cruel, deceitful and wholly irreclaimable." Victorio, meanwhile, set up camp in the Candelaria Mountains outside Chihuahua and conducted raids on the local silver miners.

In January of 1880, Victorio headed north and swung by Ojo Caliente. Captain Rucker and his soldiers tracked him into the San Andres, finally catching up with him on February 3. According to a story in the *Arizona Star,* Victorio's position was "strongly fortified in a narrow and rough canyon."

The troops were received by a heavy fire, under which several horses and men fell. Perceiving their advantage, the Indians charged the troops, who gave way, and retreated in pell-mell order; the Indians in turn became the pursuers and drove the troops across the river. In the retreat rations and bedding were abandoned, which the Indians secured.

On March 23, 1880, Colonel Hatch led his Ninth Cavalry, the army's first unit of black troops, known popularly as the Buffalo Soldiers, from Texas to New Mexico to dispatch Victorio. Hatch sent ahead an order that all Indians be returned to reservations. "I shall be forced to consider all Indians not at the agency hostile."

On March 29, according to newspaper reports, Victorio's men stole 20 horses from Hillsboro while Lt. Beyer and his troops guarded one side of town and Lt. Wright and his Indian scouts guarded the other. Subsequent accounts, probably exaggerated, presented Victorio parading his warriors down Hillsboro's main street as townspeople cowered in fear. Whatever happened in Hillsboro, several forces pursued Victorio into the San Andres, setting the stage for the battle that gave Victorio Peak its name.

Captain Carroll found Victorio first. On April 7, 1880, after a long march, Carroll and his troops had stopped for water at a creek that turned out to be contaminated with gypsum. By the time they staggered into the Hembrillo Basin, they were tired, sick, and desperate for water. As soon as they reached the springs near the base of Victorio Peak, Victorio and his men surrounded them. A battle raged throughout the night, with Carroll's forces taking heavy losses.

At dawn McLellan and his squadron arrived and quickly sent word to Colonel Hatch to bring reinforcements. According to the report later filed by Hatch, McLellan "discovered Captain Carroll, surrounded by Indians, within a semicircle upon hills of higher range."

> The hostiles had thrown up rifle pits on the crest of this range, covering three-fourths of a circle around Carroll's command, where nature had not furnished them with shelter; they had left their rifle pits and were moving down the ravines in strong bands with the intention undoubtedly of destroying Carroll. There was no time to be lost, and McLellan, realizing this, at once charged with his entire force, taking the hostiles by surprise, driving them back, and keeping up a very heavy fire as they retreated up the cañons.

Hatch estimated that Victorio had three hundred Apaches with him and that thirty were killed. The Las Cruces newspaper opined that Victorio had 53 men and that one was killed. The custom of inflating the number of enemy casualties is probably as old as war. Hatch neglected to mention in his report that as he and his troops rode into the basin, Victorio and his men managed to sneak by undetected.

Could Victorio have been hiding an enormous treasure, as reporter Howard Bryan suggested? Undoubtedly, Victorio stole plenty of valuables in his legendary marauding career, but he also did business with traders. Would he have been more likely to hoard his valuables or trade them for food and weapons? The possibility of a small cache left hidden away seems much more likely than a large one.

Whether he abandoned any treasure or not, Victorio and his band headed for the Mogollon Mountains, where, on April 29, they raided Cooney's mining camp. A month later, they were attacked by the cavalry's Apache scouts under the command of Henry Parker. The scouts killed several of Victorio's men and shot Victorio in the leg. The outcome might have been worse for Victorio if Parker's forces hadn't run out of ammunition. The battle with Parker marked the beginning of the end for Victorio. Though he continued to win most of his battles, he lost the war of attrition.

In November, in the mountains outside Chihuahua, Colonel Joaquín Terrazas and the Mexican Army finally cornered Victorio. "About midnight," Terrazas later wrote, "the death song of the Indians on the peak began to be heard, continuing with agonizing cries for more than two hours." Victorio and his men did more than sing during the night. They dug trenches in the mountainside to fortify their weak position while Terrazas waited for daybreak to attack. At first light, Terrazas and his troops overran the Apache defenses. Victorio was killed and scalped for the bounty along with 77 other Apaches, including women and children.

The saga of the Apaches in the Old West ended in 1886 when the U.S. government gathered all the Apaches in the New Mexico territory—including those who had lived peacefully on the reservations and those, like Henry Parker, who had served as army scouts—and banished them all to a reservation near St. Augustine, Florida. Geronimo, according to legend, offered in exchange for his freedom to reveal the location of the richest gold deposit in the world—somewhere in the Guadalupes, according to J. Frank Dobie's version of the tale. Geronimo found no takers. Though the promise of far-off gold had fooled the white man for nearly four hundred years, no one fell for it this time.

In 1894, the Apaches were sent from Florida to Fort Sill, Oklahoma. In 1911, some were allowed to return to New Mexico. Stories circulated among prospectors and treasure buffs that the oldest Apaches still remembered where great hoards of treasure lay hidden. Many ONFP supporters believe that Doc Noss as a young boy was briefly jailed at Fort Sill and shared a cell with Geronimo. Implausibly or not, they maintain that the chief confided to young Doc the secret location of the treasure.

If people wish to believe in the existence of a fabulous fortune, they don't need conclusive proof. A possibility, however slim, can be enough to convince the faithful. It's a remarkable sensation, that feeling that treasure lies almost within reach. The Spaniards understood, centuries ago, when they first journeyed to New Mexico in search of gold. They believed for the sake of believing. In Spanish, the word *to wait* also means *to hope*.

Top: Victorio Peak. Right: Doc Noss in black.
Above: Babe Noss at rock house near peak.

Doc and Babe and the Cheyenne Mining Company, 1941.

Babe, Doc, and Letha Guthrie in Hot Springs.

*Ben Samaniego
in armor found at Victorio Peak.*

Above: Babe holding gold bar. Written on back of photo: "Me holding a 20 lb Bar of gold Bullion & old Buster and O. G. Turner a miner 1941."
Below: Doc and Babe with miners and investors.

Dorothy Delonas, Letha, and companions at Upper Noss Shaft.

Tony Jolley.

Artifacts purportedly taken from Victorio Peak.

View of Hembrillo Basin, with Victorio Peak on left and Geronimo Peak on right.

Babe at boundary of White Sands.

Doc, fatally shot in Las Cruces, 1949.

Dan Rather at the peak.

Below: Terry Delonas at the peak during Goldfinder, 1977.

Victorio Peak from above.

Map from The New York Times.

Top: Norman Scott at White Sands Missile Range.
Above: Judy Holeman and Terry in the ONFP office.
Left: Terry at White Sands Missile Range.

Clockwise from top: ONFP crew with military police; Terry at peak with General Wharton; a meeting at the ONFP house; Letha at the peak.

Top: Base camp, nine miles from the peak.
Above: The Guzzler, maneuvering toward the
Lower Noss Shaft. Left: Alex Alonso in the
fissure, displaying T-star plank, probably
carved by Doc.

Judy, Dorothy, and Terry in the fissure.

Above: Descent into fissure. Left: Kelly Fischer, Alex, and Gene Klier in fissure.

Cherrington crane near base of peak.

Hard rock mining.

Alex planting geophones.

Top, left: The scoopertram
entering the drift.
Above: Inside the drift.
Top, right: Deeper in the drift.

Map showing windlass.

Terry at peak.

Letha, Martin Cherrington, and Dorothy near the peak.

Left: John Washbourne recording data for seismic survey.

View from the rim of the
Hembrillo Basin.

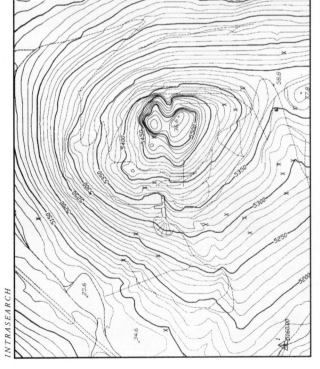

INTRASEARCH

Terry at peak with Guzzler.

Topo map of Victorio Peak.

15

Into the Fissure

It doesn't matter how slowly you go,
as long as you don't stop.
—Confucius

Fall 1992

Terry hid behind a magazine on the bumpy flight to El Paso. His seatmates, a gabby software salesman from Scottsdale and a grandmotherly school teacher from Canutillo, might have enjoyed the Victorio Peak saga, but he didn't feel inspired to recount it, preferring instead to eat dry peanuts and flip the pages of the airline magazine.

His left leg throbbed. It was badly burned as a result of the Kaposi's Sarcoma treatment. His doctor in Venice Beach covered the lesions with a topical agent that burned away the skin. About this mysterious topical agent, the doctor said only that it was highly toxic. Once a lesion was burned off, the doctor applied antibiotics to the burned area to prevent infection. Only a few lesions remained, though Terry's leg was now a livid patchwork of new skin and scars.

He counted himself lucky. Last week he'd gone out on a sailboat to help spread the ashes of his first close friend to die of AIDS. Another man on the sailboat said he'd now lost 17 friends. Terry flipped to an ad for a Florida beach resort. The water appeared altogether too blue, its airbrushed sparkle as phony as a cheap toupee. Work at the peak had resumed a month ago, with Lambert Dolphin taking yet more ground-penetrating radar readings that appeared to pinpoint Oren's Cave. Dolphin had exuded confidence. "We're going to hit a hole-in-one on the first try," he'd predicted. Instead—wrong sport, wrong result—they'd struck out. "As of now, the radar sucks," Alex Alonso had declared after drillers sank twelve holes at a cost of almost $50,000 and found no cave, no treasure. It was only after the drill rig was hauled away that Terry had realized how much he'd been counting on a quick discovery.

At least they'd made preparations for a longer search, building a base camp nine miles from the peak to save four hours of daily commute time. The crew slept in trailers or tents, ate breakfast and dinner in a converted carport, and worked ten-hour days. The constant companionship had brought them together as a team, but it had also increased friction. The failure of the drilling had further raised the tension.

Terry blamed himself. By the end of the first stint, it had become clear that his cousin Jerry was not a good fit as Director of Field Operations. Terry had replaced him with a contractor from North Carolina who'd been recommended as a "gung ho guy with the know-how to get things done." Jack Faircloth had impressed Terry with his energy and charm, but once in charge he'd alienated several members of the crew, volunteers who in many cases owned their own businesses and didn't appreciate being yelled at. Terry had already flown back once to calm the crew and counsel Jack. This time he planned to stay in Las Cruces and play peacemaker as long as necessary. The search needed a leader who could give direction without giving offense, and until Jack learned how to do that, Terry's KS treatment could wait.

He felt like a character in a soap opera—he'd been written out of several episodes and now he was rejoining the show. Even though he dreaded the pandemonium of the ONFP house, California had kept him too far from the action. When Jack and Alex had clashed, Terry had heard several conflicting accounts of what happened, including the rumor that a woman had come between them. He expected melodrama from his own life, but not from the search.

The crew was now excavating the peak's main fissure. Alex had proposed the idea, and Jack had handled logistics. It would be Terry's job to promote cooperation. Otherwise, he told himself as he slipped the in-flight magazine into the seatback pouch in front of him, the project would fail.

"So what brings you to El Paso?" the software salesman asked.

Terry managed a smile. "Ever heard of a place called Victorio Peak?"

Later, when Judy met him at the gate and asked how he was feeling, he said, "Great, great!" When he asked how things were going at the peak, she answered with the same unconvincing words.

Alex swung the pickax down on a basketball-sized boulder and broke off the outer third. Another hit cracked the middle. Another deepened the crack. A final hit split the boulder in two.

Harry Albright shoveled the pieces into a small wheelbarrow that Mike Levine pushed across the narrow floor of the fissure to a chute at the edge of the Lower Noss Shaft, where he dumped the rocks and dirt.

The next boulder was twice as big. Alex heaved the pickax over his head—careful to avoid hitting the fissure wall on the upswing—and slammed it down again. The project's Director of Video Documentation and DataCam Exploration was doing manual labor, breaking rocks not in the hot sun but in the cool recesses of Victorio Peak. Sweat drenched his Hard Rock Cafe T-shirt. The muscles in his back tingled with an ache that had become almost satisfying in its familiarity. There was an appeal to this work he couldn't deny, especially after the uncertainty of the drilling operation. Every inch they lowered the floor of the fissure brought them closer to the bottom, closer—so they hoped—to the discovery of Doc's passage to the treasure. They could measure their progress in the growing pile of rocks and dirt at the bottom of the Lower Noss Shaft, as well as in the artifacts they uncovered: a wagon wheel with the spokes removed, presumably used as a windlass; a section of Doc's ladder; a tape measure; a battery; a canteen; a shovel; a shovel handle; an ax handle; two soda cans.

Dust rose thick in the fissure, but Alex hadn't worn a surgical mask since the second day. Too suffocating. Harry Albright had given up his mask too. He said he didn't have that many years left anyway. Gene Klier—precariously perched at the top of a nearby ladder, rewiring a broken light—always wore a mask. Mike Levine sometimes did and sometimes didn't, depending on his state of mind. Today, evidently, he felt no fear of miner's lung.

"What we need is a vacuum cleaner," Mike said as he returned with the wheelbarrow. "A giant dustbuster to suck this stuff right out of here."

"Give Electrolux a buzz," Alex said. "Maybe they carry a jumbo model."

"You think so?" Mike asked.

"Gene would know," Alex said. "Gene knows everything."

"Actually, the idea sounds feasible," Gene said. "I believe there is such a thing as a vacuum cleaner truck."

"Let's get one," Harry said.

"Make sure it comes with extra hose attachments," Alex said. He enjoyed the banter. It made the work go faster.

The project had attracted an entertaining cast of characters. Harry Albright was here thanks to a cup of coffee. In 1979, while recuperating from minor surgery, he'd read a book about the Victorio Peak treasure, and the story so inspired him that he phoned his son and suggested they go for a spin. In Hatch, New Mexico, 1,800 miles later, they inquired at the local police station about where to find Babe Noss. The police chief referred them to the retired postmaster, who informed them that Babe had recently died but that her daughter Letha lived in Clovis, a mere three hundred miles away. When Harry and his son knocked on Letha's door, she met them with suspicion, talking through the peephole for a good ten minutes before inviting them in for a cup of coffee. Harry liked to say that it was the best cup of coffee he'd ever had because it introduced him to the greatest adventure in the world. Now in his early sixties, he was a lean, muscular old salt with close-cropped white hair, a white beard that reminded Alex of Charlton Heston as Moses, and a penchant for casual profanity.

"Goddamn rat in my trailer keeps eating my Vitamin C," he said now, simply for the sake of conversation.

"How does it unscrew the cap?" Mike Levine asked.

Mike was a thirty-five-year-old businessman from New Jersey, a skinny ex-preppy who liked to play hunches. One day a friend had brought him ONFP's ten-minute treasure tape. The friend had sat next to Terry Delonas on a flight to California and Terry had given him a copy. Mike's clothing store was about to go broke; the video seemed like a sign from on high. Mike and his friend had invested $10,000, and Mike had volunteered to help Terry with the project. He'd arrived in Las Cruces ahead of the rest of the crew and rented the ONFP house.

"I leave a bunch of pills out by the sink at night so I won't forget to take them in the morning," Harry said. "Rat won't touch the goddamn Decon, but it can't get enough of that C."

"According to recent studies," Gene declared from atop his ladder, "the benefit of Vitamin C in large doses is vastly overrated."

"Thank you, Dr. Science," Alex said.

Slight of build and socially awkward, Gene kept quiet most of the time, but now and then he'd pipe up with an outrageous statistic or an incontrovertible fact. He reminded Alex of a character in a sci fi movie: the sober scientist, earnest to the point of being comic.

"I don't know about those studies," Harry said, "but the rat looks healthy as a horse."

The ground underneath the second boulder consisted mostly of hard-packed dirt that gave easily to the pick. Alex was breaking up the dirt for Harry's shovel when he swung into a piece of wood. He let go of the pickax and it remained upright, its point lodged in whatever was buried under the surface. "Spooky," he said, dropping to his knees to clear away the dirt from what turned out to be the remains of a wooden platform.

"If there's gold underneath that thing, give us a signal," Mike said.

"I'll piss my pants," Alex said, scooping away the dirt with both hands. It wasn't the most dignified position to be in, but at least it was fun—unlike the drilling operation, which had been miserable from the start. High winds, horseflies that stung like bees, temper tantrums—he hated to think about it. The best that could be said for the drilling operation was that it had brought them into the fissure.

The drill rig had arrived three days late; the fuel truck and the rod and tool truck had arrived two days later. After less than an hour of drilling, a chain had broken, and repairs wasted another day. The first hole went down 305 feet without hitting a void. The second hole hit two voids, but that was when the trouble really started.

Jack had told Alex to check out the voids and Alex told Jack to ask him nicely. It was a joke—a joke with a point—but Jack refused to play along. After a day of brooding, Alex agreed to bring out the DataCam, but the drill crew ran into trouble sleeving the hole and the DataCam couldn't be used anyway. The whole dispute had been pointless, but Alex had moved out of Jack's trailer and turned his attention to exploring the main fissure with Gene.

This great crack in the limestone cap, two hundred feet from top to bottom, had once held the earthen walkways that Doc had followed down to the passageway that led to the treasure room. Doc's ill-fated attempt to widen the passage with dynamite had collapsed the walkways; the rubble from that blast now filled the floor of the fissure. Alex and Gene had entered the fissure through the Ova Noss Intercept hole, which cut into the northern hemisphere of the peak near the west end of the saddle. They'd descended a series of handmade ladders to the top of the Lower Noss Shaft, which Babe had excavated bucket by bucket in the early 1950s before the army evicted her. Bill Childers and his crew had secretly and illegally completed the excavation in the late 1980s, taking the shaft down to where the limestone ended, then tunneling west under the shale in search of Doc's elusive passage. When Alex had edged his work boots to the brink of the precipice and peered into the darkness of the Lower Noss Shaft, what registered for the first time was the possibility of failure. Then Gene had shined his flashlight on the remnants of Doc's ladder above them and sparked a revelation.

"We're here," Alex had said, "because we believe Doc's story."

"Allowing for exaggeration," Gene had replied.

"If Doc's story is true," Alex had said, "the passageway has to come off this fissure somewhere. How hard do you think it would be to clean this place out?"

It was a rhetorical question, but Gene had answered without hesitation. "Factoring in prep time, logistical problems, unforeseen catastrophes, I'd figure one hundred days. That's one hundred *work* days."

"Thanks for the distinction," Alex had said.

By the time the drill rig departed, the ONFP crew had constructed ladders, strung lights, hooked up a generator, installed a fan to improve air circulation, added new shoring, and purchased hard hats, flashlights, miner's lamps, and surgical masks. Instead of hauling the rubble out of the fissure, they decided to drop it down the Lower Noss Shaft—the illegal diggers had already looked there and found nothing. Concentrating their attention on the east end of the fissure, they divided into three-man crews and worked in alternating shifts.

The treasure hunt was not a big-budget operation with extra supplies on hand for every contingency. When the generator ran out of gas, they siphoned enough for the rest of the day from Jack's truck. When a shovel broke or a light bulb burned out, they sent Jerry into town to buy replacements.

Working in the fissure was often claustrophobic and filthy. The space between the fissure's curving walls varied from as little as eighteen inches to as much as eight feet. Alex compared the job to excavating a building after an earthquake, a very narrow ten-story building with rubble filling the bottom four floors. They needed to get down to the first floor to find the exit. And they *would* find it, Alex felt confident. The artifacts convinced him that they were on the right track, and the brute simplicity of the work somehow reinforced that conviction. Down on his knees, scooping out dirt by hand, he remembered digging for treasure in his backyard as a kid. This was the way it was supposed to be.

He let out a whoop that echoed against the fissure walls when he tugged the last plank loose and discovered a pair of figures carved into it: the letter "T" and a five-pointed star.

"What does it mean?" Mike asked.

"It's like a message from the past," Alex said.

"T-star," Harry said. "Like a cattle brand."

Gene climbed down the ladder to examine the carving. "Whoever did it had a sharp knife and a steady hand," he said.

"Maybe Terry will know," Alex said. "He's coming out tonight. We'll show it to him."

"Aren't we supposed to give it to the archeologist?" Mike asked.

Alex raised a finger to his lips. "Ssshhh," he said and stowed the plank next to the ice chest.

Terry drove out to base camp with the dinner brigade: his mother Dorothy, his aunt Letha, and Judy. The assorted dishes rattling in the back of the station wagon unleashed a combination of familiar smells—baked chicken, mashed potatoes, apple pie—that brought back memories of childhood. He often felt like a child around his mother and his aunt, though more often he felt like the only adult.

The project had reunited Dorothy and Letha, both in their seventies, both set in their ways, both fierce in their loyalty to Terry. Letha had devoted

much of her life to the pursuit of the treasure; for Dorothy, that pursuit had
been a source of embarrassment, even shame—until her son convinced the
leaders of Congress and the U.S. Army to give the family another chance.
Letha was suspicious of strangers; Dorothy was eager to please. She still dyed
her hair; Letha hadn't bothered for years. The two sisters fussed and feuded
and finished each other's sentences, though they seldom agreed on anything.
When Dorothy urged Terry to slow down, Letha insisted that it was better
to hit the gas in soft sand. Terry tried to maintain a steady speed. The prospect of getting stuck in the desert with his mother and his aunt kept his
mind on the road.

Base camp currently housed a dozen volunteers in a motley collection of
trailers, campers, and tents. A western-style windmill drew water into a round
tank that served Dick Hill's roaming cattle. The crew had cleared and fenced
a small stretch of desert next to the windmill, dug a waterline, hooked up a
generator, converted a portable carport into a mess hall, brought out five
Porta-potties, installed gas tanks and pumps, rigged up an outdoor shower,
nailed a basketball hoop to the windmill, and christened the camp with the
Spanish word for solitude. A hand-painted sign pointed the way.

Driving into Soledad at sunset, Terry couldn't help thinking of the prison
in California with the same name. The camp's resemblance to a prison was
undeniable, yet he felt lucky to be here. The desert looked beautiful in the
rosy twilight. The enormous vault of translucent sky dwarfed everything
beneath it.

Morale seemed high as the crew devoured dinner and lavished compli-
ments on Dorothy and Letha. Everyone liked the idea of cleaning out the
fissure with a vacuum cleaner. Jack Faircloth promised to make inquiries.
Later, most of the crew gathered around the campfire for roasted marshmal-
lows, and Alex brought out the T-star plank.

"That's Doc," Terry said. "Sometimes he referred to himself as Tom Starr."

"An alias?" Alex asked.

"More like a code name," Terry said.

Letha explained that Tom Starr had been a notorious Oklahoma outlaw.
Doc had claimed they were related.

"So why did he carve it into this plank?" Alex asked.

"I think it's a good sign," Mike said.

"It's definitely not a bad sign," Harry Albright said.

It occurred to Terry that the project had inspired an almost medieval obsession with signs, omens, portents—maybe because there was so little else to go on. In the absence of a discovery, they all needed encouragement, however dubious the form. Even a sign was a sign.

"The ignition temperature of a marshmallow is approximately one thousand two hundred forty-five degrees Fahrenheit," Gene Klier remarked as his marshmallow burst into flames.

"Better blow on it," Alex said.

Terry leaned back in his lawn chair and listened to the fire crackle and pop.

"A herd of deer came through the basin today," Oren Swearingen said.

"A red tail hawk circled the peak last week," said Patricia Heydt.

"The other day I spotted what I think was an oryx up near the east rim," Andy Pruitt said.

"What's an oryx?" Dorothy asked.

"African pig," Letha said.

"More like an antelope," Gene said. "A herd was transplanted to this desert."

"Sometimes I have the feeling I could see anything out there," Alex put in.

"There are mornings," Harry said, "when I expect to see a mule pulling an ore cart down along the old Santa Fe trail."

"Yeah, I've been out there hiking over a bluff," Bob Wood said, "and imagined finding an Indian camp on the other side."

"Camels roamed this desert in the eighteen hundreds," Gene said. "The army brought them over. Failed experiment. The camels spat at the officers."

"There're a few officers I wouldn't mind spitting at," Andy Pruitt said.

For Terry, the conversation was a gift, the crew proudly filling him in on what he'd missed. Judy caught his eye from across the fire and tapped her watch. His mother appeared ready to doze off, though Letha looked like she could talk all night. "That mountain has more mysteries than Molly McGuire," she said with a throaty laugh.

Terry stood up and stretched, then walked out through the gate past the windmill and the row of parked vehicles into the open desert. He wanted to be alone for a minute. He wanted to see the night sky free of the lights of base camp. When he looked up at the moon and stars, he thought of Moses in the wilderness. Vision quests. People went into the desert to be stripped of illusions. What would he discover, he wondered, if not treasure? His thoughts about discovery had always revolved around history, the redemption of his grandmother, incredible riches. Standing under the desert stars, he wondered if there might be another kind of discovery, one beyond his powers of imagination.

Heading back toward base camp, he discerned the lumpy silhouettes of his mother, his aunt, and Judy huddled beside the station wagon. The sound of their laughter surprised and pleased him. The situation here was better than expected. The T-star plank had generated a wave of excitement that would carry the crew for a few days, perhaps until they found the real thing.

The truck-mounted vacuum cleaner known as the Guzzler sucked up dirt and small rocks faster than anyone in the crew had imagined possible. Debris hurtled up the 300-foot-long conduit of flex hose and PVC into the Guzzler's ten-cubic-yard tank at a speed of 40 miles per hour. The noise was deafening. 130 decibels, according to Gene Klier's estimate. Louder than a DC-10 at takeoff.

Since the Guzzler's arrival a dozen days ago, everyone in the fissure crew wore earplugs—even Alex, who had also gone back to wearing a surgical mask because the Guzzler stirred up so much dust. As a concession to macho fashion, he tied a bandanna over the mask, so he looked more like an outlaw than a surgeon. He also wore a hard hat for protection from falling rocks.

The noise, though, was what dominated the work. "It jams your brain," he'd explained to Terry. "You need total concentration just to tie your shoes. The noise overloads your circuits. You can't hear the sound of anything you do."

"I used to work in a nuclear power plant," Terry reminded him, as if nothing more could be said on the subject of noise.

Terry was taking care of business in Las Cruces at the ONFP house while Alex guzzled at the east end of the fissure with Gene, Jerry, and Mike. Hunched over as if to dig a hole, Alex held the mouth of the flex hose—five inches in diameter—with both hands and ran it over the rocks and dirt that Mike had broken up with a pickax. If he lost his grip, the hose would whip loose and careen around the narrow fissure until wrestled under control. If he vacuumed up a rock larger than a softball, it would get caught in the hose or rip a hole in it, and the Guzzler would lose suction until repairs were made.

The Guzzler required frequent repairs, not only for clogs and punctures, but also for separated sections of hose. Duct tape held the hose together. When rocks or damp soil obstructed the hose, the crew radioed the Guzzler operator to turn off the machine, then tapped their way up the hose in search of the obstruction. Once found, the appropriate section of hose would be disconnected, the obstruction removed, and the hose taped back together again. The crew went through a dozen rolls of duct tape every few days.

At the moment, though, the rocks and dirt were flowing. Mike waltzed in with the pickax as soon as Alex needed him, Jerry carted off the large rocks and dumped them down the Lower Noss Shaft, and Gene, back at the west end of the fissure, hammered a piece of shoring against an overhanging rock. In quarters this tight—there were places where the walls pressed so close that Alex had to turn sideways to fit—cooperation was a must. When the fissure was jammed with too many people—or the *wrong* people—work sputtered along. Alex remembered a day last week when he'd raised the pickax over his shoulder in preparation for a particularly hard smash and almost knocked out the volunteer who'd crowded in behind him. Another few inches of backswing could have cracked open the man's hardhat, if not his skull. Now, in contrast, everyone seemed to move to the same efficient rhythm, and he could practically see the floor of the fissure going down.

Then a hatchet-shaped rock hurtled into the hose and the roar of the Guzzler rose to a higher pitch. Obstruction. The rock had evidently gotten hung up where the flex hose connected to the first section of PVC, about twelve feet overhead.

Rather than have the Guzzler turned off—which inevitably interrupted work for a minimum of half an hour—Alex parked the hose mouth-down on the floor of the fissure and picked up an eight-foot length of two-by-four. Sometimes a hard whack sent the rock on its way. He knocked the plank against the joint, but nothing moved inside. He tried again, a little harder this time. On the third hit, the joint burst like a piñata and the flexhose flailed down in a shower of dirt and rocks. The hatchet-shaped rock missed Alex by inches. He leaned against the plank for support while Mike radioed the Guzzler operator.

After the Guzzler powered down, Gene strolled over for a look-see.

"No biggie," Alex said, pulling down his bandanna and mask.

Jerry, as usual, was more dramatic. "That rock could have sliced off your nose," he said. "Then what would you have done?"

"Duct-taped it," Gene said.

Alex involuntarily sniffed the air as if to reassure himself that his nose was attached. "Just another day at the office," he said.

Despite the Guzzler's many breakdowns, it had revolutionized the excavation of the fissure. The day after its arrival, General Wharton had helicoptered to the peak to inspect the operation. Terry had driven out to show the general around. The two of them had stood at the bottom of the fissure and watched Alex vacuum up rocks and dirt for a full five minutes. A surgical mask had hidden the general's expression, but he'd flashed Alex an enthusiastic thumbs-up before climbing back to the surface, where, according to Terry, he'd spoken sharply to his financial officer: "Why do we have so many MPs out here? These people are not criminals. They're here to do a job. We need to stay out of their way and let them do it."

Only one MP had been assigned to the peak the next day. Alex credited the Guzzler. Its skull-rattling roar was enough to convince anyone that ONFP meant business.

In less than two weeks of guzzling, the crew had unearthed several pieces of Doc's old shoring, half a dozen .38-caliber shell casings, a Phillip Morris cigarette pack, a 1945 penny, an eerie assortment of bleached bone fragments, and a pair of five-gallon buckets that Babe had used in the 1950s. The Guzzler picked up a bucket's worth of debris every ten seconds. A full day's work for Babe and her crew took the Guzzler less than an hour.

Unfortunately, the Guzzler was due back at the rental agency in Phoenix. Several members of the crew had already headed home for Thanksgiving. Tomorrow, work at the peak would cease until after New Year's.

"I hate to quit when we're on a roll," Alex said.

"I'll have this fixed in another minute," Gene said. He'd stripped off the used duct tape, pushed the flex hose back into the PVC, and was now re-wrapping the joint with yards of fresh tape that crackled as it peeled off the roll.

"Did you hear the one about the cowboy and the lesbian?" Jerry asked. "Seems this cowboy goes into a bar and walks up to a woman in the tightest blue jeans he's ever seen. 'You a cowgirl?' he asks. 'I'm a lesbian,' she says. He takes off his cowboy hat and scratches his head. 'What's a lesbian?' 'A lesbian is someone who likes to touch women, lick women, and make love to women.' She kind of grins at him. 'You a cowboy?' 'Well,' he says, 'I thought I was a cowboy, but now I think I might be a lesbian.'"

Jerry laughed alone.

"Done yet?" Alex called to Gene.

Jerry's jokes astounded Alex. Last week he'd told an AIDS joke in front of Terry. Supposedly, Terry had explained to his cousin that he was gay and had AIDS, but Alex could imagine Terry treating the subject so delicately that Jerry missed the point. He couldn't believe that Jerry really understood Terry's situation. As far as he was concerned, Jerry wasn't mean-spirited, just clueless.

He'd told the AIDS joke during a Sunday afternoon barbecue at the ONFP house. Terry had calmly finished his dinner and even joined the crew in front of the TV to watch football. Later, Terry had spoken to the crew about Ralph Monroe. Ralph had died of cancer on Halloween night. Terry had praised Ralph for his contributions to the project and for his belief in the essential goodness of people. Terry had emphasized Ralph's compassion. Jerry had listened along with everyone else, but if Terry was trying to send him a message, it hadn't gotten through.

"What's a Mexican backhoe?" Jerry was asking when the Guzzler started up again and drowned out the punch line.

Alex muscled the shuddering flex hose back into position. His arms vibrated, even the loose change in his pocket shook along with the Guzzler as he scanned the floor of the fissure for over-sized rocks. Tomorrow the Guzzler would depart, but today, at least, they were making solid progress. Every minute of work brought them closer to the treasure. Even if they only found five gold bars, he told himself, that would be enough.

· · ·

Patricia Heydt first sneaked onto the peak in 1957, an experience she described as "beyond words—and I am rarely at a loss for words." When Operation Goldfinder rolled around in 1977, she convinced a fellow English teacher to apply for a press pass—and to bring her along as his assistant. She met Ova Noss and found her "absolutely charming." Years later, a newspaper article about Norman Scott's renewed interest in the peak prompted her to write him a letter volunteering to help with historical research. In the spring of 1992, she heard from Terry, who'd just obtained Scott's files, which included her letter. Terry, never at a loss for a fancy title, invited her to serve as the project's Chronologist—unpaid, of course. She not only accepted, she persuaded her husband Richard to join the project as well. The two of them invested $10,000, and she began to keep a record of events in a daily log.

Typed each night on an ancient Smith-Corona, her logs included a weather report, the evening's dinner menu, and a quote of the day, along with a summary of whatever activities she deemed worthy of mention. Despite omissions, both inadvertent and intentional, the logs offer a glimpse of daily life when work resumed in mid-February with a skeleton crew.

> February 16, 1993, Tuesday
>> Weather: Cloudy, windy, cold
>> Menu: Tossed salad, hamburger-rice-onion-bell pepper mix, pudding
>> Quote of the Day: "We few, we _very_ few, but we happy few."—Alex
> 9:30: Jack, Alex, Gene, Evan, Mike depart base camp with archeologist and Sgt. Miller.
> Base Camp: Pat organizes kitchen. Richard & rancher Dick Hill repair windmill, remove stumps, install kitchen shelf. Propane delivered, 900 gallons @ .78 per gallon.
> Peak work: Going up last section of road, work team loses load of PVC pipes. Has to hand carry them up. Begins placing 20' sections in fissure. Some discussion of which end goes in first.
>
> February 20, 1993, Saturday: TERRIBLE wind hits, dust storm, torrential rain. Awning support tears loose. Ice and water chests scattered around. Generator cover blows to portapots. Two leaks in kitchen roof. Waves from water tank splash generator. Weather reports 40-50 mph winds, higher gusts. Blows until midnight, then rain.
>
> February 21, 1993, Sunday: Guzzler arrives w/driver, Butch. Harry Albright &

Greg Engstrom arrive. Dead rat on kitchen floor. Richard & Pat elated. Buried without ceremony. Beautiful sunset.

March 1, 1993, Monday
  7:30 Leave base camp.
  7:57 Arrive at Peak.
  8:35 Begin guzzling.
  8:45 Guzzler off, blockage. Worked on hose.
  9:10 Guzzler working.
  9:35 Guzzler off, on at 9:40, off at 9:50.
  10:10 Guzzler on but not guzzling.
  10:30 Crew sawing pipe, working on new fittings.
  11:20 Guzzling.
  11:30 Generator problem, Guzzler off.
  11:45 Guzzling; 11:55 off.
  12:00 Guzzler on; 12:10 off.
  12:15 Crew out of fissure for lunch.
  1:35 Guzzler on and running.
  1:43 Off, then on, then off, then on, then off.
  2:00 Guzzler on, then off, then on.
  2:20 Guzzler off.
  2:27 Guzzler on; 2:40 off, then on; 3:15 off.
  3:25 Guzzler on; 3:50 off.
  4:20 Guzzler on, then off; 4:45 on again, off, on, off, on.
  5:10 Guzzler off for the day.
  5:20 Leave Peak

March 4, 1993, Thursday
Menu: Pork chops in a delicate mushroom sauce, properly boiled potatoes, salad, hot biscuits, archeologist's mother's cobbler. Pat types lists, does bookkeeping, cleans kitchen, mends Gene's pants, cooks dinner. Richard builds ladder to reach top of fuel tank, installs kitchen sink.
Crew splits in two to keep Guzzler going. Replace pipe, bust rock. A tough day.
Quote of the day: "Our success will be measured by our triumphs over our failures."—Alex (amended to "*abundant* failures")

March 10: Ethnic night—lasagna, garlic sticks, tacos, beans, tortillas, potato salad, guacamole salad (aka leftovers).
Letha arrives base camp. Jerry works w/ Richard on RV's electrical system. Now working. According to Jerry.

Pat places "no smoking" signs in RV's. Jim, guzzler operator, objects strongly, saying he needs some amenities if he is to work out here. Pat discusses with Alex, decide Jim can room with Bob Wood (yet to arrive), also a smoker. Jim immensely relieved.

March 22: A beautiful day. Hills beginning to turn green again. Wildflowers starting to bloom. Pat returns from Albuquerque, bringing new griddle and can of daffodils. Meets Trina, new cook, & Helen, Trina's friend, on road in. Trina to return to camp tomorrow afternoon.

Bob Wood runs metal detector in area surrounding 100 year old road. Locates horseshoe. Fissure crew brings out piece of board not unlike picture frame molding.

Alex & Gene enter Soldier's Hole, go to Dome Room. Mike, Fred, Jerry, Bob, Dorothy, Pat are outside, above Dome Room. With walkie-talkies two groups try to center in on exact location of Dome Room by pounding on various external rocks. Crew thinks has delineated location of Dome Room.

9:30 Raining, then hailing. Outside crew flees to vehicles.

10:00 Alex & Gene still not out of Soldier's Hole. Concern growing. Some of ceiling sifted down on them. Jerry takes walkie-talkie back to spot where radio reception was best. No response. Basin now completely socked in with clouds. Cannot see Kaylor Mountain on east rim.

10:20 Alex & Gene emerge. Unharmed. Were exploring. Ferocious cold wind. Tennessee man has requested to come out next week with his generator detector. Claims can find gold at great distances with incredible accuracy.

Quote of the Day: "We are guarding Carlotta's underwear."— Harry

NOTE: We MUST start keeping the lunch meat COLD.

April 5: Issue of whether or not to keep Trina as cook discussed (she is not able to return this week). After much discussion, vote is taken. Majority votes to ask her not to return. Pat will take up cooking again until replacement found.

April 6: Worst dust storm to date. At 1:00, can see no horizon because of storm. Dust and wind rip up number of things. Sand where we have never seen it before.

Two more symbols discovered on north wall. One an arrow pointing down with a circle below it (circle may have a dot in its middle). Second is a number, perhaps a year—1791, 1721, or 1781. Underneath number is a line. Symbols occur very close to other two just discovered.

•   •   •

Pat's daily logs didn't always tell the full story. In the case of Trina the cook, Pat chose to omit certain details she found unsavory. Trina had played National Public Radio at breakfast, at a time when NPR was airing a series on gays in the military. Some crew members had taken offense at the broadcasts and at Trina, who proclaimed that being gay hadn't stopped Alexander the Great from conquering the world. When the grumbling reached Jack Faircloth, he put the matter to a vote. Harry Albright refused to participate, not because he was appalled that a person's sexual orientation could be grounds for dismissal, but because the whole subject, he said, was too disgusting for words.

Terry, in California for further KS treatment, learned of the vote from Alex, who also reported the reasons the crew gave: they preferred silence in the morning, they preferred soft music, they were afraid that Trina's girlfriend, who was legally blind, might not be washing the dishes properly. "Besides," Alex said, evidently quoting a less enlightened crew member, "she just wouldn't stop playing that damn lesbian radio station." Trina was voted out, Terry understood, for being gay. They had never met, but Trina's ouster reinforced his decision to volunteer nothing of his private life.

He returned to Las Cruces in late April to deal with another problem that the daily logs discreetly ignored. The relationship between Jack Faircloth and the crew had worsened. Jack had issued an ultimatum: "Either Judy and Alex go, or I go."

Terry brought along a trusted friend and advisor, retired Air Force colonel Wallace Wickham, to help resolve the conflict. First they talked to Alex. "If you want me to work with the guy, I'll work with the guy," Alex said. Then they talked to Judy. "I can handle Jack," she said. They spent three days talking to Jack, secluding themselves at the Las Cruces Holiday Inn. Terry began by apologizing for his many absences, his failure to "put out the fire before it spread." Jack responded with a list of grievances that all amounted to the same thing: lack of respect from the crew. Terry emphasized that volunteers differed from professionals—they responded better to encouragement than criticism. Jack asked for more authority. A show of support from Terry would let the crew know who was boss. Terry extolled the virtues of a more team-oriented approach. Jack accused Terry of trying to please everyone. Wick emphasized that they both had the best interest of the project at heart.

Eventually, they reached an understanding—or so Terry believed until he was about to leave Las Cruces. He'd just gotten into Wick's car when Jack strode out of the ONFP house. Terry rolled down his window to shake hands, but instead Jack slipped him a sealed envelope. The letter inside— which Terry read to Wick on the way to the interstate—reiterated Jack's previous complaints, as if the three-day counseling session had never taken place. "You have greatly compromised my ability to function in the capacity as the on site Project Director, as per your appointment," Jack wrote. "When my ability and authority is able to be subverted or circumvented with your participation, then I can no longer deal in those areas in which this has occurred." The letter was signed, "Your friend, Jack," but it struck Terry as anything but friendly.

"You think it's a resignation letter?" Wick asked.

"I think we could treat it that way," Terry said.

After considering the matter for several weeks, he notified Jack in writing that his resignation had been accepted. By then, Jack had gone to North Carolina, and the ONFP crew had excavated down to the bottom of the fissure without making a discovery. "East end phase of fissure complete," Pat wrote in the daily log, as if the failure to find Doc's passageway consti- tuted a major accomplishment.

For lack of a better alternative, the crew began to excavate the west end of the fissure. The Lower Noss Shaft, which they'd filled with rocks too big for the Guzzler, now had to be emptied. Gene sharpened the pickaxes; Jerry stocked up on earplugs and surgical masks; Alex poured over Doc's accounts of his descent to the treasure room until he found reason to believe that the passage lay not at the east end of the fissure, but the west.

Despite this timely reinterpretation of scriptures, the crew's morale plum- meted. No one wanted to take charge at the peak, and work muddled along as the June heat arrived with a vengeance. Terry shuttled back and forth be- tween Newport Beach and Las Cruces. His KS treatment, now finished, had lowered his resistance. A sore throat settled into a deep chest cough. He was out picking up a prescription when Judy fielded a call at the ONFP house.

"I'm Dr. Young and I find tunnels," said the voice on the other end of the line. It was the Ph.D. from the Department of Defense, the dowser with the L-shaped brass rod.

His survey of the peak would be the "major development" Terry trumpeted to a certain pair of fiction writers, intrepid or not, who drove five hundred miles to get the scoop.

16

Boats Against the Current

*…for a transitory enchanted moment man must have held his breath
in the presence of this continent, compelled into an aesthetic contemplation
he neither understood nor desired, face to face for the last time in history
with something commensurate to his capacity for wonder.*
—*F. Scott Fitzgerald*

Robert Boswell

Dave and I became friends in what might seem an unlikely fashion: we were dating the same girl. She was twenty-two, beautiful, sexy, sexual, and a smart-aleck. Pretty much perfect for the boys we were at that time.

I was working as a counselor in San Diego, but I had applied to the graduate creative writing program in Tucson. I was ready to give up my job, sports car, and beach apartment to move to the desert if they let me in. I wanted to give myself a chance to become a writer. Also, I liked the idea of returning to school. I hated the 8-to-5 slog, even though I had a good job and lived on the beach.

To review:

    I wanted to be a writer and did not want to be a counselor.

    I wanted to be a student and did not want to be an adult.

These were separate sets of wishes, but they overlapped nicely.

I met the beautiful girl in question while visiting Tucson one weekend. A friend introduced us, and we hit it off in a big way. Dancing, sex, barroom bravado—the whole works. She came out to the beach later that month and spent a weekend with me. We did our long distance romance-thing and neither attempted to tie the other down.

Until she met Dave. It's not really a coincidence that he was a student in the same program that I was about to begin. She was an undergraduate writer and went to the readings and parties. The friend who'd introduced us was a writer. She called me to say this guy David Schweidel was interested in something monogamous, and I either had to make a serious play for her or fold my cards. By this time I had a semi-serious relationship in San Diego that was growing less semi- and more serious by the day. I folded without so much as a bluff.

Time passes (it always does). I show up in Tucson to start the MFA program, settle into a bungalow apartment roughly the size of a tool shed (though not as well ventilated), and stay up all night in the heat, wearing nothing but boxer shorts, typing stories and poems on an electric typewriter that elevates the letters "e" and "s" and barely registers the "n." My manuscripts look avant-garde, but otherwise my work is no good.

Aforementioned femme fatale shows up at my tool shed to welcome me to town. It's a smoochy don't-get-dressed-I-like-you-in-boxers welcome, and she agrees that if I'm to remain in my underwear she should be in hers. (You have to love this woman, no?) We drink beers in our briefs, but nothing transpires to earn the evening an R rating. She has boyfriend, I have girlfriend, etc. Yet that evening is all I need to justify quitting my job. I have succeeded where Gatsby failed: I am, once again, a boy.

Later, when the girl in question finds a way for the boys in question to meet, she expects (desires) fireworks, fanfare, and fisticuffs. Instead, we decide we sort of like each other. Dave is also from the Southwest, also studying writing, also tall and skinny, also plays basketball. What's not to like? Except that he wears glasses, favors flip-flops, and is left-handed, we are the same person.

We don't become close friends until I tell him that I'm going to meander through Central America over the summer because I have a (new) girlfriend who's in the Peace Corps in Costa Rica. On the spot, he says he'll come along. For three months we bum around Mexico, Guatemala, Honduras, Nicaragua, and Costa Rica, taking buses, trains, and taxis up and down the continent, making up an itinerary as we go. It turns into an adventure that leads to our hiking through jungles and rain forests, investigating Mayan sites during and after visiting hours, trolling seafront dives in port cities straight out of a Bogart movie, encountering wild animals on their wild turf, enduring men in uniform pointing automatic weapons at various important parts of our anatomy, and conversing with local radicals and foreign journalists who are trying to make sense of the violence and insanity of the region.

As writers, we're asking questions and taking notes. As boys, we're thrilling on the danger and having fun with both local and foreign females. A boy on an adventure is a specific kind of tourist. A boy wants to engage both his imagination and his body. An ancient ruin engages the imagination, but it's better if there's a 10-mile hike to get there, ideally in a rain storm. If there are beautiful (or even mildly attractive) girls from Oslo who feel harassed by a cab driver (all he's actually saying is that he can't make change for their Kroners) and they like the idea of traveling for the day with these men (boys), all the better.

The sex act with Norwegian girls, though always welcome, is not required. As much as anything, a boy's adventure is about *possibility*.

For three months, Dave and I have an extraordinary adventure. We will both write novels set in Central America. Mine will be about an expatriate American running a hotel. His will be about two pals going to Guatemala and getting in over their heads. Both are about boys having an adventure in an adult world and how the gap between the boyish exploits and the adult reality closes.

When Dave and I return to Tucson, it's clear to us that this trip is only the beginning and we will have many more great adventures—that we will be productive boys for many years to come. However, on the first day of the new semester, I meet Antonya Nelson in one of my classes. By the end of the semester, I'm in love with her. The next summer, instead of hiking through rain forests with Dave, I'm getting married. Marrying Toni is the smartest single thing I have ever done; however, intelligence did not play into the decision. I was in that head-over-heels state of stupidity that makes even the word "decision" sound ridiculous. I knew she wanted children, and I had to accept it (difficult), flee the relationship (impossible), or make her miserable (a viable alternative). Ultimately I decided that in order to be with her, I was willing to grow up.

Time (that fucking S.O.B.) kept passing. Ten years later, a guy with a farfetched story about treasure gives me the opportunity to go onto restricted federal land to see a "treasure mountain" riddled with caves. I have no interest in writing this man's story, but I want to see the Hembrillo Basin, rumored to be a place so beautiful (by high desert standards) as to warrant preservation as a national park. I call up another friend of mine from graduate school—Stuart Brown, a poet who has become a Rhetoric professor—and we go out at dawn to the site. We crawl through caves, hike over mountains, four-wheel drive along a steep road. In one of the caves, the passage is so tight I have to keep my arms above my head or I can't squeeze through it.

The story of Doc and Babe is the perfect boys' adventure: while hunting, our intrepid hero stumbles upon an opening in a mountain and decides to check it out, discovering a treasure of stupendous magnitude. The story of Terry Delonas is the perfect boy's quest—to vanquish the doubters and bring honor to the family name, our hero takes on Congress, the U.S. Army, and that flimsy leviathan we call *reason*. I telephone Dave, who's living in Berkeley. I cast it all in adult terms. We're writers, after all, and this is one wild-ass story. But the overlap is once again perfect.

Saddle up, I'm telling him, I've got another adventure for us. For maybe the last time in our lives, there's an adventure commensurate to our capacity for wonder.

PART IV

(Overleaf) Drill rig descending toward Victorio Peak.

17

Fieldwork

New Mexico: Land of Enchantment
—Motto on the state's yellow license plates

September 1993—David Schweidel

My leave of absence began in mid-September. I moved into Casa Schweidel, booted up my laptop, stared at the blank screen. It occurred to me, waiting for genius to strike, that this was a writer's dream. Not just a room of one's own, but a house, with a Mexican tile floor, viga ceiling, great light. My laptop hummed expectantly. The clock above the breakfast table ticked louder and louder. My thoughts, for a brief eternity, got lost in the clock. Two months could tick by this way. Slow, then over.

I set to work on my notes, putting them into a timeline. From the Anasazi era to *right now*. The timeline covered whatever seemed pertinent—fact, opinion, rumor. When accounts conflicted, I included all versions. The goal was to compile the full story, fill in the many gaps.

The timeline gave me a focus—which I needed because *the last big push* had been pushed back. Terry was still in California, as was Judy Holeman. When I talked to Judy on the phone, she sounded tense. Everybody's *dying* to get back, she said, then quickly amended her choice of words. Can't *wait* to get back.

I asked about the files at the ONFP house, crammed with Freedom of

Information Act documents, letters from Doc, the treasure hunters' daily logs. When could I see those files? Judy said she'd check with Terry. A few days later, she put me off again. A certain strain in her voice left me wondering whether Boz and I had fallen from grace.

Terry arrived in Las Cruces on Day Nine of my unpaid leave. Boz and I met with him on Day Ten. The lunch place at the strip mall served the local version of California cuisine. We chatted over sandwiches on sourdough and salads of bitter greens. The conversation turned when Terry said that the search should be over by Christmas, one way or the other.

How do you feel about that? Boz asked.

Real good, Terry said. He looked close to exhaustion. His beard-in-progress struck me as a form of escape, a scruffy mask, as if he'd grown tired of being himself.

Boz brought up our book contract—or, rather, our lack. With the end so near and so uncertain, he explained, publishers preferred to wait. They want to know what kind of book they're buying. If you find a fortune, Boz said, it's commercial. If not, it's a tougher sell.

What about you guys? Terry asked. Are *you* just going to wait? These next few months will tell the story.

That's why I'm here, I said. I took a leave of absence from my job. Unpaid.

So you'll both keep working on the book? Terry said.

As long as we have access to the peak, I said. And the files.

It's great to have you on the team, Terry said—or words to that effect. What I remember clearly is that we all relaxed. Leaned back in our plastic chairs and ordered dessert.

Two weeks into my leave, I caught a ride to base camp with one of the treasure hunters—Mike Levine, whose car, in June, I'd helped dig out of the sand. He talked non-stop, as if to make the car go faster. The crew's dinner cooled in the back seat. Horse racing was Mike's topic, the importance of bloodlines—nothing too intimate, but the mood was comfortable, a little manic. We were running late with the food.

I used to subscribe to *Blood-Horse Magazine*, he said. Read it like the Bible.

Sun shrinking toward the horizon, big moon rising in the east, there was plenty of light to write by as I opened the notebook on my lap. Boz and I had concocted an interview form I wanted to try out.

Mind if I ask a few questions?

Mike volunteered that he was from Springfield, New Jersey; 37 years old; five feet ten inches tall; 150 pounds. Most of the treasure hunters, I would come to learn, added an inch or two of height, but only Mike padded his weight. He was that skinny.

Marital status: single. Children: one. Education: Sarah Lawrence drop-out.

What was your first impression of the peak?

Awesome. Hot as hell.

He described how he'd gotten involved in the project, what sort of work he'd done. His worst moment, he said, was getting stuck in Stink Hole.

Best moment?

Haven't had it yet.

We left the freeway and headed across the desert toward the nearly full moon. The backpack at my feet held a dop kit and a change of clothes, steel-toed work boots and extra pens. My plan was to spend the night at base camp, work the next day with the crew. Just me. No Boz.

I'd majored in anthropology in college. The main character of my latest unpublished novel was an anthropologist. So I knew the principles of par-ticipant-observation. Live and work with the natives. Absorb the native point of view. One of my professors had done her fieldwork in the Philippines. She'd lived with the Ilongot people for more than a year before discovering they were headhunters.

The sun dipped below the horizon, lit up the last high clouds. I scribbled a phrase in my notebook—*enormous vault of sky*—while Mike elaborated on the Stink Hole incident. And my dread—have I mentioned my dread?—lifted. I thought of nights in the desert back in high school, how, after the campfire died down, the sky filled with stars. The longer you looked, the more you saw. I'd grown used to city sky.

By the time we arrived at camp, I was ready to be there. After dinner, the crew gathered outside for the nightly briefing. The western horizon, accord-ing to my notes, *still glowed with a trace of fading reddish light.* We stood in a circle. Someone remarked that meetings went quicker when everyone stood. Alex Alonso reviewed tomorrow's assignments and introduced newcomers— me and a shy investor from Seattle who apologized in advance for snoring.

I hadn't thought, until then, about snoring.

My trailer-mate was Glen Swearingen, whose older brother Oren happened to be away from camp for medical reasons. Glen kept his trailer remarkably neat. He had seven cowboy hats hanging on pegs and a pinkish bald spot, I discovered when he hung up the eighth. I hesitated to ask the interview questions. Trailer etiquette seemed to require that Glen offer me a drink. We were uneasily sipping shots of Seagram's when Mike Levine ducked in with the *Atocha* video.

For Glen, I think, the video was an easy way to entertain a stranger.

For Mike, the video was the equivalent of a holy relic. I never get tired of it, he said. I watch it whenever I need a lift.

It was a National Geographic special. The Spanish galleon *Atocha* had set sail from Havana in 1622 with a cargo, according to the bill of lading, heavy in silver and gold. A hurricane had sunk the ship somewhere in the Florida Keys, where it remained for the next 363 years, until treasure hunter Mel Fisher and his crew, after a long and calamitous search, located the wreckage. They eventually recovered $400 million worth of treasure, most of which went to Fisher's investors. Fisher himself retained a small interest, and his crew received shares based on seniority.

Watching the *Atocha* video with Mike Levine was like watching *Rocky* with a wannabe heavyweight champ. Mike felt every punch. To him, it mattered that the big strike had come only after 16 years of setbacks—accusations of fraud, an SEC investigation, four deaths.

There's a lesson there, he said.

He paused the video at the moment of discovery, when one of Fisher's divers found a reef that sent his metal detector into a frenzy—47 tons of silver in the form of neatly stacked bars.

That's what I'm waiting for, Mike said. If they could do it, so can we.

I didn't quibble with his logic. Glen studiously sipped his Seagram's.

That night, before sleep, I thought about the Stink Hole incident, how it could be presented. There were details I didn't know yet, conclusions I still hadn't reached, but a first, dreamy draft wafted into shape.

The MPs fell into three categories—Boz and I later wrote—snoozers, prison guards, and converts. This one was a convert. He'd begun by asking questions. Then he'd started working with the crew in the fissure. On break, he'd roam the peak in search of hidden openings. One morning he spotted a small crevice, a natural drainage point on the south side of the limestone cap where runoff seeped into the mountain through a hole that reeked of rotten eggs.

The smell intrigued Mike Levine. Doc had mentioned a sickeningly sweet sulfuric smell. Mike and the MP spent a full day chipping away at the hole until Mike could stand in it up to his neck. A narrow crack at the bottom led deeper into the mountain. Mike enlarged the crack with an impact chisel until it was wide enough for him to fit.

He stripped down to shorts and shoes. The MP lowered him by the heels. Flashlight in hand, Mike extended his arms as far as he could and hauled himself into the crack. The flashlight shined in his face. The passage was so cramped that he couldn't turn the flashlight around. When he tried to back out, a protruding rock just inside the entrance kept gouging him. He finally managed to extricate himself with a helpful tug from the MP.

Even though it was past quitting time, Mike insisted on going back for a good look. The MP again lowered him into the hole. Mike angled his head inside the crack with the flashlight pointed the right way this time and saw that the passage continued for twelve to fifteen feet, narrowing slightly and then opening into what looked like a room.

"This is it!" he called. "We've found a way in."

He skipped dinner that night and watched the Atocha video. For inspiration, he said. Good mojo.

Early the next morning a crowd of volunteers gathered at Stink Hole. The MP lowered Mike into the crevice. Mike pulled himself inside, past the obtruding rock, and inched his way toward the room, limestone scraping both his chest and his back. After twenty minutes of agonizingly slow progress, he flopped into the room, a limestone chamber smaller than an elevator. He shined his flashlight into every corner. The only way out was the way he'd come in.

He crawled around the room in search of a rock that might slip loose to reveal another tunnel. He tapped the flashlight against the walls and listened for a hollow sound, but heard none. The room was a dead end.

The passage seemed narrower when he slithered out, the rocks sharper. His shoulder caught on an obstruction and he barely managed to twist his way past it. Then he got stuck again. His breathing became ragged. He felt larger somehow, ungainly. He heard a voice shouting, but no words registered. If he kept sweating like this, he told himself, he'd soon be skinny enough to ooze through. He lost track of time, twisting and squirming until he found himself on his back. The drops of sweat that trickled into his mouth tasted as salty as tears. He dug his heels into the limestone floor and pushed himself toward the opening. A hand tugged at his shoulder. Sunlight blinded his eyes. When he tried to drink from a bottle of water, his hands shook uncontrollably. The MP gave him a ride back to base camp and he took the rest of the day off.

A week passed before he regained his spirits. "Discovery is imminent," he announced one night at dinner. "If Mel Fisher could find the Atocha in the middle of the ocean, we can find a lousy cave. It's going to happen. Tomorrow could be the day."

No one at the table voiced any disagreement. No one pointed out that the Atocha and its treasure had left clear traces in the historical record—unlike the treasure of Victorio Peak. No one mentioned that Fisher had found several other treasures before finding the Atocha. The crew accepted Mike's assurances because they all believed as strongly as he did. Their hopes might not soar as high, their doubts might not dip as low, but they shared the same basic faith, and not even failure could shake it.

When I woke the next morning, the G-rated pin-up gal smiling from the calendar looked disturbingly blurry. At breakfast in the mess hall, the milk smelled like cottage cheese, the grapefruit juice tasted of can, and the coffee lacked a certain robust quality I associated with the ability to think. A peanut butter sandwich washed down with Cragmont Cola left me less than acute. When I went back to the trailer to brush my teeth, Glen Swearingen was refilling his Seagram's bottle from a larger, generic container.

On the drive to the peak, I thought of D. H. Lawrence. "In the magnificent fierce morning of New Mexico, one sprang awake," Lawrence claimed, "a new part of the soul woke up suddenly, and the old world gave way to a new." My soul was still dozing as I chatted with the driver, a clinical psychologist from Albuquerque who'd once lived in the same apartment complex as Terry. He asked if I was the research assistant. I explained that I was one of the writers.

Have I read any of your books? he asked.

Doubtful, I said.

The talk, mercifully, turned to black lights. Say a guy knocked a hole in a wall, stashed a treasure in there, then plastered and repainted. The wall might look uniform to the naked eye, but a black light would show the difference in texture. Lead you right to the spot. Maybe, someone said, we could use a black light in the fissure.

Or a smoke bomb, someone else said. Legend had it that Doc once built a fire in the main cavern and smoke poured out all over the basin.

After our truck blew a shock, I ended up walking the last quarter mile to the peak, past the artful arrangement of cow bones and skull, the hand-lettered sign that said, over the signature of Padre Larue, "Abandon All Hope, Ye Who Enter Here." A cool breeze stirred the sagebrush, rustled the cotton-woods' reddening leaves. The peak rose in all its battered mystery.

I had a choice of the day's projects. Two of the crew were headed off to survey tunnel points detected by the distinguished dowser. A few more went to dig at a spot called N-3. Gene Klier was getting ready to put up shoring in the Dome Room. Nearby, a little orange bulldozer had begun blading a new section of road.

I hiked up to the entrance to the Lower Noss Shaft, where most of the crew stood waiting for the Guzzler, due any minute. The generator that ran the lights in the fissure was on the blink, and men hunkered around it in postures of reflection and concern. My technical expertise tapped out at *are you sure it's plugged in?* so I scrambled down to the Dome Room, put on a hard hat, and followed Gene Klier inside.

This was my first time in the Dome Room. It scared me. Even in the fissure, where enormous rocks loomed overhead, there was a sense of relative permanence. The rocks *looked* ready to fall, but they'd probably looked ready for centuries. Here in the Dome Room, as Gene and I gazed up, there was a sense of imminent disaster, buried-in-boulders in a New York minute.

The summer rains caused a lot of shifting, Gene said. Lot of collapse.

At the word *collapse*, I looked up again. Between us and the impending avalanche stretched sections of chain link fence bolted to the steadier rocks.

It'll probably stop the little ones, Gene said, as if in answer to my thought.

What about the big ones? I asked.

We're glad OSHA's not around, Gene said.

You feel safe in here?

Gene shrugged and set up his ladder. I ventured down the narrow passage that burrowed into the mountain. The idea, as I understood it, was to extend this passage all the way to the treasure cave. Now, after maybe thirty slow steps, the passage ended in a wall of rock. The lamp on my hard hat cast an eerie light. I ran my hand over the rough face of the wall. What if *I* found the treasure? I thought of Mike Levine trapped in Stink Hole. I thought of Doc alone in the mountain in the dark. The man was a liar, a con man, a quack. His story defied belief. Except here. Here in this shadowy passage, under these hovering rocks, how could I doubt? A bat whizzed by my head. Hadn't Doc mentioned bats? Somehow, the bat seemed like supporting evidence. Here, and only here, even a passing bat served as proof.

A few minutes later, I asked Gene what I could do to help. He set me up shoveling dirt in the narrow passage, filling in an area where the level of the floor dropped more than a foot. I moved dirt from the highest spots to the lowest. Meditative work. After a while, Gene and I went back up to the Lower Noss Shaft for a soda and a bag of chips.

The Guzzler still hadn't arrived. The generator wasn't working. Several of the crew were standing around, unsure what to do. Alex Alonso, the *de facto* boss, asked Gene to look at the generator. I pulled out my notepad. *THE GUZZLER NO COMETH*, I wrote in all caps. The only good thing was that people had time to be interviewed. Some I interviewed one on one, others in a group, and everyone seemed to enjoy being listened to, having their words written down.

I jotted notes to myself in the margins of the interview forms. *The secret of VP is in the eye of the beholder. Every participant in the project runs the risk of being branded a liar or a fool. And the vulnerability shows. But these are not wild-eyed fanatics. They're just willing to believe in something that most other people don't believe in. They're not a cult, but they do need signs to keep their belief in miracles alive.*

Late in the morning, Alex clambered to the top of Antenna Ridge to call Judy on the cellular phone. He trudged back looking bummed. The Guzzler was still in Phoenix, he said. Battery problem. Several of the crew left at noon. Gene eventually got the generator going, and a few of us worked in the fissure till the generator quit again. This time Gene couldn't fix it. We climbed in the dark up and out of the fissure. The afternoon glare hurt my eyes. It occurred to me, squinting against the harsh light, that *the last big push* might be a bust. My unpaid leave was a quarter gone, and discovery seemed a long way off.

That evening, driving back to town with Mike, both of us covered with Victorio Peak dust, I brought up Jack Faircloth.

What do you know about Terry's health? Mike asked.

It ain't good, I said. I knew about the Prozac, the bronchitis, the cancerous growth removed from Terry's leg, but I grew up in a card-playing family. Never show your hand.

Mike gave me a look, as if to say, you don't know shit. But the moon was full. The radio was broken. There was nothing to do but talk.

Last fall, Mike explained, Terry's health had been poor. Real poor. Stress was the worst thing for him. And running the show at the peak was not exactly his bag. So he brought in Jack. Jack was organized. A tough negotiator. Jack made things work. Once Terry put him in charge, though, the power went to his head. He rubbed people the wrong way. He yelled. Especially at Jerry. And he wasn't part of the family.

I left my notebook in my backpack. The light was dim. Mike didn't use the phrase *off the record*, but I understood that he was trusting me not to make him look bad.

A woman came into the story. Terry's close friend, Alex's ex-girlfriend, attractive, smart, not someone Mike trusted, liked to stir the pot.

Any romance between her and Terry? I asked.

Mike again flashed me that you-don't-know-shit look. No, he said. Nothing like that.

The story swerved toward soap opera. Terry had told Boz and me the PG version.

What do you think of Jack? I asked.

He'd be a nice guy if he wasn't such a prick.

That was the line I quoted to Boz and his wife when we sat down at their kitchen table. The kids were already in bed; the dog lay curled in front of the fridge; one of the cats jumped into my lap. Between bites of micro-waved enchilada, I rehashed my twenty-four hours at the peak.

The talk skipped from Jack Faircloth to *Tristram Shandy*, from Glen Swearingen's liquor to Heisenberg's Uncertainty Principle. After a few beers, we hit the question of what belonged in the book and what didn't.

We won't know, Boz said, till we finish a draft.

Our quick and easy blockbuster no longer seemed like a slam dunk. The treasure hunt was more of a mess than we'd thought. No one knew what to do. No one wanted to take charge. Yet the story of the mess compelled me. It seemed as fabulous and elusive as the treasure itself.

18

At the Crossroads of Science and Magic

One cannot know with certainty
how the process of observation
alters what is being observed.
—Heisenberg's Uncertainty Principle,
a layman's version

October 1993

On a slow Sunday night at the El Paso International Airport, Alex Alonso (and a note-taking observer) waited for the dowser's flight. Terry had assigned Alex the delicate task of breaking the news about the backhoe. The dowser had asked for a backhoe to investigate several shallow tunnels he'd "discovered" during his June survey. A good backhoe rented for $1,000 a week. Alex had convinced Terry that there was a cheaper way to test the dowser's accuracy. An investor was bringing a drill rig that might do the job for free. Terry had urged Alex to be diplomatic, but dowsing smacked of magic as far as Alex was concerned, and he wanted no part of it.

The terminal was nearly deserted. A vacuum cleaner mourned in the distance. Alex passed the time imagining the movie he and Terry would make if the treasure panned out. Terry worried about the screenplay, but for Alex what mattered most was getting the right look, capturing the vastness of the desert, the enigmatic glory of the peak. The movie would open inside a dark barn from the point of view of a boy—Doc at age twelve—peering through the slats of a stall at a magnificent horse. The horse stirs as young Doc swings open the stall and climbs on the horse's back. With Doc barely holding on, the horse gallops from the barn and down the road past a staid couple driving up in a horse-drawn buggy. The man shakes his fist at the boy stealing his horse.

In the next scene, young Doc is thrown into a jail cell at Fort Sill with a group of fierce-looking Indians. He's obviously scared but he acts tough as he retreats from the many threatening figures, until he reaches a dim corner where a voice speaks from the shadows. The voice belongs to Geronimo, who gradually emerges into the light. Passengers, Alex noticed all of a sudden, were flocking toward baggage claim. He spotted the dowser next to a stout gentleman with an uncanny resemblance to Santa Claus—no red suit, but a magnificent white beard, ruddy cheeks, pot belly.

"Any reindeer on the flight?" Alex asked the dowser as they shook hands.

Dr. Kent Young explained that the Santa look-alike was a professional model who'd flown in to do Christmas ads for a local department store.

"Could he tell if you'd been naughty or nice?" Alex asked.

Young ignored Alex's wisecrack. "My backhoe all set?"

Alex manufactured a frown and admitted there had been a few complications. The archeologists had asked for a written request describing the exact location of each backhoe site. "We expect to have one by Wednesday at the latest," Alex said with an exaggerated shrug.

"That's unfortunate," Young said.

Alex patted him on the back like a natural-born diplomat.

On the ninety-mile drive to base camp, Alex broke a long silence with a friendly question.

"So how'd you get into dowsing, anyway?"

"Against my will, if you really want to know."

"Does the Defense Department go for it?"

"They're skeptical."

"No kidding?" Alex said.

Young hesitantly began to recount his story. Alex couldn't study his face, but his voice rose as the story went on, and his gestures grew vehement.

When Young had been assigned to duty in South Korea in August 1976, dowsing was a practice he regarded with contempt. He'd immersed himself in the latest advances in tunnel-detection technology and helped design two state-of-the-art systems—the Automated Earth Resistivity System and the Ground-Penetrating Electromagnetic Search System.

"Those sound great," Alex said.

In 1978, Young had served in a group that located a North Korean tunnel built for the suspected purpose of invading South Korea. A dozen years later, employing several sophisticated geophysical tools, he'd found a cocaine-smuggling tunnel in Douglas, Arizona. A dowser tried to assist in that operation, and Young had run him off. In 1991, however, a dowser in San Luis, Arizona found in five minutes the same tunnel that Young had spent several days trying to locate.

"I thought, 'Man, this is *too* good,'" Young said. "But my curiosity had been aroused."

Young had borrowed a dowsing rod and driven to a Bureau of Reclamation aqueduct on the Mexican border. The aqueduct ran ten feet underground, but using only the dowsing rod he was able to track its route. He began conducting further experiments to fine-tune his dowsing results. Early in 1993, at an abandoned mine owned by the Colorado School of Mines, he successfully located a tunnel 180 feet below the surface and drilled into it on the second try. At the University of Arizona's San Xavier mine, he located and mapped tunnels at five different depths.

"So how did your buddies at work react when they saw the brass rod?"

Even in the darkness of the car, Young's discomfort was unmistakable. "I didn't run into serious opposition until I found things that weren't in the intelligence reports." Young had notified the DEA about drug tunnels coming out of Mexico, but no one in authority had believed him until the Mexican police stumbled on a tunnel in Tijuana in May of 1993. Then the DEA had called him in to locate the same tunnel on the U.S. side of the border. The dowsing rod had drawn no objections because he'd drilled into the tunnel on the first try. "If it's not in the intelligence report, it doesn't exist, as far as the DEA is concerned. The same was true in Korea. Despite the fact that dowsing has been one hundred percent effective for every target I've tried it on."

It occurred to Alex that despite Young's obvious confidence, his voice sounded strained, as if he expected people to ridicule his efforts. "You have to admit it's pretty amazing—finding tunnels with that gizmo," Alex said.

"It's pretty amazing the needle of a compass points north," Young said. He attributed the disrepute of dowsing to the "Ouija Board" dowsers who didn't know how to interpret the signals they received. "Just because the rod swings doesn't mean you're directly above your target. You have to learn how to read the signatures you're picking up." Young reached out as if to grab Alex by the arm, but instead he slapped the seat between them. "The thing to do is get a backhoe to the peak. Everything else is just talk."

As the mile markers flashed by, Alex realized that in the past year and a half he'd seen more than one potential savior arrive with a bang and depart with a whimper. Yet he couldn't dismiss Young, not without giving him a chance. He'd heard the strain in Young's voice, the over-insistent self-confidence. He'd recognized the all-too-familiar fear of being regarded as a crackpot.

Maybe this time was different, he told himself, different from all the other late night airport runs. He thought of the man who looked like Santa. He hoped Young was the real deal. Lately, there hadn't been much to celebrate.

Monday, October 11, 1993. The workday began at seven-thirty sharp when Greg Engstrom stood at the gate of Camp Soledad and blew his whistle once. Dr. Young and the ONFP crew piled into their assigned vehicles. Clouds of exhaust sputtered into the clear desert air. Then Greg blew his whistle again. The MP who was supposed to escort the convoy to the peak had not yet arrived.

"Murphy's working overtime," Jerry Cheatham grumbled as he climbed out of his Blazer.

The MP had assumed that Columbus Day was a holiday, a phone call to the base revealed. The MP was now en route, but there would be a two-hour delay.

"I take full responsibility," Greg said. "I should have expected the MP not to read the schedule."

It was a typical ONFP snafu—senseless, frustrating, not exactly the crew's fault. Luckily, the archeologist arrived a half hour later and conducted the crew to the Hembrillo Basin, where Young wasted no time getting to work.

He started on the narrow dirt road that paralleled the western base of Victorio Peak. During his two-day summer stint, he'd detected five tunnels running west from the peak toward a large cavern. Now he wanted to refine those measurements for the purpose of drilling into one or more of the tunnels. The road would provide an ideal location for setting up a drill rig— it was flat and lay outside the area deemed archeologically sensitive.

Dowsing rod in one hand, surveyor's pole in the other, machete on his belt, work gloves protruding from the back pocket of his blue jeans, Young thoughtfully paced the road. "Here's your first drill point on number one," he said. Greg marked the spot with lime green biodegradable tape as Young kept on pacing. "Here's your drop dead point," Young said. Patricia Heydt and another volunteer stretched a tape measure between the two points, and Young slowly stepped off the distance again, a foot-length at a time, the L-shaped brass rod held lightly before him, pointing straight ahead like a toy pistol until it smoothly swung to the side. "Ninety feet down." Pat and Greg both wrote the number in notebooks.

"The rod and the staff will comfort us," Greg said, gently mocking the solemnity of the proceedings.

Young operated with avuncular politeness, always saying please and thank you, addressing everyone by first name. Like a conscientious doctor describing a procedure to a patient, he explained what he was doing as he went along. Each tunnel had what he called an *image* or *signature*, from which he deduced its location and depth. The center of the image was not necessarily the center of the tunnel. Because the tunnels lay close together, their signatures overlapped, which complicated the task of pinpointing each tunnel's exact position.

Pat asked frequent questions. In the four months since Young's first visit, she'd become an avid dowser and now carried a brass rod of her own. "I'd follow you just about anywhere," she said when Young finished measuring the five tunnels and set out to track the middle tunnel up a steep hillside covered with catclaw.

The short sharp thorns of the catclaw soon ripped several holes in Young's blue workshirt. Now and then he'd hack at a particularly thick tangle of branches with his machete, but mostly he just waded through it, as if immune to the cuts and scratches. His crew of four adopted a more cautious strategy, raising their arms to avoid the thorns and shimmying sideways between the branches.

Greg continued to mark the path of the tunnel with lime green tape. Young paused only once—to pull a compass out of his fanny pack and consult it briefly. He'd lost forty pounds since June, but he was still thirty pounds overweight, according to his own assessment. Nevertheless, he scrambled up the hill without apparent strain, not slackening his pace until he reached the top, a flat expanse of dry brown grass, the desert equivalent of a meadow. Dowsing rod aimed straight ahead, he walked back and forth across the meadow, then around the perimeter.

"The tunnel enters a large cavern here," he said.

After Greg marked the boundaries of the cavern, Young methodically stepped off the distance between the walls, the two-foot brass rod, not much thicker than a wire hanger, evidently revealing the intricacies of what lay below. Finally, he came to a stop.

"Pile of metal," he said. "Right here."

No one reacted for a moment. The distant roar of the Guzzler seemed to grow louder.

"What do you mean?" Greg asked.

"The responses I'm getting here are the responses of the precious metal group," Young said.

"And what group would that be?"

"Silver, gold, platinum, zinc, and copper."

The temperature was a comfortable seventy-five degrees. A few wispy white clouds floated low in the sky. The possibility that this empty stretch of dry grass covered a cavern filled with treasure exercised a powerful hold on the imagination. It was seductive for an observer to believe that the scraps of green tape fluttering in the breeze signified a monumental discovery.

Young eventually found seven tunnels leading from the cavern, each tunnel fourteen to fifteen feet wide. He followed one of the tunnels down the hill to a ravine where five more tunnels met. "We're getting into an absolute maze up here," he said, just as a jackrabbit darted out from behind a clump of mesquite and bolted across the ravine. No one commented on the disparity between the sparseness of the visible desert and the underground tangle of tunnels that Young so keenly sensed.

By four o'clock in the afternoon, Young had detected six treasure caverns linked by a vast system of tunnels. Almost every tunnel was fourteen to fifteen feet wide. Several tunnels took right-angle turns. Such tunnels could not have been formed naturally. If they existed at all, they had to be human-made, an enterprise that would have required years of labor, perhaps hundreds of years. Was it conceivable that an operation of this magnitude could have escaped the notice of generations of historians and archeologists? If Young's findings were accurate, they would rewrite the history of the Southwest.

"Mind-boggling" was the word most of the crew settled on to describe the day's events. While Kent Young and Pat Heydt scrambled up a steep hill in pursuit of yet another tunnel, several crew members rested in the shadow of a rock outcropping at a site designated as E-2.

"I'd feel better if he'd only found one cavern," one said.

"The more he finds, the harder it is to keep faith," another said.

"Don't forget the seven cities of gold," said a third. "They could have been hidden underground."

"What did people eat?" Greg Engstrom asked. "What did they do with the tailings when they dug all this up?"

"Maybe they carted the tailings away."

"But where to?"

"If it happened before Columbus," Greg pointed out, "there was no wheel."

The late afternoon breeze shook loose a few leaves from the cottonwoods in the dry creek bed. A flotilla of low clouds cast purple shadows on the rim of the basin. The angle of the sun at this time of day sharpened the contrast between shadow and light, transforming the desert into a patchwork of subtle colors.

The wife of one of the investors asked if she could take everyone's picture. She hadn't offered her opinion earlier—she was just visiting for the week, sharing her husband's adventure, trying to get a feel for what it was like to be a treasure hunter. "Sometimes I worry about all of you," she said as she squeezed the crew into her viewfinder. "What's going to keep you happy after Victorio Peak? Think of a nine-to-five job in a building with no windows."

When Kent Young came trotting down the hill, his nose and cheeks a sunburnt red despite the wide brim of his baseball cap, he beamed at everyone. "I think we may have found Fort Knox," he said.

"Let's call it Fort *Noss,*" Pat said, trotting after him.

"Geronimo insisted that he had more gold than the Great White Father, and maybe he wasn't lying," Young said, grinning jubilantly, until he noticed that no one but Pat seemed to share his delight.

Tuesday, October 12, 1993. Operating the video camera with professional nonchalance, Alex Alonso took a long establishing shot of Victorio Peak, panned the Hembrillo Basin, and then focused on the drill rig that Steve Seymour had just parked in the middle of Range Road #306. Kelly Fischer and Steve Seymour had hauled the rig behind Steve's white Mack truck all the way from their hometown of Cory, Indiana. The morning sun hung low in the pale sky, but the dowser was already long gone—he'd left brief instructions about where the drill rig should be set up and then headed off alone to explore a tunnel that ran northeast of the hill known as Ova's Bedchamber.

The drill rig occupied center ring in today's circus. Alex was videotaping. Greg and another volunteer, playing hooky from the fissure, stood by, ready to provide any help that might be needed. While Steve hooked up the hose to the compressor, Kelly wire-brushed all the fittings and liberally painted them with wheel-bearing grease. They'd never operated a drill rig before, but they seemed to know what they were doing.

"So how'd you hayseeds get into the drilling bidness?" Alex asked in an exaggerated hillbilly accent, aiming the video camera at Kelly.

"I think he's making fun of us," Steve said mildly.

"He don't know no better," Kelly said. "He's just a soybean from California."

Kelly, a 29-year-old farmer and businessman who looked like a derelict in his torn tank-top, tattered overalls, and gypsy head scarf, had pursued a wide assortment of commercial ventures, opening a lucrative go-cart track, financing a family-style restaurant, speculating in coal. The coal business had involved drilling, and rather than pay a driller, Kelly had bought his own rig, which, due to unforeseen circumstances, he hadn't used until now. Alex estimated that the rig would cost more than $75,000 new, but Kelly had paid less than a third of that price. Despite his grease-monkey attire and lazy drawl, he was quick-witted and shrewd. It reassured Alex that Kelly considered the project worthwhile. He'd invested $15,000 and donated the use of the rig.

Alex zoomed in for a close-up on the compressor, parked just off the road in a clump of mesquite bushes. The day-glo orange tag proclaimed in black letters: "WARNING This engine produces carbon monoxide, an invisible and deadly poisonous gas. Operate only in a well-ventilated area."

"You worried about ventilation?" he asked Steve, who paused a moment to gaze at the far rim of the basin and inhale the fragrant desert air.

"I reckon not," Steve said. A self-employed truck driver who'd just sold his eighteen-wheeler, he'd decided to give Kelly a hand with the drill rig because, he said, he didn't have anything better to do. This was his first day at the peak.

"How do you like the place?" Alex asked.

"Not bad," Steve said. "Different."

Kelly started the drill rig with the turn of a key and began adjusting a vast array of knobs. Steve took over the task of smearing the fittings with wheel-bearing grease, a viscous brown goo with a consistency somewhere between lard and honey.

"Tell the folks at home about your secret weapon," Alex said.

Kelly hefted the drill bit, a shot-put-sized chunk of metal covered with a thick coat of gold spray paint. "This is an extremely rare and valuable gold-seeking bit, manufactured by the Rolling Rock company."

"And customized by Hayseeds, Incorporated," Alex said.

"It's a rotary, tri-cone, four-and-a-half-inch bit. Weighs about twelve pounds."

Kelly connected the bit to the sub, a short but heavy piece of pipe that he in turn connected to the first ten-foot-long section of drill stem. He and Steve then attached the drill stem to the raised arm of the drill rig, which had begun to resemble a praying mantis.

"You sure we're set up in the right place?" Kelly asked as he lowered the drill rig's hydraulic legs.

"According to what Kent Young told us before he bugged out of here," Greg said.

The mention of Kent Young reminded Alex of last night's debriefing. "I'll need to be around to do some iterative interpretation of the drilling," Young had said. *Iterative interpretation* sounded to Alex like scientific mumbo jumbo.

"So what do you really think of all this?" Alex had asked point blank.

"Incredible," Young had said. "The signatures of these tunnels are just like

Korea. What's involved here probably took hundreds of years to accomplish."

Sitting with the rest of the crew in the converted portable garage they'd dubbed the Gold Digger Cafe, Alex had wondered why he couldn't embrace Young's findings—they reinforced every aspect of Doc's original story, yet the more tunnels and mounds of precious metal the dowsing rod located, the less credible Young became. Have you ever been abducted by aliens? Alex had wanted to ask, but instead he'd walked outside and reclined in a canvas lawn chair next to the fire, which had dwindled to a few barely glowing embers. When he'd leaned back and looked up at the glittering night sky, it occurred to him that people had been seeing pictures in the scattered specks of light for centuries.

The honking horn of the archeologist's Bronco returned him to the moment. The archeologist rolled down his window and called to Greg. "Did anyone get permission to park the compressor off the road?"

"It's not off the road," Greg said. "It's on the *shoulder* of the road."

Greg and the archeologist bickered like feuding in-laws. Their conversation sounded good-natured, but every joke concealed a barb. The compressor wasn't the point. The point was the archeologist's power to bring work to a stop.

"Where's the witch doctor?" the archeologist asked, referring to Kent Young. "I can't have him running off without an MP escort. If you guys are going to wander all over the basin, we may need to bring in another archeologist to keep track of everybody."

Greg slammed the flat of his hand against the hood of the Bronco. "We won't pay for it," he said. "Nobody else on this post is supervised like they're on a chain gang. I'm livid."

"Take it easy," the archeologist said. "I'm on your side. It's just that no one else on the post is here for personal gain."

"Wait a minute," Alex said. "We're a client, just like Lockheed. What difference does it make if the money we earn is for personal or corporate gain? Besides, we haven't even earned any money."

"Don't worry. It'll be okay. We can probably get by without another archeologist if you don't split up into too many groups."

There was something about the man's grin as he drove off that really annoyed Alex—maybe the fact that it was costing ONFP forty dollars an hour. The archeologist had just received his bachelor's degree, which, as far as Alex was concerned, barely qualified him to sit in his Bronco and read paperbacks. For a grin like that, he needed a Ph.D.

Kelly lowered the drill bit to the ground and pulled a lever. Dust flew as the drill bit began to turn. Alex videotaped the drilling of a two-inch hole. Then, while Steve enlarged the hole by hand, Kelly installed a metal ring between the drill stem and the sub to keep the bit centered over the hole. When the drilling resumed, Kelly passed around earplugs. The drill bit disappeared down the hole, descending at a rate of two feet a minute for the first eight feet, until it hit limestone. Then the progress slowed.

Alex radioed Jerry to ask for a hoe to rake the spouting dirt and rocks away from the drill hole.

"A virgin hoe?" Jerry predictably asked.

After the first ten feet, Kelly pulled up the drill bit to look for signs of wear. Half the gold paint had already flaked off. Kelly and Steve attached the second ten-foot piece of drill stem, first tightening it by hand, then with a pipe wrench the length of a baseball bat.

The hole had reached fifteen feet when Young hiked up and declared that the drill rig was set up on the wrong side of the hole, right where he needed to stand for his readings. Without a word of protest, Kelly and Steve began the process of pulling up the drill stem, towing the rig to the turnaround, backing it thirty yards between two parked trucks, and repositioning it on the opposite side of the hole.

Meanwhile, Young chatted with a pair of potential investors visiting the peak for the first time. Alex stood just close enough to listen without being drawn into the conversation. He was frustrated that Young had gone off before the arrival of the drill rig. If he had waited a few minutes, he could have made sure that the rig got set up in the right place. Now they were wasting an hour while the rig turned around—though it certainly wasn't the first hour wasted at the peak.

Alex couldn't help noticing that Young and the prospective investors all had ample bellies. They were fit otherwise, but their bellies bounced like Jell-O. Alex wondered if a bouncing belly lurked in his own future. He was the only one who'd put on weight at the peak. He'd gained twenty pounds since the project started. Last night's meal of Bodacious Chicken and pound cake hadn't helped.

The prospective investors radiated enthusiasm. One of them was a Las Cruces real estate developer who'd grown up in Truth or Consequences. His family had known the Nosses, he said. He called Doc a quixotic figure and then laughed as if embarrassed to have used such a phrase. The other investor was a rancher from Animas, New Mexico, who shyly admitted that he did a little dowsing himself. Alex caught Young's quick grimace when the rancher pulled out his own dowsing rod.

"There's water under this road," the rancher said. "The rod says so."

"Mine doesn't talk," Young said.

"But how do you explain the science of it?" the rancher asked. "Why does dowsing work?"

By this time several members of the crew had assembled, including most of yesterday's entourage, and they crowded around to listen to the interview.

"The sun is a thermo-nuclear furnace," Young began. "A non-stop fusion reaction." He explained that an electron cloud surrounded the nucleus of each atom. When the nuclei collided during fusion, the electrons dispersed. "The sun is pumping electrons into space all the time." Solar flares and sunspots provided the most graphic illustration of this process, but even when such activity diminished, a steady stream of electrons bombarded the earth.

"This stream of electrons actually flows *through* the earth, generally from north to south, pole to pole, just like the electromagnetic flow. The electrons enter and exit through the earth's crust. The veins of metal in the crust make excellent paths for the flow of electrons."

Young referred to the veins of metal as *conductors* or *illuminators*. "A tunnel, on the other hand, is essentially a perfect insulator. Electrons flow *around* it." Conductors gathered and focused electrons in a process he called *illumination*. When an insulator—a tunnel—blocked the illumination, the result at the surface was a *shadow* or an *image* or a *signature*. The location of the insulator relative to the source of illumination determined where the shadow fell.

"The brass rod responds to flux in what would otherwise be a steady flow of electrons."

The rancher from Animas interrupted with a question. "Why is it that some people have a knack for dowsing and others just can't do it?"

"I'm not sure," Young said. "I suspect it's because the body, along with the rod, is part of the antenna. Some bodies conduct better than others. Some bodies impede the flow."

A big belly must help, Alex thought. He couldn't quite swallow Young's explanation, unlike the rest of the crew. Their open faces reminded Alex of a famous photograph of tribesmen gathered around a camp fire, listening to a master storyteller.

Young himself seemed uncomfortable with the attention. He'd probably never had groupies before. Or maybe he was just hot and hungry. For whatever reason, he excused himself and headed up to the peak to grab some lunch.

So he missed seeing what happened when the drilling resumed. As soon as the drill was reinserted in the hole, water sprayed everywhere. The rancher's dowsing rod had told the truth. Under the bed of limestone lay a vast pool of water. It was all very perplexing. None of the geologists who'd surveyed the basin had predicted the presence of water here. None had predicted limestone. If there really was a tunnel under the water table, drilling into it could flood the tunnel—and perhaps even the treasure. After a brief discussion, Alex and Kelly decided to keep drilling, on the theory that wet treasure was a better problem than no treasure at all.

By mid-afternoon, the hole had reached thirty feet. Steve and Kelly were spattered with mud. So much water had gushed from the drill hole that they'd needed to dig a quick drainage trench from the road to the arroyo.

At forty-five feet, the motor began to lose coolant and the drill threatened to overheat. Kelly stopped drilling and hauled up the stem. All the gold paint had flaked off the bit, which was now the standard dull gray.

Alex hiked to the top of the peak, where he found Young explaining why it was a bad idea to drill for a tunnel hundreds of feet deep. "It's like trying to thread a needle you're holding with your toes. We need a closer target, something smaller, like E-2. We need a backhoe."

Alex marveled at Young's determination. The man was so earnest. "We'll have a backhoe by Thursday at the latest," Alex interrupted. Despite himself, despite his skepticism, he felt compelled to give Young a chance.

Later that afternoon, when the potential investors came over to say goodbye, Alex watched in disbelief as the rancher from Animas demonstrated the practice of map dowsing. The investors had spent the day touring the peak and the surrounding desert, and the romance of hidden treasure still held them under its spell. The rancher unfolded a topographical map of the basin and spread it out on the hood of the Cherokee. Then he moved his dowsing rod over it. His serene face, dark and deeply lined, seemed to possess an ageless wisdom. "I get a strong signal right here," he said.

"That's E-2," one of the crew said.

"I'm sure Doc Young wouldn't approve of this sort of thing," the rancher said. "It's not scientific."

Alex cringed on Young's behalf. If dowsing occurred at the crossroads of science and magic, then map dowsing occurred far up the blind alley of pure nonsense. It made Young look like a paragon of the scientific method.

"Mind-boggling," Alex said.

Friday, October 15, 1993. Terry Delonas stood alone on a promontory above E-2 and watched the rented backhoe gouge at the rocks below. Looking down from his high vantage, he thought of the Roman Coliseum—only instead of gladiators doing battle, it was the backhoe versus the hillside. So far, the hillside was winning.

More than half the crew had gathered to witness this contest. Terry's cousin Wes Cheatham had driven all the way from Clovis to see the action, which consisted of the backhoe lowering its scoop, lurching forward, raising a load of rocks and dirt, inching backwards, turning, dumping the load, then repeating the process, the agonizingly slow process, again and again.

Sometimes the movements of heavy machinery possessed a certain lumbering grace, but this was not such a time. Considering that Gene Klier had never operated a backhoe before, he was doing an admirable job. An experienced professional relied on instinct—the machine became an extension of the will—but Gene needed to reduce each movement to its separate components. He pulled the levers one by one. To Terry, the whole world seemed stuck in slow motion. At this rate, he lamented, it would take centuries to clear the area in front of E-2, eons to burrow into the hillside and reach Young's vaunted tunnel.

The weather had turned cooler since Terry's last visit to the peak. The clouds floated higher in the sky. Mike Levine bounded toward Terry, grinning wildly.

"Put it there, pal," Mike said, and even though Terry had heard about Mike's joy buzzer, he shook hands anyway, just to see the pleasure in Mike's eyes when the jolt shot through him.

Pat Heydt soon joined Terry and Mike. "Dr. Young has been working like a man possessed," she said. "Yesterday he was down there with a pick and shovel, digging and hacking and carting off wheelbarrows full of rocks and dirt, trying to speed things up." Pat lowered her voice. "I suspect he's despondent. He told me in private: 'Nobody cares but you and me.' He feels confident of his findings, but he's afraid of running out of time."

"I know the feeling," Terry said as his cousin Wes ambled over and a few more crew members gathered around.

Wes's surprise visit presented Terry with a problem. Like Terry's mother and aunt, Wes was a devout Jehovah's Witness. They regarded dowsing as a form of "spiritism"—"the devil's mischief." Rather than risk a confrontation over the issue, Terry had kept Young's method of tunnel detection a secret. The Jehovah's Witnesses in the family assumed that he employed the latest technology.

When Young patted the dowsing rod under his shirt, Pat Heydt signaled Terry, and Terry invited Wes along to inspect the work in the fissure. As soon as the two of them headed up the road toward the Lower Noss shaft, Young jumped down next to the backhoe and whipped out his brass rod. After taking a few readings, he grabbed his surveyor's pole and jabbed it into the face of the hillside.

"Our signal is right here," he said, poking fiercely at the rock with the surveyor's pole as if a few minutes of strenuous effort might bring him the treasure. Then he shoveled aside the fallen rocks and directed Gene to pull the backhoe in closer. With a can of green spray paint, he drew a large "X" over the target.

"The tunnel is anywhere from ten to thirty feet in. I hope we can get that far today."

Gene barely nodded, his concentration focused on the controls of the backhoe, which slowly raised its heavy scoop and then jerked forward, scraping against the green "X" until a single small rock broke loose and tumbled to the ground.

Wes Cheatham earned a living as a carpenter in Clovis. He called himself a jack of all trades. His life had not come together as he'd hoped, and in part he blamed the treasure—or so it seemed to Terry, who reflected on the different ways the treasure had affected the family. Wes's mother Letha had been obsessed with the treasure all her adult life; Wes had resented the distraction. Terry's mother Dorothy had turned her back on the treasure to devote herself to her sons; Terry had caught gold fever.

"I'd appreciate any advice you might have about the fissure," Terry said as he and Wes hiked up the road. "How to improve safety or efficiency or whatever strikes you."

"This operation moved out of my league a long time ago," Wes said.

"Just check it out," Terry said. "I value your experience."

Descending the series of steeply pitched ladders to the bottom of the fissure, Terry marveled again at the work of the ONFP crew. They'd moved a mountain, or at least a good portion of one.

"I wish Babe could see this," Wes said.

"Not bad, is it?" Terry said, though it did seem ironic that the project's biggest accomplishment was this empty space, this absence.

After lunch, as the backhoe continued its laborious assault, Terry hiked down to the drill rig where Kelly and Steve were attempting to drill into another one of Young's tunnels. In contrast to the carnival atmosphere at E-2, there was no audience here, no cameras, no undercurrent of excitement. Water gushed from the drill hole, which Kelly and Steve, caked with mud, had sleeved with PVC to divert the runoff into a shallow canal that ran down the road and into the arroyo.

"Crude but effective," Terry shouted over the clamor of the drill rig.

"That's us," Kelly said. In as few words as possible, he explained that the hole was now seventy feet deep, that progress was slow—a foot an hour— but that they were going through solid limestone, which would make a perfect roof for Young's tunnel. "So there's hope," Kelly concluded.

"There's always hope," Terry agreed. He couldn't decide if he was bolstering their morale or they were bolstering his, but he whistled on his stroll back to E-2, past the brilliant cottonwoods shedding their leaves for the winter, past the remnants of the old Henderson corral, past the archeologist snoozing in his truck. Terry didn't stop whistling till he caught sight of his cousin Wes and Kent Young, huddled together, talking fervently. Something in Terry's stomach did a slow somersault. If Wes had found out about the dowsing, the family might mutiny. Terry edged close enough to overhear a snatch of conversation.

"My oldest son is just too shy," Young was saying. "I'm afraid he'll never get up the nerve to ask a girl to marry him."

"Kids are tricky," Wes said.

Terry clambered up to the spot where he'd stood that morning and gave his stomach a chance to settle down. Below him, the backhoe pounded away at the last traces of the green "X." Gene Klier had gotten the hang of the controls, adjusting them in tandem so that the backhoe smoothly scooped up the rocks, but progress remained slow. Several tons of hillside stood between the backhoe and any discovery. Terry felt his hope going out like the tide.

"I'm afraid today won't be the day," he said as Greg strode up beside him.

"I never put much confidence in the coat hanger," Greg said. "If it's accurate, there's more gold at Victorio Peak than anywhere else on the planet."

Terry shrugged. "Somebody told me that the Aztecs were known as the cave dwelling people. I guess I was hoping their caves might be here."

"I've got a riddle for you," Greg said with a grin. "We sleep inside barbed wire. We're watched by armed guards. We break rocks all day. What does that sound like to you?"

Terry treated the question seriously. "To me, it's not so much a prison as a dream you can't wake up from. My friend Craig calls it the roller coaster. Sometimes I wonder how much longer I can stay on."

Kent Young left the peak that evening, his findings neither verified nor disproved.

19

Joys

From whichever side you approach it, the problem of sex, family,
and kinship presents an organic unity which cannot be disrupted.
—*Bronislaw Malinowski*

November 1993—David Schweidel

Terry and I were driving in a dark car. We'd been talking a long time.

You know I'm gay, he said, halfway between a statement and a question.

I thought you might be, I said. Which was true but missed the point. Supposing is different from knowing. Like surprise is different from shock.

A little background: After the dowser came and went, the crew's morale had plummeted. Then the Guzzler was called away. No Guzzler meant no work in the fissure, which meant no work at the peak. The crew had descended on the ONFP house. It was like having all the kids home from school with nothing to do. To make matters worse, the weather at the peak was perfect—the last warm days of Indian summer.

Terry had scrambled to keep everyone busy. He resurrected long-deferred projects, appointing a "Discovery, Assessment and Reaction Team"— DART—to plan the step-by-step response to an actual discovery. The crew rebuilt generators, restocked supplies, contacted drilling companies—and the TV blasted sixteen hours a day. Terry played up the possibility of an appearance on national television to raise spirits. NBC anchorman Tom Brokaw was scheduled to visit the peak in December to shoot a segment for the primetime news program, "Now."

Meanwhile, my unpaid leave was running out. The timeline had reached 395 pages but still had significant gaps. I'd compiled a list of questions to ask Terry on the drive to Socorro, home of New Mexico Tech, where the head of the Mining Department had invited Terry and company to give a talk. It was a useful distraction during this week of no Guzzler. A road trip.

When I had walked into the ONFP house that afternoon, the atmosphere felt thicker than usual. Partly, it was the build-up of steam from several consecutive showers; partly, the frenzy of too many people in too small a space.

Terry motioned me outside. He looked ready for a long vacation.

Did you hear, he asked, about the latest fiasco?

Seemed the base had taken his DART proposal seriously. A delegation of MPs had dropped by to discuss security. Which is great, Terry said. They want to be prepared for discovery. But one of the crew had insisted on a Stinger missile. A Stinger missile on top of the peak. In case thieves armed with Uzis attacked by helicopter. Everyone rolled their eyes, Terry said. Even our guys. We make such an effort not to come off as kooks, and then something like this...

He shook his head in the afternoon sun. His smile was pinched tight. His head barely swiveled. It occurred to me that his response to stress was to go rigid.

When his mother strolled out, dressed in a pink pantsuit, he spoke to her sternly: If you wanted to come, you should have told me this morning.

She gave him a hurt look.

I'm sorry, he said as if *she* were the child, but there's no room.

She lowered her chin and trooped back inside.

I invited her twice, Terry told me. Some people just want to be begged.

Living in that house must be a challenge, I said.

Terry suggested we go buy gas. I'm forty-five years old, he said on the way to the station, living with my mother, my aunt, and my cousin.

I get along better with my family from a distance, I said.

Yeah, he said. A thousand miles would be great.

The gas tank took less than a buck's worth of regular.

On the two-car convoy to Socorro, the seat in back next to Judy stayed conspicuously empty. Terry seemed to regain some of his usual ease as we sped along the open highway. He talked; I wrote. Chapter by chapter, we filled in gaps. From Babe's trailer to the Pentagon, Goldfinder to "Unsolved Mysteries." About Craig Harrison, Terry said that he was a good friend, the consummate socialite, very flamboyant, a natural entertainer. *Flamboyant* was a code word, but I didn't get the code. About finances, Terry said that the project had raised close to a million dollars. He described the few high rollers who'd invested, the ups and downs of fundraising. I could have pressed for more detail—follow the money, preached *All the President's Men*—but I didn't want to pry. Yes, I thought of it as *prying*. Reporters thrive on a kind of calculated bluntness, but it struck me as rude. My job, as I saw it, was to listen, pay attention, follow Terry's lead. He answered my last question as we pulled into the parking lot at New Mexico Tech.

The talk was a team effort. Terry outlined the history of the project, Patricia Heydt showed slides, Alex Alonso covered the actual work at the peak.

How many bore holes have you drilled? one professor asked.

Where are they, precisely? asked another. How deep?

The room was full of professors and grad students. Alex fielded their questions without a hitch.

For me, the experience was a bit like going out with the family. They can seem different in public. Terry was typically sympathetic, if a little under-amped. Pat was the ultimate schoolmarm. (If you were in my class, she told the professors, I would have assigned background reading.) Alex was the one who changed my impression. He didn't pretend to know more than he did; nor did he play dumb. He spoke to the professors in a way they understood, and he made it fun. At the end of the talk, when he gave out the ONFP phone number, almost everyone wrote it down.

After a late dinner at a chain restaurant, Terry and I wound up alone on the drive home. Alex and his merry band sped off at 100 miles per hour; we followed at a speed closer to the legal limit. Such is the highway between Socorro and Las Cruces that they stayed in view for dozens of miles, a pair of red taillights bobbing in the distance on the unbending road.

Terry and I chatted about books, movies, music, anything but the project. I don't remember what led up to the moment when he said he was gay. The subject, I'd guess, was either travel or religion. The conversation didn't stall. He said he'd lost his virginity when he was twenty-nine and a half. That *and a half* stuck with me.

I had an odd association, as we talked, to something I'd read in college. An account by Bronislaw Malinowski, from *The Sexual Life of Savages*, of a man in the Trobriand Islands who took as his lover a woman of his own clan. Same-clan sex was a no-no, the cultural equivalent of incest, yet the affair went on almost openly until a jealous villager denounced the couple in public. The woman then committed suicide. The informer was beaten by his fellow clan members and forced to leave the village. What sparked the violence, according to Malinowski, was the public charge. Most of the villagers had long known of the affair, but the knowledge didn't matter till it became public.

My mother, Terry said, didn't even know the term *gay*. What are they called, she asked one day when I was nineteen, sunbathing in the backyard in Clovis in a pair of Speedos. Are they *joys?*

Boz's kitchen table. Midnight. I wish I could quote what we said, but I only remember the gist. It didn't make any difference, Terry's sexual orientation, to us or to the book. It wasn't part of the story, as far as we could see. Our focus was the treasure hunt. And yet. Terry had *told* me he was gay. The telling felt significant. I brought up Malinowski. The power of public knowledge.

On the other hand: so what if Terry was gay? We'd already sensed it, dismissed it, even hinted at it in what we'd written so far.

We sat at the kitchen table and drank a few beers. I was due back at my day job in less than two weeks. The search seemed far from glory, as did our book. Should we put the project on hold until discovery? Or keep plugging till the big day came? Boz had a sci fi novel in progress, a collection of short stories due out. For me, the gold book was it. Sure, we had a long way to go, but we were getting there. We had the story more or less under control.

What we didn't know, as we quaffed our Coronas, was the extent of what we didn't know: that Terry had AIDS or that a disgruntled ex-volunteer had begun contacting investors, questioning Terry's fitness to lead.

The next day I added eleven pages of notes to the timeline. Most of the material came from my interview with Terry on the way to Socorro. I also described the presentation at New Mexico Tech. I even included such details as the mining department's collection of velvet paintings (Elvis, Michael

Jackson, Stevie Wonder, what's-his-name with the big white hair—Kenny Rogers—who sang the all-too-appropriate line, *You got to know when to fold 'em)*. About my conversation with Terry on the road from Socorro I wrote nothing. It had no place in our story.

20

Infusion

Please close shower curtain when done.
It helps control mildew growth.
—Post-it in bathroom of ONFP house

Fall 1993

When Terry caught pneumonia, he sought advice from the AIDS hospice in El Paso and was referred to a specialist in infectious diseases, who examined his lungs and made a presumptive diagnosis of pneumocystis, a form of pneumonia associated with AIDS. Terry had learned about pneumocystis from reading obituaries. The doctor decided that Terry was too sick to undergo the debilitating procedure necessary to confirm the diagnosis and instead recommended immediate treatment.

The antibiotic infusion therapy required Terry to make the forty-five mile drive to El Paso for ten consecutive days. On the seventh day, he invited his mother along. She dressed up for the occasion in a matching pastel blouse and skirt. Terry had come to believe that AIDS engendered certain obligations, including the responsibility of preparing one's mother for the likelihood of imminent loss. While he still concealed the truth of his condition from the volunteers on the mountain, he felt compelled to make his mother understand. Her pastel reflection in the mirrored glass of the clinic door gave him pause. She was not at all prepared for what was coming, it occurred to him as he led her to the infusion room.

The small TV set attached to the arm of his chair reminded Terry of a bus station, but the chair was thickly padded and his fellow travelers were terminal. Across from him, an elderly patient whose large diamond ring reflected the changing light of her television was seated beside a teenage girl in tattered jeans, her frail body already beginning to waste. Yet Terry found the infusion room an oddly happy place to be. There was no pretense here, no pretending. Everyone faced mortality straight on. Nothing, neither youth nor wealth nor even faith, conferred advantage. It seemed the right place to confront his mother with his illness.

His mother evidently felt uncomfortable in the elaborate chairs designed for patients and dragged over a plastic one. The medical technician working that day was new to Terry, a young black woman with pocked cheeks. Terry introduced himself and his mother, then said, "You should know that I'm HIV positive." This disclosure, for Terry, was another obligation of AIDS. He tried to gauge his mother's reaction, but she seemed to have none.

"It's on your chart," the technician said, "but I do appreciate the reminder." She studied his arm to find a new spot to attach the I.V., ultimately taping the needle to the underside of his forearm. The first of two drips was a medication to reduce nausea. Next would come the potent antibiotics to combat pneumonia.

Terry waited for his mother to say something. The technician had automatically turned on his television, and he reached over and flicked it off.

Finally Dorothy looked away from him and said, "Of course, the I.V. is on your chart. It's what you're here for." She shook her head as she scanned the room. "These people look bad," she said. "That poor girl." She nodded toward the teenager across from them. "I feel terrible for her family."

She patted Terry's shoulder. Her hand, awkward and trembling, prompted in him a powerful desire to tell her that he would be okay and the girl, too; everyone would be fine, just fine. At the same time, he wanted to force her to acknowledge that he was a gay man with AIDS and might well be dying.

"Why did you turn that off?" she said. "It's time for one of my stories."

The television came to life again with a touch.

Terry's worries went beyond health. Jack Faircloth had started contacting ONFP supporters, urging them to replace Terry as general partner. From what Terry had gathered, Faircloth varied his approach with each supporter.

The accusations against Terry ranged from negligence to outright fraud. In a phone call to ONFP's counsel in California, Faircloth evidently represented himself as an attorney considering a lawsuit against the project. To Bill Casselman, Faircloth advised encumbering ONFP bank accounts if he ever wanted to get paid. To members of Terry's family—his cousins, his aunt, his brother—Faircloth warned that Terry was plotting against the family's best interest. In the case of Harry Albright, the project's single largest investor, Faircloth had driven from North Carolina to Michigan to tell Harry face to face that Terry was unfit to lead the project. Meanwhile, Faircloth's lawyer had notified Terry that Faircloth wanted $50,000 in salary for his ten months as project director. Surprisingly, Faircloth was willing to accept equity in lieu of cash, despite his contention that the search would fail with Terry in charge.

In response to Faircloth's lawyer, Terry argued that Faircloth had never been hired as a paid employee but had volunteered to serve as project coordinator—a job he had badly botched. Terry's family had needed no reassurances from Terry; Faircloth's calls infuriated them. The ONFP attorneys dismissed Faircloth as a hothead, and the many investors Terry had heard from expressed their unwavering support.

When Harry Albright came to Terry, they'd chatted first about inconsequential things—the mild weather, the salsa at Nellie's Cafe, the price of gasoline. Then Harry said, "You know Jack Faircloth drove up to my place?" Terry nodded, unable to interpret Harry's pinched expression. "He said some things so appalling and offensive I can't repeat them," Harry went on. His evident disgust unnerved Terry, who hadn't forgotten Harry's disdain for the lesbian cook the crew had ousted.

"What can I tell you?" Terry said.

Harry didn't move. "I want to know how you are," he said.

"I'm seriously ill," Terry said. "Do you need to know the details?"

"No, I don't think so." Harry met Terry's eyes, then looked away.

"There's nothing in my life that I'm ashamed of," Terry said. "Nothing that would harm the project." He told Harry that he'd been sick for a long time. He spoke of fatigue and stress, uncertainty and fear. Then he let the room fall silent.

"You've always been straight with me," Harry said with no apparent irony. "What I can't figure out is why that S.O.B. would think I'd turn on you.

That's what I'd like to know."

It only occurred to Terry later, after Harry passed along a newspaper article about experimental AIDS treatments, that during their conversation the words *gay* and *AIDS* had not been spoken.

Despite the many expressions of solidarity and goodwill, Terry, since catching pneumonia, had begun, when possible, to avoid the crew. He'd asked Judy to have a separate phone line installed in his bedroom so he could call her in the office and find out who else was in the house. If she told him that people were waiting outside his door, he often chose to stay put. An empty liter Coca Cola bottle was stashed in the closet. He used it to urinate in when he couldn't bear to come out even to go to the bathroom. He slept as much as he could, not only to combat fatigue but also as a form of escape. Late at night, after the TV went off, he'd slip outside and walk up the street to a vacant lot, where he'd sit on a mound of dirt and gaze at the fading stars. He'd begun to think of himself as the ghost of Missouri Street.

"This is not what I want to be doing," he said aloud.

His mother looked up blinking from the TV.

"You have to," she said, "if you want to get better."

The gap between what he needed her to understand and what she was willing to consider left him suddenly exhausted. Opposite them, the old woman with the large diamond pushed herself unsteadily to her feet. The medical technician gripped her arm at the elbow. "Dizzy," the woman said.

The teenage girl was already gone.

Terry couldn't tell his mother how to respond to his illness. He couldn't even tell her of the weariness he felt. Only she could decide what to face and what to ignore.

"Do you need any help?" his mother asked. She was addressing the dizzy woman on the other side of the room.

21

Humongous Void

Poems are never finished, only abandoned.
—*W. H. Auden*

1994—David Schweidel

The new year found me back in California, back at my day job, working on the book. Certain patterns emerged more clearly from the distance of another state. The cycle of hope and failure, for instance, had been running its course for decades, probably since Babe first laid eyes on Doc. Boz and I happened to catch the dowser episode: *expert in the field—one chance with a backhoe—no luck.* The letdown was new to us, but not to the veterans of the project. They'd heard Lambert Dolphin promise a hole-in-one on the first try. They'd dug to the bottom of the fissure's east end, expecting to hit Doc's tunnel any day, any minute. That was another pattern. A breakthrough was always imminent. The next scoop of the shovel could bring pay dirt. And when it didn't, the crew relied on Terry. He was an expert at manufacturing hope.

Terry reminded me of the guy on "The Ed Sullivan Show" who spun plates. He'd balance a plate on a pole, give the pole a shake, and start the plate spinning. Then he'd start a second plate, then a third, and pretty soon dozens of plates were spinning, wobbling, teetering on the brink, but only rarely would one fall and break. Terry's response to failure, it seemed to me, was to spin another plate: DART, Tom Brokaw, the chore of contacting drilling companies.

My response to my day job was to ask for another leave, four months this time, to begin in February. If I got it, great; if not, I'd leave anyway. The search, I figured, would end by summer: they'd hit a passage to a cave, Terry would walk in and find…Chief Victorio's day planner? A pile of rusty cans? All I knew was that I wanted to be there.

January 3, 1994. The bulldozer bumped the back end of the drill rig to the edge of the road and beyond, till the rig's right rear tire slid off solid ground and spun, hundreds of feet above the floor of the Hembrillo Basin. The rig's driver leaned his head out of the window and inched the rig forward till the tire rediscovered the road. Then, head back in, he eased the rig around the hairpin and rolled down to the next impossible curve.

Alex Alonso looked on from the rim of the basin. He wouldn't have believed that a vehicle so long could negotiate a road so cramped and twisting, but the driver had already made it more than halfway down without an accident. So what if his speed averaged less than a mile an hour? He had an expensive piece of machinery to protect, a horizontal directional drill rig, the answer to Terry's prayers, a rig so advanced it could drill at any angle, even *steer* toward its target. Such a gizmo had always fallen out of Terry's price range, but now that Cherrington Corporation had joined the team, the search would be conducted with state-of-the-art equipment run by skilled professionals.

The ONFP crew stood by, snapping photos of the drill rig hanging off the edge of the road, cheering the completion of each treacherous turn. The arrival of one of the world's leading drilling companies was cause for celebration, no doubt, yet Alex felt a twinge of loss. After excavating the fissure rock by rock, he regarded the project as his own, and the idea of handing it over to strangers, regardless of their qualifications, filled him with misgivings.

Cherrington had gotten involved in the project almost by accident. Last November, during the stir-crazy phase, Terry had assigned Kelly Fischer to cold-call drilling companies. It had seemed like busy work at the time, but Martin Cherrington had been waiting for such a call since Norman Scott faxed a query in 1988. Scott had never followed up, but Victorio Peak had found a place in Cherrington's imagination. "I've got a grip on this phone so tight," he told Kelly, "I can't let go." Less than a week later, he'd flown from

Sacramento at his own expense and spent a day exploring the peak and discussing financial arrangements with Terry. They'd reached an agreement whereby Cherrington Corporation would enter the project on an equity basis.

Alex appreciated Cherrington's willingness to assume the same risk as ONFP. No discovery, no payoff. Judging from the clippings he'd seen, the corporation didn't need the business. The latest issue of *Trenchless Technology,* an industry trade magazine, featured Martin Cherrington on the cover. The accompanying story referred to him as "the father of horizontal directional drilling" and went on to explain that HDD, in the parlance, was "the most revolutionary innovation in the pipeline industry for the last fifty years," and that virtually all HDD used processes patented by Cherrington. The article ended with a flourish: "Today the name of Cherrington is synonymous with state-of-the-art, cutting edge drilling projects."

Once the rig was safely parked at the base of the peak, the driver would return to base camp and repeat this painstaking trip with the mud mixer. Crane, generator, and office trailer would follow, along with the rest of Cherrington's gear. Alex couldn't help wondering what else Cherrington would bring, what unforeseen changes.

The faint cheers of the ONFP crew barely reached him now. A few more turns and the rig would arrive at the basin floor. Alex marveled at the driver's skill. His slow, steady progress was the mark of a pro. Of course, the driver could afford patience. He'd receive a paycheck at the end of the week. For the ONFP crew, this was not a job but a way of life. They lived on the hope of a discovery *today.* Professionals paced themselves for the long haul.

Instead of drilling blindly for the treasure cave, Cherrington would bring in a Berkeley engineering professor to conduct a seismic survey, which would provide a tomographic image of the peak. Tomography, as Alex understood it, was used by neurologists to map the brain. (CAT, as in CAT scan, stood for Computer Aided Tomography.) Geologists used tomography to locate deposits of oil thousands of feet underground. The Berkeley professor would use tomography to pinpoint voids inside the peak. Cherrington would drill only after a well-defined target had been established. Drilling was too expensive otherwise.

The rig seemed to speed up when it reached level ground. The ONFP crew trailed behind. What if the seismic survey left them with nothing to do? Alex asked himself as he started down the road. The fear of being reduced to mere spectator spurred him into a trot.

January 4, 1994. My day job, it so happened, was at the University of California, Berkeley, in the College of Engineering, which made it easy to look up Cherrington's professor. We met for a late lunch at a café on Euclid Avenue. Professor Jamie Rector was a big man, energetic and friendly, low key but confident in his ability to map the labyrinth of Victorio Peak. Early in our conversation, apropos a recent book called *Bad Science*, he said that most professors in his field practiced bad science and that Terry had been lucky to find someone reliable. He described Les Smith as a nice guy but not a great mining engineer. Ground-penetrating radar, he said when I brought up Lambert Dolphin, was sixty years behind seismic technology. As for dowsing, the best he could say was that most successful water witchers were good geologists, whether or not they had a college degree. Cherrington Corporation, on the other hand, led the world in horizontal drilling.

Why, I asked, would they jump into this project?

It was good PR, Jamie supposed, a chance to test their technology in unfamiliar conditions, and hey, it wouldn't hurt to find a little gold.

What did you think of the peak? I asked. He'd already spent a few days there; he'd be going back for the seismic survey in two weeks.

It's beautiful, he said between sips of a caffé latté. Geologically fascinating.

I didn't ask about his deal with Cherrington, whether he was working for a fee or a share of the take, but my guess was a combination of both. He seemed intrigued by the idea of treasure, if not convinced. I trotted out my theory that it was easier to be a skeptic in Berkeley, easier to believe at the peak.

That's why I want to analyze the data here, he said.

Good idea, I said. You can't get coffee like this in Las Cruces.

January 19, 1994. Peering over the edge of the Dike Shaft, Alex tested the strength of the steel cable that would serve as his life line.

"Rarely snaps," Gene Klier said, looping the cable through Alex's safety harness.

As Alex climbed over the side of the shaft, the cable unspooled from a screeching winch. By the shaky light of his head-lamp, Alex searched the shaft's north wall for the first of the geophone holes Gene had drilled the day before.

"Found it," he said, speaking into his headset, but what he'd thought was a hole turned out to be a shadow.

"You've gone too far," Gene said, hauling him up a foot.

Alex noticed a dark spot even darker than the shadow. He wasn't sure it was a hole until he put his gloved finger into it. "What's the story about the finger in the dike?"

"Dutch boy," Gene said. "You don't want to know how it comes out."

Alex carefully installed the first geophone, which resembled a cross between a doorknob and an octopus, a red doorknob with dozens of red wires dangling from it like tentacles and a long spike that he inserted into the hole so that the doorknob barely protruded.

A geophone, Alex had learned, was basically just a microphone planted in the ground, as opposed to a hydrophone, a microphone planted in water. The seismic survey would employ both to measure the speed of sound waves traveling through the peak. Because sound traveled faster through rock than through air, the presence of tunnels or caves would delay the sound waves. The purpose of the seismic survey was to learn where the longest delays in travel time occurred. By setting off blasting caps on the surface of the peak and recording the arrival of the sound waves with microphones planted inside the peak, the survey would determine the likeliest location of the treasure room.

As Gene lowered him to the next hole, five feet below the first, it occurred to Alex that he needn't have worried about being left out. Instead of displacing the ONFP crew, Cherrington had given them a new focus. If anything, the adventure had accelerated.

After bulldozing the stretch of desert just south of the base of the peak, Cherrington's crew had anchored the horizontal directional drill rig, set up the crane, mud mixer, and generator, and positioned the forty-foot semitrailers that held the drill steel and served as on-site office and tool shed. The ONFP crew had installed a pump and laid a thousand feet of fiberglass pipe over rocks, around mesquite, and through catclaw to run water up from the basin floor to the storage tank. Cherrington had then attempted to drill a bore hole all the way across the base of the peak. The first few holes hit air pockets that made it impossible to continue drilling, but the third hole was successful. Twenty-four hydrophones were strung at ten-foot intervals and deployed inside PVC tubing inserted into the bore hole. Then the tube was filled with water.

Cherrington's speed and efficiency had impressed Alex, but he'd also enjoyed seeing the professionals run into the same sorts of frustrations that had plagued the amateurs for the last year and a half. Victorio Peak played no favorites. It thwarted everyone. Even Cherrington's old-timers swore they'd never seen a place fight back like this one. Alex took an almost perverse pleasure in the peak's apparent invincibility. It confirmed his opinion that hunting for treasure here was like climbing Mount Everest or catching the ultimate wave.

The ONFP crew had installed seventy-one geophones in the main fissure, sixteen in the Dome Room, and now Alex was installing the last sixteen in the Dike Shaft. An ONFP team had surveyed the entire peak and plotted the exact location of every hydrophone and geophone. A large culvert had been inserted into the Dome Room to protect the crew from falling rocks. Martin Cherrington had estimated that ONFP's prep work would reduce the cost of the seismic survey by $100,000.

Suspended in mid-air in the narrow confines of the Dike Shaft, Alex felt a rush of pride in all that had been accomplished—even if it was just *prep work,* as Cherrington called it. The excavation of the main fissure had provided the ideal site to install the geophones. The dowser's explorations had located the water needed to operate the horizontal directional drill rig. There was something dismissive about Cherrington's assessment, yet Alex found it reassuring. At least prep work had a purpose, he reminded himself as he deftly installed another geophone.

Descending to the next hole, watching his shadow slither down the wall of the shaft, Alex remembered Babe's line: "If desire makes an expert, then I'm the world's leading authority." Somehow he and the other amateurs had become as seasoned as the professionals.

· · ·

January 20, 1994. Thursday, late afternoon, I was at home packing for a trip to El Paso when the phone rang. The caller gave her name and mentioned the Milkweed National Fiction Prize. Why is she calling *me*? I wondered. It took a moment to realize that I had won, my manuscript had won, my novel would be published. I was just about to break into tears when she put me on hold. Then I let out a whoop that felt so good I did it again. Just me, alone in the living room, phone in hand. It seemed odd to have been put on hold, but I didn't mind. I felt like I'd been on hold for years.

The rest of the conversation was a blur. I kept thinking of the book-to-be, the actual book, as I finished packing, carried my suitcase to the Rockridge Station, rode the BART train to the airport. My girlfriend met me at the gate. What I remember about telling her is that her pleasure matched mine. We flew to El Paso. Boz picked us up. I got to tell him in person too. Watching his reaction was like watching myself, the same rush of joy and relief.

The next day we toured the peak, Boz and his wife, my girlfriend and I. We hiked to the top of the mountain, climbed down to the bottom of the fissure, visited with the crew. Boz introduced his wife; I introduced Linda. Her presence made a difference. I'd always felt like a guest here; playing host changed my slant. These are the people I've been babbling about. This is my Victorio Peak.

On Saturday the four of us went to El Paso for my ex-brother-in-law's wedding. My whole family was there, except for the sister who'd been married to the groom. I told everybody the good news: My novel's getting published. It won the Milkweed Prize. Milkweed? It's a small press. But one of the largest. Which reminded me of my late father's joke about the world's tallest midget.

Delight ran high. Mine included. Now all I had to do was finish the gold book.

January 26, 1994. Snow fell in feathery flakes from the gray desert sky. It was a photo op Alex would have to forego. He ducked inside the entrance to the Ova Noss Intercept, hunkered down next to John Washbourne, and squinted at the twin monitors of the seismograph. "Give me eight more hits," Washbourne shouted into his walkie-talkie to the hammer crew working their way up the main road toward the Dike Shaft.

A graduate student in mineral engineering, Washbourne was here to help Professor Rector with the seismic survey. After a single day exploring the peak and lapping up stories of Doc and Babe, Washbourne had decided to invest in the project. Judging from the survey's preliminary results, he had a chance to earn a profit. The first day of gathering data, the survey team had detected a void forty feet from the main fissure just behind the boulder known as Big Rock. The location seemed promising. Doc's dynamite blast had caused a cave-in near Big Rock, and Doc had concentrated his recovery efforts there. The void might be the remains of the tunnel leading to the treasure cave—or it might not. Alex had kept his excitement in check, but Washbourne had reacted to the phosphorescent green lines squiggling up the monitors like a kid playing pinball, as if he could influence the results with body English.

The survey, not surprisingly, had faced its share of problems. The original plan to set off blasting caps had been scrapped the first day when the signals had proven too weak, though *weak* was not the word Professor Rector had used. He'd described the signals as "attenuated" and "laterally variable." Evidently, blasting caps produced high frequency signals—300 to 3,000 hertz—and high frequency signals traveled poorly through the mountain. The solution had been remarkably simple. A twelve-pound sledge hammer struck against an aluminum plate turned out to produce a stronger signal than the blasting caps. The worst hassle was that the hundreds of feet of trigger wire running from the hammer to the seismographs kept getting caught on cacti and rocks.

"Check this out," Washbourne said now, tapping his index finger against one of the seismograph monitors. "Give me six more hits," he shouted into the walkie-talkie. The monitors remained dark.

"I don't see anything," Alex said.

"Exactly," Washbourne said. "This isn't just a little delay. This is a humongous void."

"Unless the equipment is screwing up," Alex said.

Washbourne instructed the hammer crew to move up the road to the next spot. Outside the Ova Noss Intercept, the snow seemed to fall in slow motion, each flake wispy and delicate, but the hammer crew, no doubt, was soaked. Alex pictured Gene, Greg, and Professor Rector trudging past the

Dike Shaft in the swirling snow. They probably wished they were still working in the fissure, where the survey had begun a few days earlier—in sunny, sixty-five degree weather. The crew had taken hammer blows at one-foot intervals along both the north and south walls of the main fissure. Then they'd done the same in the Dome Room. From there, the survey had moved to the roads that criss-crossed the mountain, taking hits at twenty-five foot intervals.

When the hammer crew cleared the bend past the Dike Shaft parking lot and pounded the metal plate again, the usual green squiggles returned to the monitor. The equipment was working fine.

Washbourne let out a yelp. "We've got a major anomaly here," he shouted into the walkie-talkie. "At least sixty feet across. There's no way we can miss this sucker."

"Another hole-in-one on the first try?" Alex said, but he couldn't squelch the hope that the drilling phase would go as well as the seismic survey—the smoothest operation yet conducted at the peak. "How long before drilling can start?"

"A while," Washbourne said. "We've got gigabytes of data to analyze."

By the time the survey was completed, shots would be taken from 1,124 locations, producing more than 120,000 different travel times. "The largest land tomographic data set ever acquired," Washbourne would call it. By comparing the travel times to the distance traveled for each of the 120,000 signals, the computer—once properly programmed—would construct a three-dimensional model of the peak showing the approximate size and location of the voids.

Alex understood that the number crunching would take a while, but as countless snowflakes hit the ground and melted, it never occurred to him that *a while* could stretch well into spring.

Early February, 1994. My second lunch with Jamie Rector was much like the first, same café, same easy rapport, but Jamie had changed. *He's bit*, I wrote in my notes. Bit by the treasure bug, I meant. His words were still the words of a scientist, but he spoke them with extra oomph. I heard—or thought I heard—more than just a note of pride in the success of the seismic survey. I heard *belief*. It surprised me that a Berkeley professor, an engineer, would succumb to the enchantment of the peak, and it pleased me too. I lacked the sense to consider the obvious: that I might be laboring under a similar spell.

Jamie, despite his zeal, stressed that pinpointing a target would take two full months. The expectation in Las Cruces, I knew from talking to Judy, was more like two weeks. They don't understand, he said, the magnitude of the data set.

My background in computer science consisted of two classes in college at the crest of FORTRAN. As Jamie explained the parameters of his program, all I could think of was punch cards. Stacks and stacks of punch cards. There was a mountain of data; that much I got. The exact location of every phone, geo and hydro, as surveyed by the ONFP crew. The exact location of every hammer shot. Then, for each shot, there was the time, measured in milliseconds, the sound took to travel to each phone. More than a hundred phones, multiplied by more than a thousand shots, equaled more than a hundred thousand travel times. Divide each travel time by the corresponding distance from shot to phone, do the hokey-pokey and turn yourself around, and the numbers would transform into a picture of the peak, complete with tunnels and caves. First, though, the program had to be written, debugged, rewritten, tweaked. Meanwhile, Jamie had classes to teach. Two months, he said, was best case.

My disappointment must have showed.

Don't worry, he said. It'll be worth the wait.

My second unpaid leave had by now been approved. I was about to move to Las Cruces for four months. Long enough, I'd figured, to see the search through to the end. Any delay in fixing a target would worsen my odds. We finished lunch and walked back to campus, a thousand miles from the peak, but both of us keen to its presence.

I made the drive a week later, settled into Casa Schweidel, and got to work—not on the gold book but on my novel. The prospect of having it in print, the possibility that people would read it, had awakened me to certain imperfections. It needed a thorough revision, which I wanted to finish even while diving back into the treasure hunt.

Diving, I say, because total immersion seemed required. Walking up to the ONFP house, my first Sunday back in Las Cruces, felt like climbing the high board; stepping inside, I was submerged. Hand shakes, hugs, high fives. The alternate universe. Babe's world.

These Sunday afternoon meetings mixed corporate decorum with the pep-rally spirit of a twelve-step program. Terry presided from behind a lectern. The crew politely planted themselves in plastic chairs arranged in neat rows. I sat in back for a better view.

The meeting opened with Terry introducing four investors from Indiana, here to spend a few days at the peak. Do you snore, someone asked them, or do you lie about it? Then Terry summarized the current status of the project. We've just finished a forty-day push in seismic acquisition, he said, the most complex seismic survey ever done, and it went like clockwork. In fact, the geotechnical crew all wanted to invest.

Freshly shaven, eyes clear, Terry looked right at home leading the Sunday meeting. He was quick to dole out praise. The work of our volunteer crew, he said, probably saved us $100,000. He mentioned Professor Rector, *the head of the geophysical department up there at UC Berkeley*. UC Berkeley, I happened to know, had no geophysical department, and Jamie Rector was a junior professor, at the bottom of the tenure ladder, but it seemed wrong to quibble. Besides, Terry might turn the Milkweed Prize into a Pulitzer.

When he called on Gene Klier to describe the seismic survey in more detail, Gene shuffled to the lectern, head down. His bald spot, I noticed, was getting bigger. A tuft of hair, brown-going-gray, poked up in front. No vanity comb job for Gene. I liked him for that. He spoke haltingly at first, but seemed to gain confidence. When he looked up in conclusion, Terry led the applause.

Kelly Fischer outlined next week's work at the peak: pulling out all the geophones. Greg Engstrom offered the Indiana visitors advice on footwear. Forget cowboy boots or sneakers, he said. Nylon hiking boots should be okay for a day or two. Oren Swearingen launched into a story about an eighty-three-year-old man from Tularosa who claimed to have buried gold bars with Doc. The story made no sense, I stopped paying close attention, but one phrase jumped out: *Mr. Chalk's muleskinner*. It sounded like something from a cowboy ballad or a surrealist poem. Yes, I was submerged. Me and Mr. Chalk's muleskinner.

Near the end of the meeting, Terry mentioned that Martin Cherrington was flying in for a consult. The key issue was when to resume drilling. It all depends on the data analysis, Terry said. Probably two to four weeks.

Double that, I could have said, but I just kept scribbling.

Mid-February, 1994. Terry was eating breakfast in his room at the ONFP house. The infusion therapy had proven so effective in restoring his health that he now questioned the original diagnosis of pneumocystis. Even after his recovery, though, he'd found it hard to break the habit of keeping to himself.

A gentle knock on the door: Judy. She said that Craig was on the line. Her voice sounded oddly fragile. Terry, sitting cross-legged on the mattress, plate of toast in his lap, reluctantly set the plate aside.

"I need your help," was the first thing Craig said. He'd begun having night sweats. He'd been dropping things and bumping into doorways. He could no longer tie his shoes. The doctor he'd finally consulted had given him six months to live. "Come take care of me," Craig said.

Terry pulled the crew from the peak. He didn't mention Craig. No one questioned the decision—the Berkeley brain trust was bogged down in data, the early morning temperature at the peak had dropped to ten degrees, and the high price of doing business with White Sands Missile Range made it cost-effective to suspend operations and plan a systematic drilling program.

He flew to California and reinstalled himself at Craig's house in Newport Beach. The first night back, he gave Craig a bath and then they watched television together till Terry went to bed. When he got up the next morning, he found Craig still lying on the living room couch, asleep at last, the television droning.

Terry's duties for the next two months involved little physical caretaking. What Craig needed was a friend, someone to sit with him, flatter him, challenge his charming bullshit. He tried to convince Craig to tell his parents about his condition, but Craig refused. One reason Craig had avoided conventional doctors was that he hadn't wanted his parents to know he was HIV positive. His condition, he admitted, might have been treatable if he'd seen a doctor sooner.

Terry checked in with Judy every few days. With Professor Rector in Berkeley and Martin Cherrington in Sacramento, communication suffered.

Questions arose about the accuracy of certain survey points, the reliability of a particular type of geophone, and the answers seemed to get garbled somewhere along the telephone lines. More disturbingly, as the data analysis was refined, the size of the void shrank and its location shifted. The crew, Judy reported, was itching to return to work.

Only Terry wanted the hiatus to continue.

March 1994. My days in Las Cruces settled into a comfortable routine, up early, a little yoga in the courtyard with twittering doves and winter sun, coffee, leisurely shower, and the call of the laptop. I'd write for a few hours, eat, write a few hours more. Most of my writing time went to the novel. I wanted to work on the gold book, but not until the novel was as good as I could get it. Some days I'd break up the writing with a swim at the campus pool. Boz and I played basketball Friday afternoons and Sunday mornings.

There's a hallowed bit of folk wisdom—guests and fish go bad after three days—but Boz and his wife kept a pair of thriving goldfish in a bowl in the kitchen. They also had a dog, two cats, a daughter, and a son, as well as a multitude of friends, neighbors, grad students, and colleagues who often congregated at the kitchen table, as many as a dozen people, sharing chairs, crowding into doorways, talking and laughing, raiding the kids' treat drawer for candy and chocolate. In my own household, I drew the line at plants, but I felt at home amid the chaos.

One night at dinner, Noah, the three-year-old, lined up the salt and pepper shakers next to his knife and spoon. This is mommy, he said, and this is daddy, and this is Jade, and this is me. Then he brought over the fork. And this is *you*, he said to me.

Another night Boz and his wife and I went to dinner without the kids. Fancy restaurant, two bottles of wine, a rarely achieved caliber of relaxation, and on the way home, as we turned onto their block, Toni, Boz's wife, bolted barefoot from the Trooper before I could even register the two police cars, cherry tops spinning, strafing their house with red light. Jade and Noah, Toni quickly discovered, were safe; the police's business lay across the street; but what struck me was Toni's vigilance. I had assumed that all three of us, in the wake of our blissful meal, were equally carefree, but Toni, though mellow enough to kick off her shoes, maintained her guard. The connection to her kids was constant, visceral, wired into her gut.

I had it so easy. Why didn't I get more done?

Writing every day, I made slow progress. Emphasis on *slow*? Or *progress*?

Every week or two, I'd phone Terry. Sometimes Judy fielded his calls, but whenever I reached him, he sounded upbeat. He always had a piece of good news to trumpet. A backer from Sun MicroSystems had donated a $50,000 work station for use in analyzing the seismic data. State of the art, Terry said. Alex Alonso had met with the producers of "Now." They're coming next month, Terry said. Money, for once, was not a problem. We quit fundraising some weeks ago, he said. We're trying to catch up with accounting.

He never mentioned Craig.

I still didn't know that Terry had AIDS.

In mid-April, the treasure hunters returned to Las Cruces. The data analysis, though not yet complete, had progressed far enough to yield a target, a big room just south and east of the fissure. Alex joined Boz and me for Sunday basketball. It's showtime, he said, referring not to our game but to the project. Martin Cherrington had brought his "A" team, Alex told us. Amateur hour was over. He made a face, part grin, part scowl, as if amateur hour was a time he'd miss. He played basketball like a bull, with more passion than skill.

That afternoon I attended a meeting at the ONFP house. If you want to bring guests to the peak, Terry announced, you'd better do it soon, because guests will be limited after discovery. It was typical Terry, dangling the prospect of discovery like a carrot before a mule, but this time, I let myself hope, the hype might be true.

April 25, 1994. When Kat Keany, associate producer of the NBC news program "Now," strolled thoughtfully around base camp, Alex Alonso strolled thoughtfully beside her. Early morning sunlight glinted off the Porta-Potties. A pair of cows drank at the water tank. While Terry and the public relations officer from White Sands Missile Range waited in the Suburban parked at the gate, Alex escorted Kat past the motley collection of trailers and RVs that had housed the crew for nearly two years now. The Winnebago was in decent shape, but the battered Nomad, the ancient Airstream—Alex wondered how these wrecks must look to her. Quaint, probably. Or worse. She lived in Brentwood, an eyesore-free zone. She'd covered the Clinton campaign in the last election. She was energetic, attractive, older than Alex by a few years. Her expression of polite interest was impossible for him to gauge.

"It's not much," he said with a harsh laugh, "but we call it home." A gust of wind whipped a tumbleweed up against the barbed wire fence.

Inside the Gold Digger Cafe, the cans of Spam stacked on the shelf by the door made him wince. He didn't want to be the subject of a human interest story—*"Now" presents the curious tale of a band of treasure hunters surviving on Spam.*

"Nice," she said with no detectable condescension.

Back outside, she lingered by the circle of stones that held the charred remnants of last night's fire. A lawn chair no one had put away flipped over in the wind. Alex was tempted to tell her about all the work that had gone into setting up the camp, the elaborate practical jokes, late-night bull sessions under the stars.

"This might be a good place to shoot interviews with the crew," she said. Her bright smile gave him hope that she could be won over.

Riding to the peak in the roomy Suburban, she wore exactly the same smile as the White Sands public relations officer prattled on about the difference between half-staff and half-mast, apropos the recent death of Richard Nixon. "You'd be surprised how many people at the base say *half-mast*," he said. "I'm always having to correct them. It's *half-staff*, not *half-mast*. We're the army, not the navy."

"Good point," Kat said.

"Fascinating," Alex muttered under his breath. Kat's ability to manifest enthusiasm for such blather reminded him that she was a professional. Enthusiasm was a trick of her trade. His, too, for that matter. Don't go treasure hunting without it.

He wished that Terry would speak up, but Terry seemed content to gaze dreamily out the window. He'd outlined his strategy to Alex earlier that morning on the way to breakfast at the Las Cruces Hilton. "Let the WSMR guy play host," he'd said. "Let him feel like this is *his* project."

Alex had the sick feeling that the public relations officer would blab all the way to the rim of the basin. The first look at the peak deserved silence, but the man had no reverence. He was immune to the magic. When they rounded the last curve and the Hembrillo Basin suddenly filled the windshield, he was jabbering about battlefield archeologists.

"Stop," Alex said. He meant *stop talking*, but the public relations officer stopped the Suburban, so Alex climbed out and held the door open for Kat. Terry got out with her.

The wind had picked up, gusting to sixty miles an hour, and they had to lean forward to make progress toward the edge of the rim. Terry hung back but Kat went with Alex right to the edge. The peak jutted up from the floor of the basin like a ten-gallon hat creased down the middle. A cloud of dust swirled around it. Alex sneaked a glance at Kat. Her polished smile was gone, eyes squinting against the dust.

"Great," she shouted over the wind. "Great shot."

Alex kept his mouth shut. The first look deserved silence.

The crane at the base of the peak slowly swung the next piece of drill steel toward the horizontal directional drill rig. The thirty-foot steel pipe swayed in the whistling wind while Cherrington's mud-splattered chief of operations dashed to the mud mixer, wrestled down a lever the length of a baseball bat, and sprinted back to the drill rig, where Alex and Kat heard him scream into his radio at the drill operator perched inside Cherrington's office trailer.

"It's like surgery," Alex said. "Performed in a tornado."

Sheltered from the brunt of the wind by the side of the trailer, he explained to Kat that the rig was boring a hole through the peak toward what they hoped was the treasure room—the large void pinpointed by the seismic survey just south of the main fissure. The bore hole now extended 280 feet, halfway to the target. The drilling advanced at the rate of a foot and a half per minute, or one thirty-foot length of drill steel every twenty minutes.

"See how the drill steel is hollow?" Alex said. "The compressor shoots the mud through the drill steel with enough force to power the drill bit 280 feet away. Then the mud flows back, *outside* the steel but *inside* the bore hole. Mud powers the drill. And the beauty of this puppy is that you can *steer* it." Alex raised and lowered his fists as if he were gripping an imaginary steering wheel.

Kat asked no questions and took no notes, but seemed to pay close attention.

A few minutes later, in the relative comfort of the office trailer, Martin

Cherrington munched a nonfat Raspberry Newton and described the drilling process in more detail. "You have to put yourself into the tool," he said, indicating the pair of computers being monitored by the drill operator. "It's like flying an airplane on instruments."

A steering unit attached to the drill bit sent data to one computer. The drill operator used the other computer to verify the data's accuracy. A small printer generated a log with the current location and angle of the drill, the azimuth reading, and the magnetic influence of any ferrous metals in the vicinity. The drill operator adjusted the drilling angle with the touch of a key.

"You get a feel for it after a while," the drill operator said without looking up from the computer screen.

No one mentioned that Cherrington had aborted his first two tries for the treasure room after hitting unexpected voids a few hundred feet short of the target. The mud had spilled into the voids and consequently stopped circulating. Without a constant flow of mud, the drill bit wouldn't spin. In both instances, Cherrington had been forced to pull out hundreds of feet of drill steel, jack up the mammoth drill rig, put skid pipes under it, hook it to the crane, push it with the backhoe, remove the skid pipes, unhook it from the crane, and start a new hole. There was no guarantee that this third hole wouldn't encounter the same problem.

Alex checked Kat to see if her eyes had glazed over. What she needed was not more talk about bore holes and azimuths, but a jolt of the exhilaration of hunting for treasure. He invited her to take a tour of the fissure.

As Kat carefully negotiated the transfer from one ladder to the next, easing her foot down, testing her foothold on the ladder below before letting go of the ladder above, Alex thought he recognized her look of intense concentration. There was no net in the fissure. A fall could mean broken bones, perhaps even a fatal blow to the head, despite the protection of the hard hat she'd borrowed.

Some people treated this descent as a significant rite of passage. A few weeks earlier, the director of the Santa Fe Opera had gone around shaking everyone's hand after surviving the ordeal. "Not just anyone would do that, would they?" he'd asked jubilantly, not realizing until hours later that he'd aggravated a hernia.

Kat handled the descent with relative ease. "Fun," she said when they reached bottom.

Alex aimed his flashlight up to where the floor of the fissure had been two years ago. Then he led her over to Big Rock and showed her the tunnel that now ran under it, jackhammered through solid limestone.

Big Rock itself was a two-ladder climb. The view from the top was dominated by an overhanging boulder the size of a Buick. Alex shined his flashlight up past the boulder to where the bottom of Doc's ladder came down from the Upper Noss Shaft. The light beam moved to a spot where a piece of old scaffolding had been unearthed. Alex tried to convey what the work had been like, the daunting task of retracing Doc's route to the treasure. The crew had excavated tons of rocks and dirt. "When I look at this place," he said, "I see every obstacle we've overcome."

"There *ought* to be a treasure down here," Kat said.

Alex couldn't decide if the enthusiasm in her eyes was genuine—or simply a reflection of his own.

Sunlight streamed into the Layton trailer where Alex, Kat, and Terry were fixing a late lunch. Cherrington and his crew had already eaten. The public relations officer had excused himself to go talk shop with the MP. Despite the fierce wind outside, the hump-backed trailer had warmed up to the perfect temperature for a nap.

"The siesta is such a civilized custom," Alex said as he ripped open two packets of mayonnaise and squeezed the contents onto a slice of white bread.

Terry painstakingly spread mustard on a slice of whole wheat with a little plastic knife. "We don't pay anyone to sleep," he said.

"We don't pay anyone, period," Alex said.

Kat contented herself with a bag of potato chips and a carton of cran-apple juice.

"Seriously," Terry said, postponing his first bite of sandwich, "only a volunteer crew could have accomplished so much. You can't pay people enough to work this hard."

"It's quite an operation," Kat said. "I'm excited about the possibility of bringing Tom out here."

She didn't look excited, but Alex gave her the benefit of the doubt. "Bring on Tom," he said, leaning back in the metal folding chair, propping up his boots on a corner of the table.

Terry, meanwhile, calmly ate his ham and cheese sandwich, methodically chewing each bite, as if the prospect of rubbing elbows with Tom Brokaw left him indifferent. He'd ballyhooed the "Now" program for months, but evidently the only thing on his mind at the moment was Virginia baked ham and American cheese.

It tastes like dust, Terry thought. *Everything at the peak tastes like dust.* Outside, the whistling wind and the distant pounding of the drill rig performed a hypnotic duet. Inside the creaky Layton, Terry felt the urge to curl up on the bench seat and sleep for a long time. Some days the temptation to quit ran high. The best way to fight it was to focus on the present moment: *taste* the sandwich, *smell* the mustard, *enjoy* the percussive music of the heavy machinery, the beads of sweat dribbling down the pudding cups. He had yet to attain the peace he pretended to possess, but he had learned to cultivate a certain detachment. It helped him assess his situation with a semblance of objectivity.

He was pessimistic about Tom Brokaw ever setting foot on the peak. Kat Keany seemed nice enough, but from what Terry had gathered, she lacked clout. She wasn't *the* associate producer; she was one of many. She worked in Los Angeles; NBC's center of power was New York. Her last story—about a miracle cream applied to the thighs to make fat disappear—had been canceled. "Now" normally had forty stories in pre-production, many of which never aired.

"Looks like you need new boots," Kat said to Alex. His heavy-duty steel-toed work boots were scuffed, faded, torn at the instep.

"They're three weeks old," Alex said. "I go through a pair a month."

Terry had grown almost accustomed to the ups and downs of the project. It was like being a character in a good news, bad news joke. The boots were nearly new, the boots were worn out. Every silver lining had a cloud. The good news was that General Wharton supported the project. The bad news was that he planned to retire soon. Terry expected him to renew the license agreement before retiring, but he hadn't addressed the larger issue of how much the base charged ONFP for access to the peak. Without an itemized bill to consult, Terry estimated that ONFP was paying $1,500 a day in so-called support costs, though the only support Terry knew of was one MP, an archeologist hardly worthy of the title, and a place on the base's schedule, which meant that the scheduling officer received a call from Judy, wrote "ONFP" in grease pencil on the schedule board, and faxed a confirmation. ONFP paid anywhere from $40,000 to $100,000 every few months for this nebulous support. A discovery now would render the problem moot, but a prolonged search would permit the base to bleed the project dry. Good news, bad news. And vice-versa.

Jack Faircloth had recently gone on another letter-writing binge, raising the issue of Terry's "homosexual lifestyle" and "long standing deteriorating health" and accusing Terry again of mismanaging project funds. Despite the virulent tone of the accusations—or perhaps because of it—investors had rallied around Terry, professing their loyalty not only to the project but to Terry personally.

His "long standing deteriorating health," it so happened, was better than usual at the moment. The swelling in his left leg had subsided. He needed rest, the doctors said, and a drastic reduction of stress.

Craig Harrison's health, unfortunately, was beyond help.

"A tawdry little soap opera," Kat said, "but you wouldn't believe the interest." The conversation had turned to the Tonya Harding story, which Kat had covered for "Now." She shook her expensive coif. "*Everybody* wanted to know *everything.*" She flapped her hand in the air, as if to erase the story. "What do you plan to do after this is over?"

"I don't let myself think about it," Alex said.

"I'd like to live in a monastery for a while and meditate," Terry said.

The sound of the drill rig grew louder as the wind briefly died down. Perhaps it was Kat's question or perhaps it was the tug of siesta time, but Terry felt the moment, the day, the entire project threaten to slip away. It was like staring at an optical illusion. If he lost focus, a million-dollar treasure recovery venture could turn into a farce. "When I was a boy," he said with a sudden rush of conviction, "I used to daydream about coming here, and in my daydreams there was always a crane. I didn't know what purpose the crane would serve, but I knew it was supposed to be here. When Cherrington brought out that crane, something clicked in my head. *This is just how you pictured it.* I get a kick out of that crane." Terry shrugged almost apologetically, as if to ask forgiveness for his speech. The audience he was trying to inspire, he'd realized midway, was himself.

Or so I imagined, sitting there with the three of them, eating my own dusty sandwich. How can one person know what another is thinking? Boz and I spent many hours interviewing Terry. He conveyed a strong sense of his thoughts and feelings. No matter how much he divulged, though, no matter how much we understood, pinning a particular thought to a particular moment requires a leap. Call it an educated guess, a bald-faced lie, poetic license—whatever you call this leap, it's what people do when they tell a story.

So I imagined what Terry was thinking, despite my unawareness of all I would come to learn, the extent of Jack Faircloth's maneuverings, Craig Harrison's swift plunge toward death. What struck me then was the magnitude of Terry's effort to keep the project afloat, as if only by levitation, a monumental act of will, could he prevent the whole business from sinking. What strikes me now, looking back on this interlude in the sun-baked Layton, wind shrieking outside, everyone drowsy and yawning, caught in the afternoon's ebb, is the peacefulness of this lull, the seeming legitimacy of our belief that Cherrington's horizontal directional drill rig might soon burst into a cave filled with treasure. Why not? The search, which had begun as a slapdash charade, with limited expertise, deficient equipment, and inadequate funding, had reached its zenith of science, technology, and cash flow. A professor from a top-ranked university had charted the inner configuration of the peak, a world-class drilling company was steering its way closer and closer to the professor's target, and Terry had raised enough money, evidently, to pay for any work necessary. I didn't realize it then, but this was the project's best chance. My belief in the treasure would continue to surge and wane, plummet and soar, but it would never again feel quite this reasonable.

The next day, when the drill reached the designated coordinates, the *X* that marked the spot, there was no humongous void, no treasure cave, only solid limestone. I was back at Casa Schweidel, working at my laptop. I didn't see anyone's reaction. The crew, I learned later, gathered to watch. They waited together for the breakthrough. What they expected was a big room, but the drill hit nothing but rock.

Cherrington, after a sleepless night, decided to drill on into the fissure. The bore hole should have a mere fifteen feet to go. Alex climbed down to the bottom of the fissure to capture the event on video. He trained his camera on the spot where the bit was supposed to emerge. When the drilling reached twenty feet, he put the camera down. Finally, more than an hour later, the bit burrowed out amid a cloud of debris and dust. The distance between its theoretical position and its actual position was nearly thirty feet.

Opinion varied as to what had gone wrong and who was at fault. The likeliest theory held that the point where the bore hole started had been improperly surveyed. Consequently, all subsequent points were off. Given that ONFP volunteers had conducted the survey as a money-saving measure, most of them favored a counter theory, that the survey had been accurate, but that the data, when relayed to Cherrington, had been misunderstood or misapplied or otherwise lost in translation. Either way, the bore hole had missed its target. Cherrington abruptly left the peak. Constrained by financial reversals elsewhere, no longer able to pour his resources into such an uncertain project, he and his "A" team and their sophisticated equipment moved on to a job that paid in advance.

Kat Keany would telephone Terry several weeks after her visit and say that Victorio Peak was a much bigger story than she'd anticipated, further research was required, and NBC was contemplating a Freedom of Information Act request. *Bigger story* sounded to Terry like a tactful substitute for *don't call us, we'll call you.* After "Now" expanded its broadcast to three nights a week and changed its name to "Dateline"—or, as the more cynical members of the crew referred to it, "The O. J. Simpson Show"—coverage of the Simpson trial would push every other story, including Victorio Peak, to the sidelines. Another tawdry little soap opera, Terry may have thought. His own story he could not judge.

May 1994. My fortieth birthday put me in a funk. I woke up late, with no gumption to write. I sat at the laptop anyway. The clock above the breakfast table ticked louder than ever. Linda called to wish me a happy one, but she was *there* and I was *here.* Only I didn't feel here. I felt elsewhere.

Boz was in the yard hooking up swamp coolers, and I went out to help, but my languor must have been contagious. He decided to consult a professional; I decided to go lie down. I read for a while, listened to Bonnie Raitt sing "Too Soon to Tell," heated a can of soup.

After lunch I straggled back to the laptop, stared at the last chapter of my novel, which, despite all my revisions, remained imperfect, and finally started writing: a letter to Linda. She and I had been an item for almost seven years. We were fast approaching the critical juncture when couples either split up or get hitched. Naturally, I avoided that subject in my letter. Instead, I described my state of suspended animation, the rigors of life after forty. By the time I was done, I felt a little less blah.

A few nights later, after a poetry reading on campus, Boz and Toni hosted a party, with loud music and shots of tequila and increasingly reckless dancing. Several of the treasure hunters attended. They fit right in with the crowd of grad students and profs. I spent most of the party on the dance floor, performing wild leaps.

My own life, in other words, occupied the core of my attention while the treasure hunt veered off course. Cherrington's failure to hit the humongous void seemed to me, compared to the trauma of turning forty, a mere bump in the road. He would return, I assumed, to try again. A few survey points may have been miscalculated, but the results of the seismic survey as a whole appeared valid. After Cherrington's hasty departure, the ONFP crew had used Kelly Fischer's newly acquired slant rig to drill into a smaller void located 18 feet west of the Dike Shaft, precisely where the seismic survey indicated it should be. Hope would follow failure just as failure followed hope. It didn't occur to me that Terry might view Cherrington's exit differently.

A week and a half after the party, on a sunny Thursday afternoon, I drove to White Sands Missile Range with Terry and Judy. I felt great because I'd finished revising the novel. Carrying the manuscript to the post office, buying and licking the stamps, sliding the envelope into the slot—the glow still lingered. Terry, though, seemed wound up tight. His current mission was to confront the base's environmental officer and demand a change in policy. Specifically, he wanted the base to drop its archeology requirement. Every day that ONFP set foot on the peak, they were charged upwards of $400 for an archeologist. When hordes of metal detectorists had roamed the desert, at least the archeologist had stepped out of his truck once in a while, but now that work consisted mainly of drilling, the archeologist did nothing, as far as Terry was concerned, but sleep and read paperbacks. To make matters worse, the head of the company that supplied the archeologist was the environmental officer's good buddy.

I'm ready for a fight, Terry said, and he looked ready, jaw clenched, fingers drumming against the steering wheel, almost as if throwing a punch might bring him peace.

Good luck, I said, pulling out my notepad and a five-page list of questions. With the novel in the mail, I'd dived back into the gold book. So what did you do, I asked, at the nuclear plant?

As soon as Terry started answering my questions, his jaw relaxed. He described the facility in detail. *Dolly Parton Land*, the rad techs called it, in honor of its enormous pair of domes. He conjured up a world of concrete walls and hours of boredom, shredded paper suits and scorned procedures.

Twice I left there in an ambulance, he said. Once when a heavy metal bar got dropped on me, once for heat exhaustion.

Judy listened from the back seat. Like a good umpire, she strived to go unnoticed.

By the time we arrived at the base, I'd scribbled down close to a thousand words. Terry was explaining that on Fridays before a holiday, a tech would inevitably trip the nuclear reactor, forcing all workers to stay on the job—and collect triple pay.

The environmental officer was walking toward his office as we pulled up. Got him, Terry said, and practically leaped from the car. The environmental officer glanced around as if in search of a hiding place, then darted inside the building with Terry in pursuit.

Did Terry have an appointment? I asked Judy.

She paused in the lighting of a low-tar cigarette to shake her head. I cracked open my door and reviewed my notes. When Terry stormed back, a cigarette and a half later, he started the car and launched into a heated account of the drop-in.

The EO was about as gruff as he gets, Terry said. The first words out of his mouth were, I'm leaving. Basically, he told me there was nothing he could do. He blamed state regulations. Santa Fe bureaucrats. Who am I fighting? I asked him. If it's you, I know I can't win. But if it's policy, maybe we can get the policy changed.

Terry, as he drove, kept recalling the skirmish. The EO looked stunned, Terry said, when I demanded to meet with his superior. Then I told him that ONFP was going off schedule until the matter was resolved. *That* popped his eyes open, Terry said. They're used to seeing me bow and scrape. He hunched his shoulders in a posture of mock submission.

It began to dawn on me, as he continued his tirade, that he wasn't just stressed—he was desperate. This raid on the EO stood no chance of success. Why, I asked myself, would he go on the warpath *now*? The archeology charges hadn't changed. What had changed, I came to realize, was his outlook. He'd lost hope. Cherrington's withdrawal had undermined his confidence in a quick discovery.

Judy and I mostly listened until his outrage wore off and his grip on the steering wheel loosened. Then I waggled my list of questions. Less than a page remained when we parked in front of the ONFP house. My unpaid leave was nearing its end. Months might pass before Terry and I found a better chance to finish the interview. We dropped Judy off and adjourned in separate cars to the lunch place in the strip mall that served weak espresso and tough pastries. It was almost five o'clock by the time we got settled at a table.

I turned the conversation to July '92, the first day of work at the peak. When Boz and I had written our initial draft of that section, we'd imagined Terry leading the crew. Later, we'd learned that Terry had stayed at the ONFP house. It was such a big day, I said. Why'd you hang back?

I was pretty sick, Terry said. I needed to hold down my stress.

Do you ever wonder, I asked, if working at the nuclear plant messed up your health?

I have AIDS, he said. The lines etched into his forehead seemed to express surprise.

What the lines of my face expressed I can't reckon.

I assumed you knew, Terry said.

The possibility crossed my mind, I said. But I didn't know.

The spots on my leg, Terry said. Kaposi's sarcoma.

I'm sorry, I said. I was still holding my pen and notepad, but I hadn't written a word. The revelation must seem obvious now—if a gay man is continually sick, we assume he has AIDS—but in 1994, less than a decade after the disease dragged Rock Hudson out of the closet, the clues were easier to ignore. I set my notepad on the table and lay the pen across it.

Late afternoon sunlight slanted through the window shades. If the café had air conditioning, it was doing a poor job.

Terry told me about his medical history. He'd been diagnosed with AIDS the year *before* he'd started at the nuclear plant. His health had fluctuated ever since. Now his eyes were giving him trouble. He was afraid it might be cytomegali, a virus commonly associated with AIDS. He'd called a dozen doctors, he said. None would treat him without a referral. I'm just trying to make it to Memorial Day, he said, so I can see my doctor in California.

Why wait?

He counted off the reasons finger by finger: this archeology dispute, a meeting next week in Santa Fe with the attorney general of New Mexico, the blow to morale if he bailed out.

Every day is hell, he said. I haven't had a day of pleasure from this project since we got to the peak. He mentioned the movie *Philadelphia*, the idea that a man who knows he's dying should get to do what he wants. This is not what I want to do, he said.

My notepad seemed to quiver on the table.

I provide the illusion of leadership, he said. Every day I'm frightened half to death.

A customer at the magazine rack cleared his throat. I couldn't help thinking of the last time a word from Terry had left me stunned. That conversation, coming back from Socorro, felt like one friend talking to another, but this conversation seemed more than personal.

I don't consider my sickness to be part of the story, he said. But the fact that I'm gay is a big part. It has to be in there. It's the truth. He gave me his shy shrug, the self-deprecating smile.

I nodded, murmured, asked a few questions.

After I moved to California and confirmed in my own mind that I was gay, he said, I went through a terrible period of soul-searching. In the eyes of my faith, I was the worst kind of sinner. I felt unfit to live. Someone recommended a therapist, and she asked if there was anything I wanted to do before I killed myself. And I knew. Instantly. I wanted to finish my grandmother's work. Open up the mountain and have a look. Terry's smile broadened, as if the memory still held power.

Both of us had obligations elsewhere. Out-of-town guests were arriving at the ONFP house; I was due at Jade's talent show. We walked together to the parking lot. I don't remember whether we hugged or shook hands, but I do remember speeding to the elementary school, watching from the back of the auditorium while Boz's daughter sang "Give My Regards to Broadway" with a troupe of determined first graders.

Surrounded by parents and kids, I tried to sort out my thoughts. Terry had AIDS. AIDS meant death. Why hadn't he told me before? Why had he told me now? When I'd composed my list of questions, I'd saved the most sensitive for last. I'd known that Terry's health was a touchy subject. I'd known about the treatment for his leg, the treatment for his lungs. I'd known he was gay. But I'd failed to make the obvious connection.

Later that night, after the talent show and dinner at a festive restaurant, after the many intricate rituals of putting the kids to bed, Boz joined me at the kitchen table. I gave him the lowdown. We talked about Terry. We talked about AIDS. And as we talked, our voices somber, our expressions grave, we felt our book changing shape. It seemed wrong to consider a dying friend as a character, a fatal disease as a twist of plot, but eventually we talked about how this bombshell would affect the book.

The next morning, typing up my recollections of the conversation in the café, I stalled on KS. I couldn't remember what the letters stood for. Terry had said the words, but they hadn't stuck. My uneducated guess was *Karsonomi's Syndrome*. Later, when I became more fluent in AIDS, the mistake embarrassed me. The difference between *Karsonomi's Syndrome* and *Kaposi's sarcoma* seemed to mirror the difference between memory and truth.

At the end of May, just after my return to Berkeley, Linda and I attended a wedding in Lake Tahoe, and the following day we hiked to a smaller lake called Fallen Leaf, where I asked if she would marry me, and she said yes.

August 1994. Craig deteriorated quickly at the end. Terry served as his attendant and errand runner, the one who fed him popsicles and pushed the buttons of the remote control. Craig never informed his parents of his condition, but someone must have let them know. When they moved into Craig's house, Terry moved out. Later, after Craig was transferred to the hospital, Terry would run into the Harrisons outside Craig's room. They passed without a word.

In Craig's lucid periods, he and Terry spoke of final things, death and what might follow. Their conversations turned Terry not toward the faith of his childhood but back to the everyday demands of the project. He consulted often with Judy about practical matters. He negotiated contracts with lawyers, settled petty disputes, cajoled dispirited volunteers, placated worried investors. In the hospital waiting room, while Craig wasted away down the hall, Terry spoke on the telephone about movie rights. When he overheard the Harrisons heatedly discussing a real estate deal, he couldn't summon the wherewithal to condemn them. Grief, at times, took almost unrecognizable forms.

In a matter of weeks, Craig lost virtually everything that had made him the person Terry knew. When he started struggling for his last breaths, Terry was at his bedside. He held Craig's hand and told him not to worry, it was okay to let go, then he hurried to the waiting room and summoned the family.

Craig Harrison died on August 8, 1994.

Terry did not immediately return to Las Cruces. About his own mortal fears, there was no treasure hunter in whom he could confide. He had been raised as a witness for Jehovah, but what he had witnessed in the past half year bore no relation to God. No Jehovah's Witness, which was to say no member of his family, could nurse him as he had nursed Craig without violating the tenets of the faith.

When he had first moved back to help Craig, he had wanted something tangible to bring from the peak. A bar of gold to lay on Craig's bed as a kind of offering. That desire now haunted him. It had become all too clear that Craig had no use for gold—no matter the quantity, no matter the quality, no matter the mythic source. The disease, Craig had finally decided, existed only inside. An inside job, he called it, the body's mutiny, the mind's treason, the heart's dirty trick. The blood that carried life and the blood that carried death were, in the end, the same blood. Gold offered no consolation.

PART V

(Overleaf) Victorio Peak from above.

22

Critical Thought

Suppose an individual believes something with his whole heart; suppose further that he has a commitment to this belief, that he has taken irrevocable actions because of it; finally, suppose that he is presented with evidence, undeniable evidence that his belief is wrong; what will happen? The individual will frequently emerge, not only unshaken, but even more convinced of the truth of his beliefs than ever before. Indeed, he may even show a new fervor about convincing other people to his view.

—*From* When Prophecy Fails *by Leon Festinger,*
H. W. Riecken, and S. Schachter

David Schweidel

What lies buried in Victorio Peak? Did Doc Noss discover an enormous treasure—or did he concoct an enormous lie? Before Terry told me that he had AIDS, I felt free to withhold judgment on such questions. I entertained doubts about the treasure, just as I entertained hopes. I tried to embrace all possibilities at once. Terry's revelation led me to reconsider my approach. If I could miss something so obvious, so crucial, what else might I miss? AIDS was a fact with consequences. It obliged me to exercise critical thought.

First, the sheer magnitude of treasure defies belief. The sixteen thousand gold bars that Doc estimated were stacked inside the peak would constitute more gold than has been mined in the Southwest during its entire recorded history. As for the origins of the treasure, not only did Doc and his followers propose several possibilities that seem extraordinarily unlikely—the seven cities of gold, the lost mine of Padre Larue, Maximilian's secret hoard—but Doc claimed to have found evidence—skeletons of conquistadors, a map bearing the name Padre Larue, letters signed by the Empress Carlotta—suggesting that all three wound up in Victorio Peak. This evidence, none of which has survived, further undermines Doc's credibility.

A version of the Padre Larue legend appeared in a geological bulletin published by the New Mexico Bureau of Mines in 1935, soon after Doc arrived in the state. The article would have appealed to a man with an interest in buried treasure. Doc had begun looking for treasure long before he reached Victorio Peak. In fact, he had already *found* treasure, if the statement of Melvin Rueckhaus in ONFP's petition to the Pentagon is accurate: "During 1936 Doc mentioned…having found gold which he identified…as probably the Larue treasure." Finding the Larue treasure in 1936 would constitute a miracle; finding it again in 1938 would constitute fraud. If Doc was trafficking in gold bars before he set foot on Victorio Peak, he may also have been stockpiling treasure yarns to account for the gold.

Certainly, the details of the actual discovery, though charming, ring false. Would a treasure hunter like Doc have ignored sixteen thousand bars of *anything* until Babe finally nagged him into bringing up a sample? How did Babe get around with that string tied to her ankle? More significantly, the colossal dimensions of the treasure cave—Doc described it as 2,700 feet in length—would dwarf the largest void detected by the extensive surveys conducted at the peak.

The explosion that blew up the passage to the treasure also raises doubts. If Doc lied about the treasure, the destruction of the passageway not only concealed his lie, it created an instant opportunity to make money. He could sell shares in the recovery of a "lost" treasure, whether it existed or not.

So much of the evidence that might have substantiated Doc's story has disappeared. The footlocker that vanished after Doc's death supposedly contained a "hold certificate" issued by the Denver Mint in the fall of 1939 for six gold bars valued at $97,000, as well as a jewel-encrusted crown and photographs of Doc next to a stack of gold bars. Even the negatives of the photographs disappeared when Merle Horzmann allegedly stole the box where Letha kept them. The loss of all this evidence, like the destruction of the passageway, can be viewed as tragic or convenient.

What is not in doubt is that Doc had a serious drinking problem, an uncontrollable temper, a bogus medical title, a criminal record, and an admitted habit of offering fake gold bars for sale. The family's explanation—that Doc replaced the fake bars with the genuine article as soon as he got paid—paints Doc as far more scrupulous than his verifiable history would suggest. A final troubling question about Doc: why would he leave a hundred and ten gold bars buried near the peak for ten years, a decade of bad jobs and bounced checks? The details of Doc's story, when examined from a critical perspective, would seem to add up not to a legendary discovery but to a legendary con.

Nevertheless, people continue to put credence in Doc's story. Even a paranoid can have real enemies, and even a con man can find real gold. Who more likely than Doc, combing the desert in search of hidden treasure, to stumble on a bonanza? And what better place for Apaches to stash their plunder than a little mountain riddled with caves and fissures, with a fresh water spring at its base, not far from a major trade route, in the middle of Apache country?

The many witnesses who swore they saw gold bars in Doc's possession, and the smaller number who swore they saw Doc remove treasure from the peak, lend support to the possibility that his story contains at least a grain of truth. How else to explain Tony Jolley's detailed account of digging up gold bars the night before Doc's death, or Fiege and Berlett's lie detector testimony that they too found a cache of gold inside the peak, or the gold bars that F. Lee Bailey presented to the Department of the Treasury?

Though no treasure cave has yet been revealed, ONFP's excavations have verified key elements of Doc's description of the peak's interior: the presence of earthen walkways, the sulfurous smell, the location of "Big Rock." Limestone has been discovered in areas where geologists predicted it couldn't exist. Even the underground river Doc spoke of no longer seems farfetched.

Ultimately, however, Doc's credibility depends on Babe. She hiked by his side to the top of the peak; watched him enter its depths empty-handed and emerge laden with riches. Without her tenacity and corroborating testimony, Doc and his story would long ago have faded into folklore. Yet Babe's story, too, has its dubious aspects. Babe was not one to let mere facts obscure what she regarded as the larger truth. She exaggerated, she embroidered. The crown encrusted with two hundred forty-three diamonds and a pigeon-blood ruby, the chance encounter with an insurance customer set to jump Doc's claim, the putdown of John D. Rockefeller all attest to Babe's penchant for gaudy embellishments, fateful coincidences, and snappy punch lines. In her version of history, Doc could do no wrong. She blamed the law, the government, the mining engineer—anyone but Doc. He may have run off with the unmentionable Violet, but before his death he came to Babe and patched things up, she insisted, though her declarations of undying love smack of protesting too much.

Is it conceivable that Babe only pretended to believe in the treasure? In the summer of 1939, she wrote a letter to the U.S. Mint inquiring about treasure law.

> We are residents of New Mexico and find lots of Stories about burried [*sic*] treasures such as bars of Gold and Silver—also Mexican money. Now we have in our possession an old map that tells of a rick of gold bars and Mexican money. Now we are searching in the vicinity of where it is liable to be—and what I want to know is what the United States law on a find of that kind. Can we take it to the U.S. Mint and sell it or will the government claim the treasure?

The letter reads like a naive attempt to be sly. The unmistakable inference is that she and Doc had already found *something* and wanted to know if the government would buy it or confiscate it.

Babe devoted the last forty years of her life to the pursuit of the treasure. She battled, after Doc's death, for possession of his maps and diagrams of the peak. She continued to conduct excavations until the army evicted her; then she fought the army in quest of renewed access and sued the state and federal government to protect her legal rights. If her life proved anything, it proved the strength of her belief in the treasure.

Yet the strength of a belief may not correspond to its degree of truth. Sometimes a person will cling harder to a belief precisely because of the scant evidence to support it. Psychologists use the term *cognitive dissonance* to refer to this paradoxical process. The more reason to doubt, the stronger a belief must grow to survive. People who insist, for instance, that the world is flat or that aliens conducted experiments on their cattle maintain such beliefs only with great effort.

Perhaps the fierceness of Babe's conviction derives not from certainty but from its opposite. Perhaps she put so much faith in Doc's solemn word that the question of what she actually witnessed became irrelevant. In her desire to share the thrill of discovery, to convince the skeptics, she injected herself into the action. She made Doc's story her own and never wavered from it.

If Doc's credibility depends on Babe, Babe's credibility depends on Terry, his unflagging confidence in her character. Whoever trusts Terry by extension trusts Babe, because he swallowed her story whole, without resolving its contradictions and inconsistencies. In making his case to the Pentagon and to the public, Terry has relied on shaky evidence. The statement of Melvin Rueckhaus, for instance, has been quoted as if it referred to Victorio Peak gold. The assay included with the petition values Doc's gold sample at $5,000 *per ton,* though the gold in the peak is usually characterized as pure or nearly pure. Terry simply presents the evidence, neither falsifying nor correcting the likely misimpressions. Unlike Babe, Terry acknowledges his doubts—but not often, and not to an audience of believers. Terry's trust in his grandmother is based less on evidence than on blood, the feeling in his gut when he listened to her wondrous stories.

So what really happened? What is the likeliest reconstruction of events? My best guess is that Doc found a cache of Apache plunder that included a small number of gold bars. He began hauling out as much as he could, perhaps burying a few bars in the surrounding desert. Babe accompanied him on several trips to the peak, but he refused to let her see the treasure room. Why would Doc exaggerate the size of the treasure? Because he wanted to impress Babe? Because he was already setting up his con? Regardless of his reason, Babe balked at being kept at a distance and began playing up her part in the discovery.

Meanwhile, Doc sold some of the gold on the black market at well below the price set by law. Babe wrote to the U.S. Mint in an attempt to learn what the government would do if the find was reported. She assumed that the bulk of the treasure remained buried inside the peak. Doc knew better. He destroyed access to the treasure on purpose.

Thereafter, he and Babe backed up each other's tale of the treasure that got away. Its value, in memory, grew larger and larger. Doc's desertion prompted Babe to put the claim in her own name. His death inspired her to declare that they had reconciled—though her son Harold testified against

Doc at Ryan's trial. Babe promoted her romantic reunion with Doc as a way to cut out Violet, but eventually she convinced herself of their love's everlasting glory.

Babe's daughters echo Babe's accounts with uncanny fidelity, often using the same phrases, for instance comparing the ancient gold bars to a "Baby Ruth candy bar." It's as if Letha and Dorothy inherited the memories their mother borrowed from Doc.

What about Tony Jolley's memories? Did he and Doc really dig up and rebury 110 gold bars? If so, why would Jolley leave them hidden in the desert for twenty years and then retrieve only ten of them? Most likely, Doc enlisted Jolley to help with a scam he was running on Ryan. Perhaps Jolley used the episode years later as a cover story to explain income from a less reputable source.

Leonard Fiege and Thomas Berlett passed lie detector tests administered by the Secret Service. Did they stumble on the remnants of the cache Doc discovered? If so, why couldn't they find it again? Did the army steal the gold?

Babe accused General Eddie of stealing the Victorio Peak treasure in the early 1950s. Others suspected that the army removed the treasure in 1960. Lyndon Johnson, according to persistent rumors, stole the treasure during his presidency. F. Lee Bailey accused the army of stealing the treasure in the mid-1970s. One story of theft would be more convincing than so many. Like the mythical seven cities of gold, which migrated thousands of miles west after the discovery of the New World, the allegations of theft have migrated in time every decade or so. This sort of peregrination typifies folklore, not fact. Suspicion of the army will likely persist, however, given the army's enigmatic bureaucracy and the public's love of a juicy conspiracy.

The mystery, in other words, will linger. The path of critical thought led me to the edge of reasonable doubt, but not beyond. I clung to the grain-of-truth theory. Boz was more skeptical. He believed that Victorio Peak never held any treasure.

23

The Difference Between a Tunnel and a Drift

*Victorio Peak would be more accurately described
as a hill, rather than a mountain.*
—From an environmental assessment of
Victorio Peak, prepared by EcoPlan, Inc.

1994-95—David Schweidel

The treasure hunt entered the hard rock mining phase in late September, when ONFP contracted with a Denver mining company to dig a 220-foot tunnel from the Dome Room to the largest of the voids detected by the seismic survey—the same void Cherrington had missed. The tunnel, according to estimates, would reach target in four weeks at a cost of $138,000. Work began on October 13, 1994, with completion expected by Thanksgiving.

The ONFP crew invited me to a bachelor party at the peak—they even offered to chip in for my flight—but wedding biz kept me in Berkeley. I married Linda on October 15. Boz stood up front. His wife Toni read a poem. Sixty guests attended. Terry sat in the middle of the third row.

The first seventy feet of tunnel went quickly, advancing fourteen feet a day through solid limestone on the dike's north side. Then, just short of the dike, the two-man mining crew hit shale, which slowed progress to six feet a day. At the dike itself, they hit rubble. Speculation arose that the rubble was not a natural phenomenon but the product of army dynamiting. Jamie Rector, over lunch in Berkeley, suggested a simpler explanation—that the rubble resulted from the peak's long history of slumps and fractures. Regardless of the rubble's origin, so much shoring was required to protect the miners from falling rocks that progress came to a stop. After advancing three feet a day for several discouraging days, the crew fell back to the seventy-foot mark and started a new route. Thanksgiving arrived with the tunnel less than halfway to its target and costs already exceeding the initial estimate.

I flew down in early December to see the tunnel. Kelly Fischer gave me a ride as far as base camp. We breakfasted on taquitos from Whataburger—Kelly's treat—and talked, between bites, about life in Indiana, the value of work, what it was like to operate a tractor at age ten. Gene Klier delivered me from base camp to the peak. He was frustrated, he said, because last night he'd made a special trip from Las Cruces, hauling a heavy generator over a muddy road at midnight so the mining crew would have the generator when they left for the peak in the morning at seven sharp, and then the MP had held them at base camp till after nine o'clock due to what Gene called a typical army screw-up.

The first time someone leaves the cap off the toothpaste, you don't get frustrated, Gene said. But when it keeps happening, you go crazy.

My philosophy is the opposite, I said. If something keeps happening, you need to adjust. Only your family can bug you just by doing what they always do.

It occurred to me when Gene winced that the army, for him, might have become too much like family, the unwanted in-law who never fails to spoil the picnic.

How long, I asked, have you been out here?

Twenty-four months.

The sky was overcast, a somber gray, but the culvert that served as the entrance to the Dome Room gave off a glossy light. I remembered a TV show I'd watched as a kid—*The Time Tunnel*—wherein the hero tumbled through the eponymous tunnel like an astronaut in space, weightless, against a psychedelic background of shifting shapes and flashing lights. The show was cheesy, but the low-budget special effects held a certain magic for me, as did this corrugated-metal culvert, with its uncanny sheen, dazzling despite the lack of sunshine. When I followed Gene inside, the clang of our boots against the metal brought to mind what Terry had said about freaky music. Yes, I could still hear it, along with the roar of the generator pumping fresh air into the tunnel and the sound of a small engine puttering up ahead in the darkness. The light of my miner's lamp cast a shadowy glow on the rough tunnel walls, the hard-packed floor, the limestone ceiling close enough to touch with my outstretched hand.

Seventy feet into the mountain, the tunnel forked. The left fork, Gene explained, had been abandoned. Too much rubble. Too much time and expense to keep the sky from falling. He aimed his headlamp at the elaborate shoring. It's not a total waste, he said. The miners use the left fork to dump the muck.

As if on cue, the puttering engine grew louder.

Scoopertram, Gene said.

We edged to the side of the tunnel to let the scoopertram pass. It looked like a cross between a golf cart and a miniature frontloader. The driver rode sidesaddle, partially enclosed by a metal-mesh cage, from which hung a pair of fuzzy dice. In the event of a rockslide, the cage would provide no more protection than the dice. The driver bobbed his headlamp in greeting as he motored by.

Gene ushered me farther up the right fork. He kept to the side to avoid the widening stream of mud. The miner at the end of the tunnel, a large man spattered with mud from his boots to his hard hat, chided Gene for being dainty.

This is Arnold, Gene said. Also known as *The Beast*.

Arnold's hand dwarfed mine.

I'm Dave, I said. I'm not known as anything.

Dave's a writer, Gene said.

I flashed my notepad like an ID badge. Hard rock mining is new to me, I said. I just want to see how the work is done.

Arnold handed me his drill. It weighed close to a hundred pounds. I didn't drop it, but I didn't hold it long.

Mining is simple, he said. Make a mess, clean it up, mess it up again. That's mining.

Sounds a lot like writing, I said.

Gene headed back down the tunnel. Arnold went back to work. He was drilling a series of holes into the wall at the end of the tunnel. The holes were slightly larger than a stick of dynamite. At the center of the wall, Arnold drilled the holes close together, in a diamond pattern. Moving out from the center, he spaced the holes farther apart. The drill was six feet long and rested on a six-foot hydraulic jack. To start a hole high on the wall, Arnold braced the drill and jack against his chest, aimed the tip at the chosen spot, and wrestled to keep the drill in place until the hole was deep and straight enough that he could trust the jack to support the drill's weight.

The other miner, meanwhile, puttered back and forth in the scoopertram, clearing away debris from the previous blast. He finished as Arnold was drilling the last hole. Then they started planting the dynamite. The tunnel was quiet now. We took out our earplugs. Arnold introduced me to the other miner, Lon, a courtly Southern gentleman from the hills of Tennessee. Today was Lon's last day at the peak. He said he hated to leave.

The space around the dynamite was packed with fertilizer. Evidently, the nitrogen in the fertilizer added power to the explosion. Best bang for the buck, Arnold said. While Lon set the fuses, Arnold began carrying his equipment out of the tunnel. When all the separate fuses had been connected, Lon asked if I wanted to light the master fuse.

How long will we have before the dynamite goes off?

Two and a half minutes.

I don't remember what I used. Probably, Lon let me borrow his lighter. What I do remember is the etiquette after the fuse was lit. Arnold and Lon seemed to make a point of slowing down. They casually inspected the dark recesses of the tunnel, picked up the last few remaining tools, and sauntered out. I followed, forcing myself not to run, the voice in my head screaming *go, go, go!* Outside, the overcast sky was the same lusterless gray. Arnold and Lon busied themselves with menial chores. Lon washed his hands. Arnold tinkered with his drill. They stood far apart, turned away from the tunnel, as if the impending explosion deserved to be snubbed. I braced myself, my eyes on the shiny culvert. Two and a half minutes couldn't possibly last this long. Then a muffled boom. The ground shifted underfoot. My adrenaline surged. I wanted to slap Arnold on the back, shake Lon's hand. *Wasn't that cool?* But they just went about their work. In half an hour, when the air in the tunnel cleared, Lon would climb aboard the scoopertram and haul away the muck, Arnold would drill another set of holes, they'd load and pack more dynamite, light another fuse. Make a mess, clean it up, mess it up again. In the meantime, though, we gathered at the ice chest and popped open a round of orange sodas.

I wish I could stay, Lon said. It's like making love with a woman and the doorbell rings and this time you have to answer it.

Arnold said nothing. He and Lon were parting ways. I knew because I'd attended a meeting in Las Cruces the day before. Terry and their boss had reached an agreement whereby the mining company would withdraw from the project, and ONFP, after the Christmas holidays, would tunnel on with their own equipment and crew. Both Lon and Arnold had been invited to work for ONFP—at reduced pay, with equity—and Arnold had agreed, but Lon had reluctantly said no.

The reason, he explained now, was that he didn't want to quit his boss. The mining world is small, he said. I can't afford to get blackballed. At a different stage in my life, I might take the risk. But not with a wife and kids. No can do.

He dropped his soda in the trash bag, dried his hands on the cleanest corner of a dirty rag. Arnold expressed his sympathy with a shrug. A light drizzle began to fall from the gray December sky, plinking against the gleaming culvert. I wondered what was stranger, that Lon didn't want to leave this scraggly patch of desert, or that I understood why.

A funny thing happened on the way back to California. I stopped in El Paso to visit my mother. While there, I got a call from my far-flung sister. This sister is the seeker in my family. She's practiced transcendental meditation, walked barefoot over hot coals, even tried to levitate. She had recently moved to a small town in Washington to live near her spiritual leader, a "channel" for the spirit of an ancient warrior from the lost continent of Lemuria. It would be fair to say that I tend to be skeptical of my sister's cosmic ventures, and yet I also respect her fearlessness, her sense of wonder.

She was calling to ask my advice, which she'd never done before. Friends of hers had met a man selling shares in a treasure, and not just any treasure, but the legendary treasure of Victorio Peak. She and her friends were interested in investing. Would I talk to them if she set up a conference call?

Sure, I said.

My sister, like many people, revels in coincidence. There are no accidents. Everything happens for a reason. I hold a different view, but the treasure hunt, I have to admit, seemed to attract coincidence like a trailer park attracts disaster. At a party in Berkeley, for instance, I was expounding on the project's long history when a good friend, someone I'd known for years, confessed that her father had been stationed at White Sands Missile Range in 1961 and was, in fact, Morton Jaffe, the colonel who'd called the Noss treasure "a fake and a myth" and lied about the army's top secret search. His attacks on the Noss family had struck Babe as particularly virulent and personal, and some suspected that he had absconded with recovered gold. My friend, however, remembered no sudden influx of wealth, no abrupt rise in her own family's standard of living. (When she told her father about my book, he wished me luck—but added that I should find a better subject than "those crooks.") For me, the involvement of my friend's father in the saga was an uncanny coincidence. For my sister, it was Fate to meet Terry at my wedding and then, *out of the blue*, to be offered the chance to share in his treasure. My sister loves pyramid schemes, chain letters, unlikely opportunities to get rich quick.

The conference call was low tech. My sister and her friends put me on their speaker phone.

How did you hear about the treasure? I asked.

It just seemed meant to be, they said. They'd run into a man named Augie Delgado, they said, and they weren't too sure about *him*, but Augie Delgado had introduced them to Bill Brown, and they'd gotten a good hit off Bill. Bill had great energy, and Augie was enthusiastic, too, and they both sounded like there could be a discovery any day now, and there would never be a better time to invest. Is that true? they asked. You were just there, right? What do you think?

I had already contacted Terry and asked if ONFP had a sales rep in the state of Washington. Terry had groaned, and apologetically explained that his cousin Jerry had a friend, Bill Brown, who was a very enthusiastic supporter of the project, sometimes *too* enthusiastic. I've tried to stress the importance of not overselling, Terry had said, the need to emphasize the risks.

So I told my sister and her friends that Bill Brown was evidently legitimate, but overzealous.

What about the treasure? they asked. When are they going to find it? Do you think it'll happen soon?

The speaker phone seemed to amplify the sound of their breathing. I could picture them on the other end of the line, huddled around the phone, waiting for my verdict. I felt a responsibility to Terry not to slight the project and a responsibility to my sister to dispel any illusions.

I've been involved in this project for a year and a half, I said, and discovery has always been imminent. Yes, it *could* happen tomorrow, but more likely it will *never* happen. There *might* be an enormous treasure, but there might be no treasure at all.

You mean the army already stole it?

I don't think so.

Then it's still there.

The original treasure may have been a hoax. Or a big exaggeration.

Do you think we should invest?

Not if it's money you can't afford to lose. The only way this is a good investment is if you have a few hundred dollars to spare and you just want a connection to the project. It's a fascinating story. The people are great. But I'd say the chance of making money is very low. A real long shot.

Of course I don't remember the conversation word for word, but I tried to emphasize the risks. I certainly didn't oversell. My sister and her friends thanked me at length. I felt a little guilty for bursting their bubble.

My sister told me later that they all invested. I didn't ask how much.

One day early in the new year, Terry drove out to the peak. The corrugated-metal culvert at the entrance to the Dome Room reminded him of something he couldn't quite place as he rolled a pair of foam earplugs into the shape of pellets and popped one inside each ear. Maybe an old TV show, *The Twilight Zone*, a time-travel episode. Slipping a miner's lamp over his hard hat and stepping into the culvert, he idly wondered what era he'd choose: Doc and Babe's heyday, or perhaps the distant future.

The culvert was eight feet in diameter so there was no need to stoop, but he ducked anyway. His boots clanged loudly against the metal until he entered the hard rock mining tunnel itself, which was surprisingly roomy. The height varied between seven and nine feet; the width, between six and ten. He didn't have to walk very far before everything beyond the beam of his miner's lamp was shrouded in darkness.

The strong smell of diesel fuel compelled his attention. A small generator pumped fresh air into the tunnel, but the diesel fumes extinguished any hint of freshness. Overhead, an inflatable plastic pipe—a sulfurous yellow in the light of his miner's lamp—carried the meager supply of air. At least the limestone ceiling looked solid at this point. No boulders threatened to fall. The tunnel was cool, dark, and quiet except for the distant whine of the generator at the entrance.

At the seventy-foot mark, where the tunnel forked, the limestone changed to rubble and the overhead shoring changed correspondingly. Timber sets no longer sufficed. In the worst spots, three layers of shoring overlapped. Even the numerous rock bolts, driven into the ceiling with a pneumatic drill, seemed inadequate to the task of holding back the tonnage of loose rocks. Parked in the left fork was the scoopertram, unattended. Beyond it lay the pile of rocks and dirt removed from the blast area after the last round.

Terry took the right fork. A trickle of water ran along the hard-packed dirt floor. He followed the trickle as it widened into a muddy stream two or three inches deep. When he heard the miners talking at the end of the tunnel, he stopped. He wasn't ready for conversation. As a little boy, he had imagined walking down a tunnel like this, arriving at the heart of the mountain. He remembered the sound of his grandmother's voice, the thrill of contemplating what it would be like to retrace Doc's footsteps.

One of the miners emerged from the darkness. Terry shook his muddy hand.

"This is remarkable," Terry said. "Just being in this tunnel."

"Yeah," the miner said. The beam of light from his head-lamp dipped toward the floor. "Only it's not a tunnel. It's a drift."

Terry smiled at the distinction. "What's the difference?"

"A tunnel goes somewhere," the miner said. "A drift dead-ends. You have to go out the way you came in."

Terry nodded. He moved aside to let the miner pass. The excitement he'd felt a moment before had ebbed. He stood alone in the drift as if waiting for the feeling to return. He'd intended to walk on to the end, but when he heard the scoopertram start up, he turned around and went back the way he'd come.

The drift, true to its name, did not head straight for its target. Instead, it meandered through the mountain.

One reason was safety. The danger of falling rocks made some areas almost impossible to shore. The drift veered away from those areas.

One reason was eagerness for a quick discovery. The hard rock mining crew kept hitting fissures that led deeper into the peak. Often, they would detour into those fissures to conduct further exploration. If they could find a natural passage to the treasure, their job would be done.

One reason may have been fear of failure. If they arrived at the target and discovered nothing, then what?

So the drift gradually turned into a labyrinth. The zigzag strategy baffled Jamie Rector. "It's like looking for your car keys where the light is good," the professor told me in Berkeley, "instead of where you dropped them."

Terry spent more and more time in Newport Beach. He got involved in the clinical trial of a new protease inhibitor that required him to be available once a week for blood work. When a tumor developed in his left leg, he had it treated with radiation.

"I'm fighting my own battles," he said in a phone call. "Just trying to stay alive."

Judy Holeman kept me informed of developments in New Mexico. Most disturbingly, the high cost of doing business with White Sands Missile Range was on the rise. "They're trying to make up the budget deficit with our project," she said. "It's abuse of power, no question. They're running their own little banana republic."

In protest, Terry decided to stop replenishing the escrow account from which the base withdrew its fees. ONFP had already paid the base more than $750,000.

Meanwhile, in May of 1995, my novel was published. In September, my first child was born. Six months later, at the end of my wife's maternity leave, I quit my job to stay home with our daughter. Progress on the gold book slowed to a baby's crawl.

The treasure hunt progressed no faster. The drift drifted on; the army threatened to evict ONFP for nonpayment. Then, in March of 1996, the hard rock mining crew blasted into a tunnel ten feet wide and forty feet high, filled with debris that included a pair of army earplugs and several large bone fragments, possibly human. Wind blew through the tunnel. According to the crew, the wind meant that the tunnel was connected to a void, most likely large, that "breathed." ONFP issued a press release describing the tunnel as "probably the route Doc used."

Less than a week later, the army terminated the search. The balance in the escrow account was zero.

Terry tried to pressure the army through the media. Judy sent me a clipping from the *Las Cruces Sun-News*:

> Did the Army close down Victorio Peak because the treasure hunters got too close to their goal? Or did the treasure hunters decide to announce a major breakthrough when they knew they'd soon be shut down over a billing controversy? It's hard to tell, but here's what appears to be the status of the fascinating saga at this point....
>
> It appears WSMR officials have impeded the Noss group with overly stringent requirements and grossly inflated charges for security, scheduling and environmental and archaeological monitoring. It is this issue over which work at the site has been halted. The Army wants an escrow payment of $140,000 that would bring to nearly $1 million the amount the partnership has had to "reimburse" WSMR.

The eviction, for Boz and me, fit a familiar pattern. *Cut off from the treasure*—again. *On the verge of discovery*—again. The cycle of hope and failure was making another loop.

Between diaper changes and games of peekaboo, I worked on the gold book. Boz had already finished his chapters; I continued to anguish over mine, half a page one day, half a sentence the next. Some days I deleted more than I wrote.

On April 7, 1997, ONFP filed a complaint in the U.S. Court of Federal Claims against the United States of America, as represented by the Secretary of the Army, the commanding general of White Sands Missile Range, and others. The eleven counts in the complaint included failure to bill ONFP only for actual costs incurred, failure to bill ONFP at agreed-upon rates, failure to provide an accounting to ONFP, and failure to act in good faith.

During the discovery phase of the proceedings, White Sands Missile Range turned over thousands of pages of files related to Victorio Peak. Among these files were documents indicating that officials at the base had intentionally overcharged ONFP and diverted excess payments into a slush fund totaling more than $450,000.

Boz and I finally completed a draft in the winter of 1998, but it satisfied neither of us. My second child was born in June. Which may explain the haze surrounding certain subsequent events. ONFP lost its suit. I packed all my notes into boxes and stashed the boxes in the garage. I could hardly write anyway. Writing required immersion, and being a parent required constant presence on the surface. While my wife worked full time, I made pink playdough at pre-school, sang "The Farmer Plants His Crops" at gymnastics plus, performed the assorted contortions of any bona fide stay-at-home dad. The end of the millennium came and went. My boxes of notes gathered dust.

24

The Rock of the World

It's tiring, this endless revision
of our idea of a world
which is itself being continually revised—
—Tony Hoagland

Robert Boswell

Treasure Island ends with a description of what each character does with his share of the treasure. It's a traditional way to conclude, a "where are they now?" wrap-up with the added element of major loot. When a treasure story ends without doubloons or jewels, without gold bars or silver ingots, the wrap-up is, to say the least, a little more complicated.

One thing is certain: all the people from this book still dream of stepping into a cave of riches. All the men who worked in the fissure and the drift, who drilled into an underground stream, who planted geophones and swung their metal detectors, still believe in the treasure of Victorio Peak. Nothing will ever persuade them otherwise. If you come across veterans of the peak in a café or tavern, at a bookstore or the Elks Club, in a corner of the library where a historian is giving a talk on the Lost Dutchman Mine, they will be eager to talk about their experience, and they will tell you their truth: "We were *this* close. I could *feel* it." They all believe they were a small part of a great and secret history.

Who am I to say they're wrong?

History, after all, is not what it used to be. The past is changing by the minute. I'm not thinking about the spin doctors who reconfigure the past in order to control the present; rather, I'm thinking of how each of us when we enter adolescence reinterprets the adults we've known all our lives, how we shift away from our childish beliefs—a shift that may lead to disillusionment and depression—and which, if we're lucky, is supplanted by an adult understanding of the major figures from our past and of our own childhood experience. And this understanding continually changes as we mature and go through the ever-surprising muck and wonder of adult life.

Cultures go through perceptual shifts as well. New ideas become pervasive and lead us to reconsider the past. If there were a Hall of Fame for changing the past, Sigmund Freud would have a wing of his own. Karl Marx would be in there, along with Einstein and writers like Joyce and Faulkner and Alice Munro and García Marquez. Some punks and yahoos and mean-spirited bastards would have to be given their plaques as well, but I'm not going to talk about them. In fact, I'm not really interested, at this moment, in any of that crowd. Rather, it's the phases themselves that interest me.

On June 17, 1972, in Washington, D.C., a security guard named Frank Wills found duct tape on a door to the Democratic National Committee's office at the Watergate Hotel. He called the police, and in doing so ushered in the postmodern era. It had been looming for decades, evident in the works of certain authors, artists, and architects, but it did not become the dominant cultural mode in America until the Watergate scandal enacted the terms by which postmodernism operates. (You won't find this definition of postmodernism anywhere else. I'm making it up.)

The modernists, who'd had dibs on the collective imagination for many decades, believed in an inspired leap in the progression of human thought. Virginia Woolf put it best: "In or about December, 1910, human character changed."

Postmodernists avoid this kind of heavy lifting. Postmodernism is an aesthetic of juxtaposition. Modernism dwarfs it, and the comparison between the two—almost inevitably a comic one—is what powers the postmodern engine. Example: Have you ever noticed how postmodern buildings that look wonderful downtown seem ridiculous when they appear in some "industrial park" out near the airport? The buildings downtown often literally bear the reflection of modern buildings on their mirrored walls, while the ones out in the sticks, juxtaposed with cow pastures, remind you of an actor caught in the wrong costume.

If modernists were a dour, brainy bunch who set out to reinvent the culture, postmodernists were a self-reflexive and ironic crowd that looked at the culture's "grand narratives" and poked them full of holes. Enter Watergate. The grand narrative of American democracy as embodied in the office of the President of the United States was suddenly chockfull of holes and ready to deflate.

The Victorio Peak story entered its postmodern phase in 1973 when John Dean, testifying at the Watergate hearings, mentioned F. Lee Bailey and his claim of "an enormous amount of gold." Suddenly, Doc's wacky story *seemed* more credible because Doc and Babe began appearing in sentences that also included F. Lee Bailey, the Watergate scandal, or *The New York Times*. The relatively simple question of whether a slick but uneducated con man had stumbled upon a fortune or merely concocted a scam gave way to a half-dozen fragmented stories of technological glorification, governmental conspiracy, and celebrity hot-dogging. If it was possible that the President of the United States had ordered a crew of bumbling yahoos to break in to Democratic headquarters, then almost anything was possible, even the wild tale of gold in an obscure New Mexico mountain range.

Victorio Peak emerged as a five-hundred-foot metaphor. Terry Delonas saw the peak for the first time thanks to Operation Goldfinder, and Goldfinder became his model for postmodern treasure hunting. It left him with a vision of his story as a battle against the U.S. government; the mountain itself would be no more than a pawn in the right technological hands.

That Terry saw himself as a knight on a quest while he lobbied Congress and script-doctored an episode of "Unsolved Mysteries" defines something about the postmodern mindset.

I don't see Terry as a knight. My own inclination is to cast him as a postmodern Gatsby. His romantic attachment to wealth as a form of redemption finds its corporeal embodiment in his grandmother rather than in young Daisy, a substitution made palatable by the unlikely combination of Terry's being homosexual and a Jehovah's Witness from Clovis, New Mexico. To resurrect Babe's love (to return to the past), he uses his personal resources to build a metaphorical mansion—a treasure hunting expedition that would put everything Doc ever mustered to shame.

Here's what Fitzgerald writes about young James Gatz on the brink of inventing Jay Gatsby:

> …his heart was in a constant, turbulent riot. The most grotesque and fantastic conceits haunted him in his bed at night. A universe of ineffable gaudiness spun itself out in his brain while the clock ticked on the wash-stand and the moon soaked with wet light his tangled clothes upon the floor. Each night he added to the pattern of his fancies until drowsiness closed down upon some vivid scene with an oblivious embrace. For a while these reveries provided an outlet for his imagination; they were a satisfactory hint of the unreality of reality, a promise that the rock of the world was founded securely on a fairy's wing.

Was Terry, like Gatsby, doomed to fail? If the mountain of his imagination had as its foundation a cunning con man's fable, no amount of work or faith or money could make it true.

The ultimate postmodern treasure story has no treasure, of course; only advertisements for itself.

In the year 2000, when the debacle of the Presidential election failed to poke holes in the grand narrative of the presidency, postmodernism died in this country. It's dying around the globe. Everything that has ever happened is in turmoil. The lenses in your glasses are changing while you read.

Which means, among other things, the story of Doc and Babe is once again up for grabs. And, too, the story of Terry Delonas and his crew of volunteers. They've entered the bubbling cauldron of history.

25

Freaky Music

Each of us is born with a God-shaped void.
We fill it with whatever seems to fit.
—Anonymous

David Schweidel

When I was twenty years old, I worked as a waiter at a steak and lobster restaurant in El Paso. My first night on the job, a customer ordered Johnny Walker Gold on the rocks. Johnny Walker *Gold*, he repeated with special emphasis, either for my benefit or his girlfriend's. When I returned with his drink, he took one sip and made a sour face. This is not Johnny Walker Gold, he insisted. I hustled the drink back to the bartender and explained what had happened. The bartender made a face of his own. You watched me pour, he said. You saw the bottle. Actually, I wasn't paying attention, I said. The bartender sniffed the customer's drink and strained it into a different glass, with fresh ice cubes. He set the glass down on my tray. I didn't argue. I'd been advised to stay on the bartender's good side. So I served the drink a second time. The customer seemed to eye me with suspicion as he raised the glass to his lips and ventured a tentative swallow. Then he turned to his girlfriend. Now *this*, he said, is Johnny Walker Gold.

One morning in the twenty-first century, while soaking in a hot shower, I had a thought, which led to another, which sparked yet more, until it dawned on me that I was *having thoughts*, entirely unrelated to pre-school or play dates or the logistics of drop-offs and pickups. My inner life had returned, and soon after I went into my garage and pulled out the draft of the gold book. It was a treasure story without a treasure, Johnny Walker without the gold. I could bury it in a cardboard box or serve it in a different glass.

My neighborhood in Berkeley is rich with trees—gingko, redwood, Japanese maple. When I started working on the gold book again, I also started taking more walks, not just for the exercise but for the effect on my thoughts. Sometimes, indoors, the story seemed too big, too unwieldy to grasp, but outside, walking among oaks and sequoias, I could almost get hold of it, almost see it whole. I tried to turn it around and study it from every angle, to discover the thread that tied everything together: the Guzzler and the cytomegali virus, Watergate and Esteban the Moor, Jehovah's Witnesses and mule deer.

One question preoccupied me. Why would any sane person, in the face of repeated failure, keep searching for such an unlikely treasure? I'd pause in front of a magnolia tree or a liquidambar and jot down reasons in my little notebook:

> *lure of sudden riches*
> *magic of the desert*
> *satisfaction of the work itself*
> *escape from day jobs and ordinary domestic duties*
> *thrill of solving a mystery*
> *possibility, however slim, of making history*

The impulse to search for the treasure seemed comprehensible enough, but not the impulse to *keep* searching.

I remembered an article an anthropologist friend had given me about a religious group in the Midwest in the 1950s. The leader of the group received a prophecy (via automatic writing) from a planet called *Clarion*: destruction of the earth was imminent, members of the group should spread the word and await further instructions, which included, eventually, removing all metal from their clothing and rendezvousing, at an appointed place and time, with flying saucers bound for Clarion. A few industrious graduate students infiltrated the group and then studied what happened *after* the flying saucers failed to show. What did believers do in the wake of such a letdown, after quitting their jobs and selling their houses, pulling their kids from school and getting rid of their pets? Instead of rejecting the prophecies as a hoax, most of the group redoubled their proselytizing efforts and seized on new clues to recalculate the correct time and place. Failure, in other words, only strengthened their belief. It was a matter not of judgment but of faith. Judgment alters when the evidence alters, but faith transcends evidence.

The Clarion prophecy impressed me as obvious hokum. How could anyone swallow such bunk? Doc's story, though, despite its farrago of what seemed like calculated lies and foolish exaggerations, still held, in my mind, a degree of credibility that I wanted to believe was based on judgment, not faith—sensible, rational judgment. Terry had talked about people who sounded reasonable for the first ten minutes, but if you let them go any longer, they went Loony Tunes. I don't want to be one of those people, Terry had said.

I didn't want him to be one of those people either.

It occurred to me, as I walked my neighborhood and worked on the gold book, that Boz and I, in our portrait of Terry, had highlighted his reasonable side. The more fanatical aspects of his story we'd painted in muted shades or left entirely out of the frame, like Doc's *other* treasure buried in the Caballo Mountains. We preferred to see Terry as someone like us, reasonable, but how could any reasonable person ignore the brunt of his own experience, refuse to face the obvious truth, and continue, despite a history of conspicuous failure, to pursue an impossible goal?

When I told Boz I was working on the gold book, he wished me luck in the manner of a grizzled squadron leader dispatching a plucky volunteer on a mission that meant sure death. The phrase *you crazy bastard* may have been used. The important thing, for me, was to have his permission. During the hazy, sleep-deprived years of letting the gold book lie, I had tried to figure out what the story needed. The problem, I decided, was not the absence of treasure. Finding a pot of gold at the end of the rainbow was a fairy-tale plot. Searching for a treasure and not finding it should be the existential mother lode. What the story lacked, I eventually decided, was a character who changed, who came to recognize the futility of the search, someone reasonable, like Boz and me. So I wrote the writers into the story, chapter by chapter, while my older daughter took yoga, karate, gymnastics, soccer, swimming, drama, circus, and trumpet, and my younger daughter graduated from pre-school and started college—no, kindergarten—and my wife supported us, and local housing prices doubled, and our own house, a rental, less than a block from the Hayward fault, slid farther and farther off its foundation.

One day it hit me that searching for a thread to tie the whole story together was as daft as searching for the treasure. Another day it hit me that the absence of treasure *was* the thread that tied the whole story together. An actual treasure required no spiritual gyrations, but a phantom treasure depended on faith. I'd rush home from my walk and write my latest revelatory riff. *A treasure story without a treasure is like a fish story without a fish. The big one always gets away.* Or this: *Victorio Peak has a void at its heart. For Terry, raised on Rod Serling, citizen of the* Twilight Zone, *what better to fill the void than freaky music? Terry heard it at the top of the peak. He heard it in his grandmother's stories. He heard it in the halls of Congress and even in the copy machines at American Savings and Loan. The treasure might be phantom, but the freaky music was* real, *inaudible, perhaps, to the human ear, but perfectly recognizable to a more primitive locus of intelligence. If you hear the freaky music, you know you're supposed to be there.* After finishing one of these cadenzas, I'd rise from the computer, hardly noticing the dust balls in the hallway, the dishes stacked in the kitchen sink, until the illusion of total understanding faded.

On a sparkling day in December, I stopped to admire the gingko around the corner. Most of the year it blended with the surrounding trees, green among evergreens, but when its leaves turned yellow, a shade more like butter than gold, it came out of hiding, unveiled its brilliance, which reminded me, oddly, of Terry, selling car wax in Santa Fe, closeted even to himself, then waking one morning to the shimmering remnant of a dream, inspired to move to California and write a screenplay in the hope of reclaiming the family treasure, a treasure as unlikely as the path he would follow, winning an act of Congress, raising a million dollars, leading a flock of loyal followers to the brink of discovery. If he failed to write a fairy-tale ending to his grandmother's legendary saga, at least he succeeded in becoming its hero for a while. What else, I asked myself, should he have done with his life?

I returned to my rented house with Terry on my mind. If pursuit of the treasure had stretched him beyond what might otherwise have been his limits, what had the project done for *me*? My Victorio Peak phase had seen publication of a novel, marriage, fatherhood, membership in the PTA, and thousands of hours of work on a story I couldn't leave behind.

If Terry was unreasonable, what was I?

Be it treasure or best seller, the second coming of Christ or the presence of weapons of mass destruction, when people invest in a belief, they usually hold on, no matter the evidence. Cub fans, every spring, insist that this year their team will win the World Series. If such steadfastness is unreasonable, it is also standard operating procedure. America venerates the leap of faith, the underdog who ignores conventional wisdom, common sense, the laws of gravity, and, despite a history of belly flops, takes off yet again into the void. We celebrate the bravery of the leap, and rarely acknowledge the cowardice, the willful stupidity. It's easy to recognize the heroism of voyaging out into the desert, marching off to war, but what about the valor of refusing, of staying home and making dinner?

What would you do if your best friend invited you on a treasure hunt?

By then it was time to pick up my daughters at school and drive them to gymnastics.

Robert Boswell

One day in June of 1993, Dave and I climbed to the top of the peak with a bundle of rope. I tied a loop around my waist and then we looked for a boulder around which to loop the other end. There was nothing secure, so Dave wrapped the rope around his waist.

I climbed through the "bottleneck" and dropped into the fissure's thin air.

We had been told that sections of the slanting walkway were still in place. This walkway had always seemed unlikely to me—dirt and rocks wedged between the walls, filling the narrow opening, and slanting downward to a hole that would permit the spelunker to drop to the next walkway, a pachinko machine for humans. I wanted to see the remains. I wanted to stand on the earthen walkway.

The drop from the opening to the bottom of the fissure was over two hundred feet, and beyond a certain point, all I could see was darkness. I worked my way down to what really did look like a bit of walkway. It was about four feet long and two feet thick. The bottom side was made of packed earth and rock. The topside was smooth. It was just as Doc had described it.

I felt a very specific thrill that had less to do with Doc Noss than it did with the larger history of the region. The cave had likely been used by native people, perhaps for a very long time. This mountain had been a secret place and perhaps a sacred one. That history got lost in the ensuing treasure fever.

Standing on the walkway was probably my best moment at the peak, but not the only good one. I took my brother and mother out there, and they were astounded by the fissure. I took my wife and some of her family. I took my daughter and a few friends. Dave and I spent a lot of enjoyable time talking about the peak and the book, and we both marveled at Terry's faith in his family's defining story and how the truth of that story clearly meant more to him than the possibility of riches. There was a spirit to the core group of treasure hunters, embodied particularly by Terry and Alex and Judy, that I admired and enjoyed and, yes, *treasured*.

Yet if I had it to do over again, I would stay the hell away from Victorio Peak.

I was skeptical of Doc's tale from the beginning, and I never came to believe in the treasure (though I hoped ONFP would prove me wrong), but I was far from clear sighted. I still played the fool. I believed the crew would reach the great room inside the mountain—the room that radar and sonar and psychics and dowsers all swore had to be there. I fell for the omnipotence of technology. I, too, dismissed the power of the mountain.

This book has been more than a dozen years in the making. That's longer than Odysseus took to get home from the war—and he went to hell and back.

26

Endings, Real and Imaginary

The "path" comes into existence only when we observe it.
—Werner Heisenberg

The story ends in 1995, when Terry finds himself alone in the drift. A drift differs from a tunnel, he has just been told, because it has no outlet. The dim light and stale air seem to confirm that the passage leads nowhere. It will not take him where he wishes to go. He will never enter the cavernous room of his imagination, never lay eyes on the family treasure, never fit his boots into his step-grandfather's dusty footprints. The hallowed spot where Doc Noss met his fortune will remain forever lost.

The story ends in 1994, when Terry has his heart-to-heart with Harry Albright. "You've always been straight with me," Harry says. The words *gay* and *AIDS* are never spoken.

The story ends in 1998, when the treasure hunters reunite in El Paso for Alex Alonso's wedding. The lawsuit against the army has not yet been decided. I stand with Terry at the edge of the dance floor as Alex straps on an electric guitar and serenades his bride with an Eric Clapton ballad. Terry mentions under the music that distant relatives of LBJ have contacted him with a tale of seventy-nine tons of gold stored in a warehouse in New Jersey. "Who knows?" Terry says. "There might be some connection." Alex plays a slow guitar solo, couples sway before us, and I try to comprehend how Terry can still believe in phantom treasure. Despite the failure of metal detecting, the failure of ground-penetrating radar, the failure of the excavation of the fissure, the failure of the brass rod, the failure of horizontal directional drilling, the failure of the seismic survey, the failure of hard rock mining, he still believes that one day soon, with a little luck, there will be a breakthrough, a discovery. I can't help shaking my head in dismay—and admiration. He's right back where he started—the army refusing to permit a search—yet he manages, somehow, to keep the faith.

I plan to file for bankruptcy in a few months, he tells me. His health, he says, is fair.

The story ends some time in the future when Boz and I visit Terry in his trailer in a Southern California beach town. His trailer is smaller than Babe's (if you count her add-on cabana rooms) but neater, although the desk is covered with letters and faxes and handwritten pages torn from yellow legal pads. I imagine a counter lined with prescription vials and homeopathic remedies, a refrigerator stocked with wheat germ and carrot juice, Brewer's yeast and bottled water, perhaps a small but expensive round of French cheese. I also imagine a single bed. Terry thanks us for coming, as if *we* are doing *him* a favor. We thank him for inviting us, or letting us invite ourselves. What we talk about, I'm not sure, best sellers and movie deals, most likely, appearances on *Oprah*, maybe a few endearing anecdotes about my daughters, but I do know that when conversation falters, we hear the sound of the ocean, wave after wave, lapping, crashing, as open to interpretation as the desert's vast spaces.

I like hearing the ocean, Terry says. It reminds me of Babe.

The story ends when we forget it—or the story goes on, the way Terry, when he finally comes out of the drift that is not a tunnel, has to go on being Terry. He has to hike to his car and drive back to Las Cruces. He has to walk into his house and eat dinner with his family.

"No matter how old you are, I'm still your mother," Dorothy Delonas says as she fetches him a steaming plate of fried chicken, tater tots, and green bean surprise.

Succumbing to a childish impulse, he curls his right hand into a telescope and watches her set down the plate as if from a great distance. He feels present, yet far away; at home, yet out of place.

Family dinners inspire in Terry an uneasy mixture of pleasure and anguish that these are his closest kin. He sits at the head of the green dinette table, his aunt Letha on his right, his cousin Jerry next to her, Judy at the far end, Alex Alonso opposite Jerry, and Terry's mother, serving herself last, on Terry's left. Surrounded by family and friends, unable to shake the spell of the drift, he asks himself what in the world he is doing here. Returning to New Mexico from California always feels like returning to his fate—fried chicken, tater tots, green bean surprise—so unhealthy, so lovingly prepared.

The conversation skips from Jerry's new house to the private detective who has volunteered to do a little snooping for ONFP. When Letha launches into the story of her arrival in New Mexico, Terry bows his head and listens with his eyes closed.

"It was back in 1938, and Mama called and said that Doc had found a treasure. My husband told me not to go. I had three little kids. Wes wasn't even a year old." Letha would have been twenty-three in 1938, her hair a brilliant red. "My grandma knew a couple that was driving to California. I put up gas money. Me and the kids rode in the backseat."

Letha addresses herself to Alex, the only one there who might not have heard the story before. Alex hunches forward as if he too were squeezed into that backseat, bouncing across the dusty Texas panhandle.

"We pulled into Las Cruces about four-thirty in the afternoon. When we got to Mama's house, Doc had the biggest pistol I'd ever seen pointed at the biggest cop I'd ever seen, and Mama was running around asking everyone in the crowd to sign in her book. There was maybe twenty or thirty people gathered in the front yard. I was humiliated. The nice couple helped me unload my boxes and my kids, and then they left real quick.

"Pretty soon a second cop come along and Doc held the pistol on him too. He gave Doc a little chunk of gold that Mama showed everyone, and more people signed the book. Then we piled into Doc's van and headed for Albuquerque."

Terry opens his eyes now, plants his elbows on the table, and rests his chin between the palms of his hands.

"They filled me in on the way. Seems that just the night before, Doc had gone to a dance hall to pick up a man named Tony Corriego who was going to do some work at the peak. Tony was busy dancing so Doc sat down and had a drink. Well, the boyfriend of the girl Tony was dancing with hit Tony in the mouth, and then some friend of Tony's joined in, and a brawl broke out. Doc tried to slip away, but the police arrested him and made him spend the night in jail."

Letha's hands accompany her story like a pair of interpretive dancers. Color rises in her cheeks.

"Now at that time Doc had a great big cat almost as big as a coyote that he'd found starving in the mountains. He'd shot a rabbit and fed it to the cat, and the cat was very devoted. Strays'll do like that sometimes if you take care of 'em right. But this cat was pretty fierce to anyone but Doc."

Terry closes his eyes again. His mind forms an image of the cat.

"Now Doc's vehicle was a step van—"

"The bread wagon," Terry interrupts.

"The bread wagon," Letha repeats. "It had double-doors in back but no windows. Anyway, the cops was always interested in Doc's goings-on, so after they put him in jail, they shot the lock off the back of the bread wagon, and when they opened it up, the cat lunged right at 'em. They shot it stone dead and just left it there in the back of the van, bleeding all over the groceries Doc had bought for the trip to the peak. And they stole a chunk of gold he'd found on his last trip.

"Next day, when Doc gets out of jail and picks up his van, he finds the cat dead and the gold gone. He goes home and has Mama send word to the cops that he's drunk and causing trouble. When they come to the house to arrest him, he gets the drop on 'em and sends the one cop for the gold piece while he keeps the other cop covered. That was Tiny Davis, the biggest cop I ever saw. Babe called out everyone in the neighborhood to hear Tiny Davis confess what they had done. When the first cop brought back the gold piece and paid Doc for the bloody groceries, everyone knew Doc was on the level. That's why Mama had 'em sign in the book. We still got that book somewhere, don't we, Dorothy?"

"We do," Dorothy says. "I don't know where."

"I remember telling Doc, 'You just made you a couple enemies for life,' but he didn't seem overly concerned. And I thought, *My God, New Mexico.* That was my introduction. The first day I set foot in this state."

As Terry opens his eyes, Letha's hands settle on the edge of the table. He sees in her shining face a clear impression of the young woman she must have been.

"Tell about when Mama and Doc found the Spanish word map," Dorothy says.

"I better put on some coffee," Judy says.

Terry remembers the book with all the signatures stashed in a cluttered corner of Babe's trailer. He remembers Babe digging through the layers of accumulated scraps and tokens, triumphantly unearthing whatever prize she sought, a cherished relic of her days with Doc: the book with the signatures, the sword, a pencil sketch of the Upper Noss Shaft. How did she cram so much into that trailer? It was barely big enough to hold *her.* She'd moved through that trailer like a giant. She was huge and Doc had been huge, their discoveries and blunders epic in proportion.

"I was ignorant," Letha says. "There's no other way of explaining it."

Terry pushes back from the table, crosses his legs, and settles himself as comfortably as possible in his plastic chair. Alex catches his eye and exaggeratedly mouths, *My God, New Mexico.* Judy watches from the kitchen doorway, her expression tender, full of concern, until Terry shakes off her attention.

"Doc told me to be on the lookout for signs," Letha says. "I thought he meant signs with words on 'em, like road signs, and I said, 'Doc, I don't see no signs,' and he said, 'Young 'un, you just got to know how to look,' and we tramped down by a spring…"

APPENDIX

*(Overleaf) What would you do if your best friend
invited you on a treasure hunt?*

Endnotes

Chapter 1: A Postmodern Treasure Story

This is mirage country.

From *New Mexico, a Bicentennial History* by Marc Simmons:

The high, dry country of New Mexico is the birthplace of America's tall tale. The land's heady mixture of winelike air, sparkling sunlight, and bare-earth colors dazzles the senses and stimulates the imagination, so that the separation of fantasy from fact becomes a difficult, sometimes impossible, chore. Here, where space stretches far and often resembles the moonscape, golden mirages and extravagant yarns of lost treasure have found compatible breeding ground.

For more than four hundred years, virtually every trading caravan between Old Mexico and New risked falling prey to the Jornada's nasty heat, dry water holes, and roving Apaches.

From *Commerce of the Prairie* by Josiah Gregg:

This region [the Jornada del Muerto] is one of the favorite resorts of the Apaches, where many a poor arriero [muleteer] has met with an untimely end. The route which leads to the spring winds for two or three miles down a narrow cañon or gorge, overhung on either side by abrupt precipices, while the various clefts and crags, which project their gloomy brows over the abyss below, seem to invite the murderous savage to deeds of horror and blood.

The system of caves, according to Doc and Babe, held Spanish armor, statues of saints, swords, a crown, a chest of jewelry, twenty-seven skeletons....

From Chester Johnson's 1963 report of the State Museum of New Mexico:

M. E. ("Doc") Noss, a chiropodist living in the Hot Springs area, reportedly discovered a cave or crevice at the top of Victoria [*sic*] Peak in the San Andres Mountains through which he said he was able to descend 187 feet. He then proceeded along a passage to a "room" 2700 feet long. The room, he claimed, contained a large treasure: several stacks of Spanish-made gold bars; chests of jewelry; Spanish armor; swords; crowns; the statues of several saints; and Wells Fargo chests. Noss also reported that there were twenty-seven skeletons in the room, and later he brought one out to prove it.

One witness claims to have gone with Doc into the treasure room.
The witness was Serafín Sedillo.

Doc and Babe's descendants admit that Doc was a bit of a con man who went on to traffic in fake gold bars....
From an interview with Letha Guthrie, on the subject of whether Doc tried to pass off fake gold bars as real:

> It's true. He did rig up some phony bars at the end. That's because so many folks took the bars without paying. He was going to give them the bad bar, get the money, and then give them the good bar. Pulled that on a doctor in Clovis. The guy welched on paying him. Then they screamed, "I got taken." But if they had given Doc the money, Doc would have given them the gold.

In the fall of 1939, in an effort to improve access to the treasure, Doc hired a mining engineer to set off a dynamite blast at the worst bottleneck.
The mining engineer was S. E. Montgomery.

In 1958, four airmen stationed at nearby Holloman Air Force Base crawled into a foul-smelling cave in Victorio Peak....
The four airmen were Tom Berlett, Leonard Fiege (not an airman, technically, but a captain), Ken Prather, and Milt Wessel.

Subsequently, in partnership with Holloman's judge advocate general, they badgered the army for three years for permission to recover the treasure.
The Holloman judge advocate general was Sigmund Gasiewicz.

When Babe learned from a local rancher that the army was jumping her claim....
The local rancher was H. L. Moreland.

Chapter 2: Swinging Bachelor

"Since I was five, I knew."
Much of Terry's dialogue in this scene comes from statements he made to the authors.

Chapter 3: Soon to Be a Major Motion Picture

We talked for more than an hour, excavating history or sharing a delusion, until friends of theirs arrived, an elderly couple with close ties to the treasure story.

The elderly couple was Jack Woods and his wife.

Near the end of the interview, three treasure hunters trudged in, dirty and exhausted.

The treasure hunter with the laundry was Alex Alonso. The other two were probably Mike Levine and Jack Faircloth.

Chapter 4: Petition

Poised on the threshold of his makeshift office, Terry Delonas hesitated.

This scene is based on the recollections of Terry, Alex Alonso, and Judy Holeman.

Terry had thanked Alex for the office in a formal letter of welcome: "Congratulations on your decision to join forces with the Ova Noss Family Partnership. I guarantee it will ruin your life."

Neither Alex nor Terry could find a copy of the letter promising to ruin Alex's life, but both vividly recalled it.

At the cluttered desk, a young man she didn't recognize typed on a computer keyboard at an inhuman pace.

The young man was Howard Englund, also known as Monkey Boy.

Chapter 5: Clovis Boy

"Doc and I was out with some friends hunting mule deer," Babe began, standing over the dinette booth in the cramped trailer. The boys had stopped in to see her Saturday morning before reporting to work.

Much of Babe's dialogue comes from video and audio recordings, as well as from depositions and trial transcripts. The details of this particular Saturday morning are based on Terry's account of his many such conversations with Babe.

"We had to eat before sundown on account of the bugs," Babe explained, adding that Doc and his bulldog had almost missed dinner.

Doc's bulldog was named Buster.

He lugged out a gold crown that Babe later cleaned in her kitchen sink. She was standing at the trailer's sink as she recounted this episode, and Terry tried to imagine her scrubbing a priceless crown instead of his dirty breakfast plate.

From a video-taped interview with Babe Noss, on the subject of Doc's discovery:

And he also found a crown, and he didn't know if it was stolen off some king's head or how it got there, and so he brought it out, and I cleaned it partially in my sink, and then we found a jewelerman in El Paso, his name was Lombardi, like that Guy Lombardi, the famous musician (I don't know if there's any relation), so Lombardi—Doc stayed right with him while he was giving it a bath, and cleaned that up, and it weighed seven and a half pounds, and it had 243 diamonds and one pigeon blood ruby, and Lombardi told Doc that the stones were very valuable....

Chapter 6: Gridlock

"What I do from now on is my affair," Scott said in a telephone conversation with Ralph Monroe, "and what you do is your affair."

This quotation and those that follow come from a transcript of a tape recording of this conversation made by Ralph Monroe.

Chapter 7: Goldfinder

Seventy pairs of taillights bobbed toward Victorio Peak in the chill March dawn.

The procession included journalists from *The New York Times*, *The Washington Post*, the *Los Angeles Times*, *Rolling Stone*, *The London Daily Mail*, the *National Enquirer*, *Time*, and *Newsweek*.

When a White House aide had asked for a sample of the gold, Bailey's clients produced a small, cigar-shaped bar about seven inches long, dotted with bubbles.

Bailey's public relations consultant, Wayne Smith, delivered the bar to White House aide Todd Hullin, placed it on Hullin's chair, leaned a quarter next to it for scale, and took two Polaroid photographs. Both men initialed and dated the photographs, and each kept one as a record of the transaction.

Three days later the general counsel of the Department of the Treasury informed Bailey that any gold found on U.S. government property belonged to the U.S. government and could not be acquired by trespassers.

The general counsel was Thomas Wolfe, who wrote a memorandum to the Secretary of the Treasury:

Title to gold located on U.S. Government property cannot be acquired by a trespasser…. The Unites States is the owner of any antiquities found on U.S. Government property…. Since the gold belongs to the United States, the United States could not purchase the gold…. The United States could make an arrangement to pay a finder's fee…. A fee of 10% would be appropriate…. We might be prepared to negotiate up to 15%…. We know of no way of providing payment clear of taxes…. Based on all the facts and circumstances, we recommend that Treasury not proceed to make an arrangement with Mr. Bailey because of the request for secrecy and immunity. Moreover, in light of our present policy on gold, we do not see sufficient benefits in acquiring the gold to balance against the long history of no gold being produced from alleged gold caches and against the use of such schemes to defraud the public.

Scott raised his megaphone. "The existence of a tunnel at the so-called Soldier's Hole site has now been ascertained. Digging in said area will presently commence."
All quotations of Norman Scott in this chapter come from videotaped footage of Operation Goldfinder shot by KENW.

Gasiewicz and two other Air Force lawyers were impressed enough by their story to join them in a partnership they named the Seven Heirs.
The two other Air Force lawyers were Ralph Garman and Edward Rice.

A trio of curious ranchers stumbled upon the operation after five weeks.
The ranchers were H. L. Moreland, Robert H. Bradley, and R. B. Gray.

One of Babe's attorneys described it as follows: "the amenities were barely over when Jaffe bluntly announced his position on the Noss treasure discovery—'a fake and a myth.'"
The attorney was Philip Koury, author of *Treasure of Victoria* [sic] *Peak*.

Soon after this meeting, another of Babe's attorneys wrote a letter to the commander pointing out the weakness of the army's position.
This attorney was Robert Martin.

The first person to explore the hole was one of Scott's assistants.
Scott's assistant was Kevin Henry.

Chapter 9: Rad Tech Delonas

When most of the water was soaked up, he placed the used paper towels in a yellow plastic bag held by a crew member called Loon.
Loon and the other rad techs in this chapter are composite characters based on Terry's account of working at San Onofre.

The current version of Terry's screenplay began with a helicopter shot of the Hembrillo Basin at sunset, the camera gradually zooming in on the top of the peak, where Babe, anxiety etched in her careworn face, paced back and forth.

The screenplay that Terry worked on was not this detailed. The authors have augmented Terry's screenplay as a device for telling Doc and Babe's story.

In Roswell, New Mexico, Doc was arrested for brandishing a gun at a waitress. He served four months in state prison.

Doc Noss, in his parole application to the state prison in Roswell, New Mexico, where he served four months of a nine-month sentence for threatening a waitress while armed:

> I drank four glasses of beer and was under the influence of the glasses. I do not remember what I said to Jo Ann after I drank the glasses in the beer garden.

Doc was a handsome man, dressed in black from his boots to his cowboy hat, with a neat string tie that somehow emphasized his strong physical presence.

From Chester Johnson's 1963 report of the State Museum of New Mexico (emphasis added):

> Joe Andregg was only sixteen when he worked for Noss, and as he told the writer in July 1963, he…"cared nothing for the gold," but he "greatly admired the man, Noss, and *his fancy black western outfit.*"

The music would stop abruptly when Doc and Babe arrived at the peak with Serafín Sedillo, a skinny teenager from Rincon, New Mexico, whom Doc had hired to help haul out the gold.

From Chester Johnson's 1963 report of the State Museum of New Mexico:

> Noss hired a local boy from Rincon, Jose Serafin Sedillo, to help him in the difficult task of bringing out the gold. Sedillo made only one trip to the treasure room with Doc Noss, but on this occasion he carried out two gold bars in his pockets. Since part of the climb had to be made with the aid of ropes, no heavy load could be brought out at one time…. When they reached the surface, Joe said he was going to keep the bars he brought out. Doc said he wasn't and would kill him first, and he drew a gun. Joe left, and did not return until after the cave was blasted shut.

Serafin Sedillo, quoted in Chester Johnson's 1963 report of the State Museum of New Mexico:

> We went in the afternoon, because Doc had learned that at 2 p.m. the sun showed through a hole in the roof of the main cave…. The gold bars were stacked up like cordwood…. I grabbed two small ones and stuffed them into my shirt…. I had a hell of a time climbing up the rope with those things.

Sedillo goes on to describe what happened after they reached the surface and he announced his intention to take the gold for himself:

> Doc said, "No, you aren't." He took out his gun and said he would kill me first. I gave him the gold and left.... The next time I come around there, a couple of years later, the cave was blasted shut by somebody named Montgomery.

In July of 1939, Babe wrote a letter to the Denver Mint, asking what she and her husband should do if they stumbled across any gold bars.

Babe Noss, in an undated letter to the U.S. Mint, received July 17, 1939:

> We are residents of New Mexico and find lots of Stories about burried [*sic*] treasures such as bars of Gold and Silver—also Mexican money. Now we have in our possession an old map that tells of a rick of gold bars and Mexican money. Now we are searching in the vicinity of where it is liable to be—and what I want to know is what the United States law on a find of that kind. Can we take it to the U.S. Mint and sell it or will the government claim the treasure?

She'd never criticized Doc in front of Terry, yet Terry still harbored doubts about Doc's character—both as a movie hero and as a man.

Terry's cousin Wes tells the story of how Doc came home drunk one night and hit Babe, then went out to the cot on the porch and passed out. As soon as he started snoring, Babe took a "lariat-rope," wound it around the cot, and securely tied him down. Then she got a "cat o' nine tails" and started whipping him. He woke up cursing, but she didn't quit till she'd whipped him from head to toe and back again.

"Doc," she said when she was finished, "you can get drunk anytime, and come home and beat on me as much as you want, but don't ever fall sleep."

A gentler side of Doc's character is suggested by this letter he wrote to his step-daughter Letha. (Doc's handwriting is neat and his spelling accurate, but punctuation, capitalization, and paragraphing have been added):

> May 25, 1943
>
> Dear Letha,
>
> I just received your letter. Was indeed glad to hear from you.... I have a couple of copper claims now at High Roles M M east of Alamogordo in the mts. It sure is nice up there. I had a government engineer out there. He left Sat 22nd. I am getting twenty thousand dollar loan on it. I am sure the loan will go through OK....
>
> Letha, why don't you come home? At least we have plenty to eat and what we want to eat. I'll see you make it. I could tell you all about my moves if I could talk to you. Don't worry. Doc is damn sure in the race and I believe I am going to win, too. The government agents are sure wanting my copper and lead. Now is our time to make it if there ever was on earth....
>
> Believe me, Hot Springs sure is a dead hole. Babe and myself are going fishing tomorrow morning to pass some time away.

Letha, come on home. You can do better here than you can ever hope to there. You worry and work hard and I know you can do better here. When we start operations at High Roles, you take over the commissary and mess hall. I'll see you make plenty of money. I expect to feed 30 men three times each day at 75 cents each meal....

Write soon and tell me how you are and what you are doing and when will you be here with us....

Your friend,

Dr. M. E. Noss

According to the report of the State Museum of New Mexico, Las Cruces grocery clerk Ben Samaniego had "followed Doc Noss to see where he got his gold" and sneaked down to the treasure room.

From Chester Johnson's 1963 report of the State Museum of New Mexico:

Another local man, Benny Samaniego, in August, 1963, told the writer that on one occasion he had "followed Doc Noss to see where he got his gold." He said that he was in the treasure room when he heard Doc and Montgomery arguing about the place to put the charge. He "was about to yell when they decided to wait until the next morning." He got out as fast as he could without trying to take anything with him. He told the writer that there were several stacks of gold bars, skeletons, armor, old guns, and statues in the room. The skeletons, he added, are tied, kneeling, to posts, as if they were prisoners that were left to die.

Babe and Letha commandeered the front row, where they shouted advice to the special prosecutor, Melvin Reuckhaus, who, despite the potential conflict of interest, also represented Violet Boles Noss, demurely seated a few rows behind Babe and Letha.

A special prosecutor tried the case against Charley Ryan because the district attorney was embroiled in the Cricket Kugler case, a local *cause celebre* steeped in sex, politics, and murder.

The first prospective juror set the tone of the trial when he testified that anyone who plugged Doc Noss deserved a medal.

This detail, along with all quotations in this section, comes from the trial transcript.

Chapter 11: DC to LC

Craig offered his review after everyone else had left: "Masterpiece Theater it wasn't."

This conversation between Craig and Terry is based on Terry's generalizations about Craig and comments about their conversation that night.

When Scott mentioned that the license agreement was being negotiated in the name of

ONFP, Jones responded with obvious derision: "That ain't the smart way to go."

All quotations in this section come from a video tape of the satellite conference.

Terry continually needed money to pay Bill Casselman and Norman Scott, as well as the cost of flights, phone calls, etc.

Though Norman Scott was no longer on monthly salary, he continued to work occasionally for ONFP on a fee basis.

Chapter 12: The Only Cure Is Gold

In the late 1930s, Doc claimed to have unearthed an ancient parchment map with Padre Larue's name on it.

From a translation of the Spanish "word map" purportedly discovered by Doc in a chest buried near Victorio Peak, dated 1797 and attributed to Pope Pius III:

> Seven is the holy number.... In seven languages, seven signs and languages in seven foreign nations, look for the seven cities of gold. Seventy miles north of El Paso del Norte in the seventh peak, Soledad, these cities have seven sealed doors, three sealed toward the rising of the sun, three sealed toward the setting of the sun, one deep within the house of the golden cave, high noon, and receive health, wealth, and honor.

Chapter 13: Fantastic Start

The MP was probably still a teenager, Alex decided when he took a closer look. A teenager who carried a gun. In answer to Alex's direct question, he admitted that he was from Waterville, Maine.

The MP from Waterville is a composite character, based on MPs who worked at the peak.

"Who needs archeologists?" one of the volunteers now asked, stirring from his lethargy.

The volunteers' comments about the archeologist in this scene were made later on in the project, in the presence of the authors.

Chapter 15: Into the Fissure

Harry Albright was here thanks to a cup of coffee. In 1979, while recuperating from minor surgery, he'd read a book about the Victorio Peak treasure, and the story so inspired him that he phoned his son and suggested they go for a spin. In Hatch, New Mexico, 1,800 miles later, they inquired at the local police station about where to find Babe Noss.

The book that Harry Albright read was *100 Tons of Gold* by David Chandler.

"What we need is a vacuum cleaner," Mike said as he returned with the wheelbarrow. "A giant dustbuster to suck this stuff right out of here."

The conversation in the fissure is based on the participants' recollections and on later conversations that the authors heard.

Chapter 16: Fieldwork

After our truck blew a shock, I ended up walking the last quarter mile to the peak, past the artful arrangement of cow bones and skull, the hand-lettered sign that said, over the signature of Padre Larue, "Abandon All Hope, Ye Who Enter Here."

The Padre Larue sign was the handiwork of Glen Swearingen.

The MPs fell into three categories—Boz and I later wrote—snoozers, prison guards, and converts. This one was a convert.

The MP who helped Mike Levine was Sgt. Terry Miller.

Chapter 19: Infusion

Finally Dorothy looked away from him and said, "Of course, the I.V. is on your chart. It's what you're here for."

The conversation between Dorothy and Terry is based on Terry's account of a trip to infusion therapy with his mother.

Chapter 21: Humongous Void

The thirty-foot steel pipe swayed in the whistling wind while Cherrington's mud-splattered chief of operations dashed to the mud mixer, wrestled down a lever the length of a baseball bat, and sprinted back to the drill rig, where Alex and Kat heard him scream into his radio at the drill operator perched inside Cherrington's office trailer.

Cherrington's mud-splattered chief of operations was Larry Bertolucci.

Chapter 22: Critical Thought

The assay included with the petition values Doc's gold sample at $5,000 per ton, though the gold in the peak is usually characterized as pure or nearly pure.

From the notarized statement of B. D. Lampros, submitted by Babe to the Secretary of Defense in 1952:

> I worked with Doc Noss to carry gold out of the mine. In 1939 I took one roughly bullion bar on my round to Douglas, Arizona, and had Hawley & Hawley to assay it, and it was found that this roughly volcanic formation bar to run over $5,000 gold per ton....

Doc's desertion prompted Babe to put the claim in her own name. His death inspired her to declare that they had reconciled—though her son Harold testified against Doc at Ryan's trial.

From "Ryan Murder Hearing Opens Here Today" in the *Las Cruces Sun-News,* March 10, 1949:

> Then four witnesses, among them Noss's stepson, Harold Beckwith, took the stand.
> All testified that they had known Doc for many years and that his reputation was bad.
> Beckwith said when he (Beckwith) was 14 years old and his mother was married to Noss, the slain man had, at one time, hit him over the head with a pistol and shouted:
> "If you don't get out of here, I'll kill you."

One story of theft would be more convincing than so many.

The phantom treasure of Victorio Peak has been a magnet for stories of theft and conspiracy.

After "Unsolved Mysteries" aired its Victorio Peak episode, Gene Erwin came forward with this story, published in *Peak of the News,* the ONFP newsletter, issue #12, March 1990:

> My knowledge of the treasure began in the summer of 1961. My wife Juanita, the children and I were on vacation in New Mexico. We went to the White Sands Missile Base to visit Juanita's brother, Captain Orby Swanner, and his family. One evening while sitting in his living room talking with my wife and me, Captain Swanner said there was something he wanted to tell us. His tone of voice was serious. Only we three were in the room. First, he pledged us to secrecy, saying that what he was about to tell us, if found out, could possibly ruin his military career. We agreed to his terms and promised not to speak of it to anyone.
> This is Captain Swanner's story: Sometime earlier there were two soldiers stationed on the Missile Range. One day they found a small entrance into a cave inside the mountain. There were several chambers with small passageways connecting the chambers. Stored inside the chambers were stacks of gold bars and chests containing other treasures. The soldiers reported their find to the provost marshal and the base commander. They were told not to speak about

their finding the gold to anyone. If they did talk, there would be severe action taken against them under the National Security Act. Captain Swanner inspected the treasure site and reported to the commanding officer. The Pentagon was notified and a cloak of secrecy was drawn around the treasure site. I asked why did the treasure have to be kept secret? The reply was that very important work was going on at the Missile Range. It was vital to national security that this work not be interfered with.... When asked what happened to the treasure, Captain Swanner said that a special team sent from the Pentagon inspected, photographed and inventoried the treasure. The treasure was then removed from the mountain and stored elsewhere.

John Ehrlichman, in a memo dated July 9, 1970, to Secretary of the Treasury David Kennedy:

> While I was with the President [Nixon] in San Clemente last week, I was called on by a Mr. Keith Alexander.... Mr. Alexander claims to have secret knowledge of the location of 742 bars of gold weighing between forty and eighty pounds each. He obtained knowledge of the whereabouts of this cache from an aged Indian who assertedly is the last of his tribe. Some of the gold was mined by the tribe and some dates back to Aztec and other ancient times.

Ehrlichman asked Kennedy if Mr. Alexander—"who appears to be a reputable geologist, but for whom I cannot vouch"—could sell the gold to the Department of the Treasury. Kennedy replied that the government would only *consider* paying for the gold. After Ehrlichman notifed Alexander that no assurances could be given, the matter was dropped.

Keith Alexander belonged to a group that called itself Project A. Three members of Project A—Dick Richardson, Joe Tipton, and Lloyd Broadhurst—claimed to have discussed the Victorio Peak treasure with then-President Lyndon Johnson, a childhood friend, according to their story. Supposedly, Johnson met with the three at White Sands Missile Range in 1964 to work out a plan for removal of the treasure. When Tipton and Richardson grew fearful that the President intended to take the treasure for himself, they broke off negotiations, which Broadhurst later attempted without success to reopen. Rumors linking LBJ to the treasure persisted, however, including one that spoke of several tons of gold bars being flown to LBJ's ranch in the mid-Sixties, and another that had Ladybird Johnson calling White Sands daily during Operation Goldfinder for updates on the progress of the search.

From a report of White Sands Missile Range security, dated March 4, 1974:

> [I]t was reported that a group had entered the range, used dynamite and removed 37 tons of gold and artifacts. Immediately two range inspectors were dispatched to the Hembrillo Basin to investigate the report.... Their findings substantiated the report to the extent that several blasts were set off at the base of a shale outcropping approximately one mile east of Victoria [sic] Peak at a place known as "the Cottonwoods." Additionally, there was evidence of a campsite, and "sign" indicated an estimated five to nine personnel with two or three vehicles, one with a small trailer, had been in the area.... No evidence was found indicating that any gold or artifacts were removed. Inquiry into this matter is being continued by the FBI.

In April of 1995, a long-time ONFP supporter was talking about the Victorio Peak project at a cocktail party in Orange County when he met a man who had served as Director of Transportation for the White House during the Johnson administration. The man claimed that a military plane flying from an obscure New Mexico location to Johnson's ranch in Terlingua, Texas had crashed in the desert with a cargo of precious metal. The man agreed to meet with Terry Delonas and tell the full story on video. Bill Casselman knew the man from his own White House days and vouched for his honesty. A few days before the scheduled meeting, the man cancelled. When asked for an explanation, he declined to elaborate.

Suspicion of the army will likely persist, however, given the army's enigmatic bureaucracy and the public's love of a juicy conspiracy.

From a report to the Treasury Department titled "Alleged Gold Hoard," dated August 10, 1961, by Secret Service agent John Paul Jones:

> Efforts to recover the alleged gold hoard were futile due to blockage of the tunnel.... It should be noted that this operation has been carried as a top secret project; and the only persons [censored] who [censored] of this mission were [censored].

Chapter 23: The Difference Between a Tunnel and a Drift

When she told her father about my book, he wished me luck—but added that I should find a better subject than "those crooks."

In all our years of studying ONFP, we found no evidence of criminal intent or criminal acts, and no evidence that anyone used the organization for financial gain. Terry never accepted a salary for his work with ONFP.

The eviction, for Boz and me, fit a familiar pattern. **Cut off from the treasure**—*again.* **On the verge of discovery**—*again. The cycle of hope and failure was making another loop.*

In the course of our research, we found that the search was often on the verge of discovery.

From the minutes of the meeting of the Cheyenne Mining Company, December 4, 1941 (emphasis added):

> Dr. Noss discussed the progress of the work, saying they were down 264 feet in the shaft, and that it was going to take some money, time, and labor yet, but he thought *within two weeks they could have it ready to open....*

From the *Santa Fe New Mexican*, April 10, 1949 (emphasis added):

> Identification of the late Dr. Milton Ernest Noss as an ex-convict today dampened nationwide interest in a treasure hunt in southern New Mexico which he set off....

The quest he left behind is being carried out by Mrs. Ova Noss, his former wife, in Hembrillo Canyon....

She was reported Friday to be on the verge of breaking through the cave-in which Doc said had deprived him of fabulous wealth. A strong wind was blowing out of the cave entrance to the mine. This was taken to mean....

From an article in *Peak of the News,* issue #19, Spring 1993, by Alex Alonso:

The unobstructed continuation of Doc's path may be only 20 feet away; and once that is reached, we may have a clear path the rest of the way to the Main Cavern. *What Doc experienced back in 1937 is within reach, maybe only feet away.*

From an interview with Terry Delonas, March 8, 1996:

We expect discovery of the treasure—or of a crime scene—*in the next few weeks.*

From "Doc's Struggle Nears Completion" by Alex Alonso, in *Peak of the News,* issue #22, Spring 1996:

By the time this newsletter is mailed, we hope to have our discovery. But then again, we remember that some of Doc's correspondence in 1941 mentioned a breakthrough in "the next few weeks."

Chapter 25: Freaky Music

I remembered an article an anthropologist friend had given me about a religious group in the Midwest in the 1950s.
The anthropologist was Gerald Berreman.

Judgment alters when the evidence alters, but faith transcends evidence.
From *When Prophecy Fails* by Leon Festinger, H. W. Riecken, and S. Schachter:

Suppose an individual believes something with his whole heart; suppose further that he has a commitment to this belief, that he has taken irrevocable actions because of it; finally, suppose that he is presented with evidence, undeniable evidence that his belief is wrong; what will happen? The individual will frequently emerge, not only unshaken, but even more convinced of the truth of his beliefs than ever before. Indeed, he may even show a new fervor about convincing other people to his view.

Who's Who

———

Albright, Harry: Michigan businessman; ONFP investor and volunteer

Alonso, Alex: inventor of DataCam; ONFP's Director of Video Documentation; de facto leader of crew; donated office space to Terry early in project

Andregg, Joe: Los Alamos electrician who, as a boy in 1938, saw Doc take gold from VP

Bailey, F. Lee: attorney for group attempting to recover VP treasure in 1970s; defender of Boston Strangler, Patty Hearst, O. J. Simpson

Beckwith, Harold: Babe's elder son; paid for Babe's fatal trip to Caribbean

Beckwith, Marvin: Babe's younger son; crashed airplane at peak; introduced Les Smith to project

Berlett, Tom: one of four Air Force men who, in 1958, claimed discovery of VP treasure

Boles, Violet: Doc's second wife, *aka* Violet Boles Noss Yancey

Boz: co-author Robert Boswell

Carpenter, Ed: Southern California financier who supported the ONFP project

Casselman, Bill: attorney for Terry in Washington, D.C.

Chandler, David: author of *100 Tons of Gold*

Cheatham, Jerry: Terry's cousin; son of Letha Guthrie; raised funds for ONFP; worked in crew

Cheatham, Wes: Terry's cousin; son of Letha Guthrie; carpenter in Clovis, NM

Childers, Bill: WSMR employee who, in late 1980s, conducted unauthorized search at VP

Daar, David: attorney for Ova Noss during Operation Goldfinder

Dean, John: counsel for Richard Nixon; Watergate witness whose testimony brought national attention to VP

Delonas, Dorothy: mother of Terry and Jim; daughter of Babe

Delonas, Jim: Terry's older brother and occasional negotiator for ONFP

Delonas, Terry: grandson of Babe; step-grandson of Doc; founder of ONFP; Clovis boy; Hamlet in a suit

Dolphin, Lambert: ground-penetrating radar expert affiliated with Stanford Research Institute

Eddie, E. E.: commanding general at WSMR in early 1950s

Engstrom, Greg: retired army major; ONFP volunteer

Faircloth, Jack: ONFP Director of Field Operations who clashed with Terry over leadership role

Fiege, Leonard: Air Force captain who, in 1958, claimed discovery of VP treasure

Fischer, Kelly: Indiana farmer and businessman; ONFP investor and volunteer

Gaddis Mining Company: conducted 1963 exploration of VP

Gasiewicz, Sigmund: Air Force attorney who pressured army to permit 1963 search at VP

Guthrie, Letha: Terry's aunt; daughter of Babe, mother of Jerry and Wes Cheatum

Harrison, Craig: maitre d' at Irvine Hilton, Terry's housemate in Newport Beach

Herkenhoff, Gordon: engineer for NM state land office who investigated Doc's claim in 1945

Heydt, Patricia: retired high school English teacher; ONFP investor and volunteer

Heydt, Richard: retired highway patrolman; ONFP investor and volunteer

Hill, Dick: NM rancher whose road ONFP used to reach base camp

Hobbs, Gordon: Washington bureaucrat who monitored the ONFP project

Holeman, Judy: Terry's co-worker and friend; virtuoso of the telephone; ONFP investor, office manager, cheerleader, and den mother.

Horzmann, Merle: secretary of Doc and Babe's Cheyenne Mining Company; "family friend" who tried to convince the New Mexico state police to arrest Doc

Jaffe, Morton: colonel at WSMR in early 1960s

Johnson, Chester: author of state museum of New Mexico report on VP treasure in 1963

Jolley, Tony: cowboy who reputedly helped Doc move gold the night before Doc was killed

Jones, Thomas John Paul: commanding general of WSMR in late 1980s

Jordan, Oscar: head of NM state land office in the 1960s and 1970s

Keany, Kat: assistant producer of NBC News program "Now"

Klier, Gene: Washington carpenter; ONFP investor and volunteer

Koury, Phil: attorney for Babe Noss in the 1960s

Larue or La Rue: legendary priest said to have discovered or founded legendary lost mine

Levine, Mike: New Jersey entrepreneur; five feet ten inches tall; ONFP investor and volunteer

Marsh, John: Secretary of the Army when Terry submitted petition

Monroe, Ralph: advisor to Terry; lawyer and accountant; early supporter of project

Noss, Milton Ernest "Doc": itinerant chiropodist who claimed discovery of VP treasure in 1938

Noss, Ova "Babe": wife of Doc; grandmother of Terry

ONFP: Ova Noss Family Partnership

Parr, Roscoe: New Mexico prospector who spent years searching for NM treasure

Pruitt, Andy: president of Washington treasure-hunting club; ONFP investor and volunteer

Pryor, David (Jr.): D.C. public relations consultant; friend and co-worker of Terry's; early ONFP supporter

Pryor, David (Sr.): senator from Arkansas; advisor to Terry on Congressional protocol

Rector, Jamie: professor of engineering at the University of California, Berkeley

Rueckhaus, Melvin: attorney for Doc and later for Doc's second wife; special prosecutor in trial of Doc's killer

Ryan, Charlie: Texas oil man who shot and killed Doc Noss

Samaniego, Ben: Las Cruces grocery clerk who found a suit of Spanish armor inside VP

San Onofre Nuclear Generation Station (SONGS): the nuclear power plant where Terry worked

Seymour, Steve: Indiana truck driver; ONFP volunteer

Shannon, John: Assistant Secretary of the Army who met with Terry at Pentagon

Skeen, Joe: Congressional representative for Terry's district in New Mexico

Smith, Les: engineer who conducted Gaddis Mining Company's 1963 excavation of VP; ONFP consultant

Swanner, Orby: army captain in charge of top secret search of VP in 1961

Swearingen, Glen: ONFP supporter and photographer

Swearingen, Oren: dentist who saw ancient map of VP and spent years searching for treasure; ONFP supporter

Victorio: Warm Springs Apache leader who battled U.S. troops

Washbourne, John: graduate student in engineering at the University of California; ONFP investor and volunteer

Wickham, Wallace: retired Air Force colonel; advisor to Terry and ONFP

Wood, Bob: Washington treasure clubber; ONFP investor and volunteer

Woods, Jack: bulldozer operator hired by Babe in 1949 and subsequent family friend

WSMR (pronounced *Wizmer*): White Sands Missile Range

Young, Kent: tunnel finding expert from the Department of Defense

Acknowledgments

————

The authors wish to thank the following people for their help during the research and writing of this book:

Harry Albright, Larry Bertolucci, Terry Boswell, Stuart Brown, Jerry Cheatham, Wes Cheatham, Martin Cherrington, Patty Contaxis, Dorothy Delonas, Jim Delonas, Lambert Dolphin, David Dudley, Greg Engstrom, Kelly Fischer, Sherry Folsom, Letha Guthrie, Sarah Hamilton, Patricia Heydt, Richard Heydt, Don Jolly, Gene Klier, Carolyn and Roger Lane, Mike Levine, Bob Newell, Jamie Rector, Norman Scott, Steve Seymour, Les Smith, Glen Swearingen, Oren Swearingen, John Washburn, Emilie White, Wallace Wickham, Kim Witherspoon, Bob Wood, Sue and Terry Wright, Kent Young, the staff of the University of California's Bancroft Library, and, especially, Alex Alonso, Judy Holeman, and Terry Delonas.

We also wish to acknowledge several books and articles that provided useful information:

Mines of the Old Southwest by Rex Arrowsmith
The Conquest of Mexico by H. H. Bancroft
The Gilded Man by Adolph Bandelier
"Romanticizing the Stone Age: The Incredible 'Tasaday'" by Gerald Berreman in *Cultural Survival Quarterly*, Volume 15, Number 1, 1991.
Spanish Exploration in the Southwest by Herbert Bolton

Treasure of the Sangre de Cristos by Arthur Campa
One Hundred Tons of Gold by David Chandler
The Story of Mining in New Mexico by Paige Christiansen
Mexico by Michael Coe
Jornada del Muerto by Brodie Crouch
Coronado's Children by Frank Dobie
New Mexico Past and Present by Richard Ellis
"In Search of a Legend" by Guy García and Michael Haederle in *People Magazine*, September 14, 1992
Commerce of the Prairies by Josiah Gregg
The Southwest: Old and New by Eugene Hollon
"How Americans Lost Their Right to Own Gold and Became Criminals in the Process" by Henry Mark Holzer in the *Brooklyn Law Review*
Turmoil in New Mexico: 1846-1868 by William Keleher
Treasure of Victoria [sic] *Peak* by Phil Koury
Gold, Money and the Law by Henry Manne and Roger Miller
Maximilian in Mexico by Percy Martin
"Martin Cherrington and HDD" by Paul Miller in *Trenchless Technology*, November/ December 1993
New Mexico's Royal Road by Max Moorhead
"Gold!" by Dan Morrison in *Spirit Magazine*, April 1993
And the Band Played On by Randy Shilts
New Mexico: a Bicentennial History by Marc Simmons
The Mescalero Apaches and *Tularosa* by C. L. Sonnichsen
Wells Fargo in Arizona Territory by John and Lillian Theobald
Victorio and the Mimbres Apaches by Dan Thrapp
The Leading Facts of New Mexican History by Ralph Twitchell
Cortez and the Downfall of the Aztec Empire by Jon Manchip White
The Desert Reader by Peter Wild

Finally, we would like to thank our families for their support and patience:

Jade and Noah Boswell and Antonya Nelson
Laurel, Kate, and Linda Schweidel